Selling Catholicism

Selling Catholicism

Bishop Sheen and the Power of Television

Christopher Owen Lynch

THE UNIVERSITY PRESS OF KENTUCKY

Publication of this volume was made possible in part
by a grant from the National Endowment for the Humanities.

Scholarly publisher for the Commonwealth,
serving Bellarmine College, Berea College, Centre
College of Kentucky, Eastern Kentucky University,
The Filson Club Historical Society, Georgetown College,
Kentucky Historical Society, Kentucky State University,
Morehead State University, Murray State University,
Northern Kentucky University, Transylvania University,
University of Kentucky, University of Louisville,
and Western Kentucky University.

Editorial and Sales Offices: The University Press of Kentucky
663 South Limestone Street, Lexington, Kentucky 40508-4008

02 01 00 99 98   1 2 3 4 5

Library of Congress Cataloging-in-Publication Data

Lynch, Christopher Owen, 1954–
    Selling Catholicism : Bishop Sheen and the power of television /
Christopher Owen Lynch.
        p.   cm.
    Includes bibliographical references and index.
    ISBN 0-8131-2067-5 (alk. paper)
    1. Sheen, Fulton J. (Fulton John), 1895-1979. 2. Life is worth
living (Television program) 3. Television in religion—United
States—History. 4. Catholic Church—United States—History—20th
century. 5. Christianity and culture—United States—History—20th
century. 6. Christianity and culture—Catholic Church—History—
20th century. I. Title.
BX4705.S612L86   1998   98-17426
282'.092—dc21

Manufactured in the United States of America

Contents

Foreword

As a high school senior I had as an assignment through the winter season from Sister Robertus, our homeroom teacher, a *précis* (her word) of Monsignor Fulton Sheen's Sunday night Catholic Hour sermon. That was in 1935-36. He was already a nationally known figure via radio and, at least in the east, for his preaching to a packed St. Patrick's Cathedral in New York on Jesus' "seven last words" from the cross. This Good Friday devotion came from Italy and was known as the *Tre Ore*, the three hours the gospels speak of that Jesus hung on the cross, from noon to three.

Two years later I had a wordless encounter with Sheen while acting as sacristan (for my board and room) in the campus chapel at Seton Hall College. He was the guest of a faculty member he had known as a graduate student at the University of Louvain—now Leuven. My clear memory was of the length of time he spent in prayer after having presided at the rite of the Mass. At some point in those radio addresses, he began to exhort listeners to devote one hour a day to private prayer. Youthfully idealistic, I was delighted to see that he practiced what he preached.

While pursuing my Ph.D. at the Catholic University of America in the mid-1940s, I audited the one graduate course Sheen's teaching schedule called for. Every chair in the room was taken well before class time, although there might have been only six or seven students following the course for credit. It was a standard two-semester history of philosophy, from the pre-Socratics to Kant, and on through the British pragmatists and modern existentialists. The well-planned lectures were delivered flawlessly. He used the blackboard in his flowing hand to good effect, chiefly for the spellings of names or terms in Latin and Greek, French and German. He stopped exactly at the stroke of the next hour. Each class was a masterful performance of the teacher's art.

Fulton Sheen resigned from the Catholic University of America faculty in 1950, and I joined it that autumn. He had been appointed national director of the Society for the Propagation of the Faith, an arm of the U.S. Catholic Bishops, to raise funds supportive of mission-sending societies. I never knew him as an academic colleague. I would have known him at second hand, however, had not my younger sister hied herself to a nunnery. In her four years after college she served as secretary to his predecessor in the Society post.

Sheen would later be appointed to the bishopric of Rochester, New York, as this book records in tracing his career. But as a resident of Manhattan he made the transition from radio preacher to television teacher more than successfully. This was because he was a consummate pedagogue. He was a bit of a showman, as the new medium required, but his years in the university classroom had prepared him for that. In my early years of preparing college and graduate classes I was not a television watcher. But whenever I caught the Bishop on the screen in the home of friends, I was reminded of the teacher I knew: the piercing gaze from deep-set eyes, the trace of a smile, the deep, well-modulated voice, and above all the clarity of exposition. He made religion acceptable to a wide audience because, like a second-century apologist, he spoke of it so intelligently, so reasonably. A better word might be so winsomely.

He responded perfectly to the country's mood in the post-war, Truman-Eisenhower years. Let Christopher Lynch tell you how and why.

Gerard S. Sloyan
Professor Emeritus of Religion
Temple University

Preface

This book is a close textual analysis of the messages of Bishop Fulton J. Sheen, drawn from forty-two episodes of his popular television program *Life Is Worth Living* (1952-57). The book examines Sheen's message in light of America's postwar success, an era that brought much social change. Many Catholics were climbing the socioeconomic ladder and leaving their ghettos for the suburbs and the corporate world. However, there were tensions between Protestantism and Catholicism over issues such as the authority of the pope, religious toleration, and doctrines regarding Mary. As a result, although Catholic teaching was always embedded in his text, Sheen chose not to speak explicitly about Catholic doctrine. He idealized the medieval era and held it out as a model for contemporary society, offering clear-cut boundaries that would eliminate anxiety in the midst of change. He ritualized the Catholic coming of age by communicating his message through television, the medium of contemporary America. By appealing to the mythos of American civil religion, he showed his Catholic listeners how to survive in society and reassured others that Catholics were truly patriotic. His message blessed the new corporate culture in the emerging secular society while implicitly stressing the need for the Catholic Church to mediate between the sacred and the secular. In doing this he helped pave the road to the ecumenism that would emerge in the next decade.

Acknowledgments

I am grateful to an Irish Catholic family that helped me appreciate a rich religious culture as I grew up in the television culture of the 1950s. To them I dedicate this book. The Passionist community inspired me with a love of the communication of religion and a critical ability that always challenges us to go beyond our own cultural boundaries.

This book never would have taken shape without the guidance of the Department of Rhetoric and Communication at Temple University. I am especially grateful to Gerard Sloyan, Aram Aghazarian, and Leonard Swidler for their careful reading. Special thanks go to Marsha Witten, whose enthusiasm and patient support challenged me to probe more deeply into the texts. She was the role model for me as professor and researcher. Tom Rosteck and Stewart Hoover helped fuel my interest in this analysis. Passionists Gerald Laba and John O'Brien provided encouragement in getting this project started.

Janet Yedes provided moral support as we journeyed through the introspection of the writing process. I want to thank Janice Fisher, Mary Conway, and Patricia Brown for their technical assistance. Bishop Edwin Broderick was very helpful in providing information on the origins of Sheen's program; I am grateful to R.D. Heldenfels for helping me locate Bishop Broderick. The Reverend Sebastian Falcone provided hospitality when I visited the Sheen Archives in Rochester, New York, in 1992. Duane Pancoast of Sheen Productions was helpful in making videotapes available. The Reverend William Graf, director of archives and records for the Diocese of Rochester, played a key role in finding pictures for this book. I am appreciative of Greg Koep for the picture of myself on the jacket.

Much thanks to my students and fellow faculty in the Department of Communication and Theatre at Kean University, who never tired when I elaborated on the rhetoric of Bishop Sheen and his culture.

Finally, I am grateful to John P. Ferré from the University of Louisville and George Cheney of the University of Montana, who gave valuable insights to strengthen the work.

Introduction

The year is 1952. It is eight o'clock on a Tuesday evening. Recently your family bought its first television set, and you are deciding what to watch: should it be *The Texaco Star Theatre,* hosted by Milton Berle? or perhaps Frank Sinatra's program? Instead you choose a new program that has become a success over the DuMont television network.

The program opens with an image of a leather-bound book denoting the program's title, *Life Is Worth Living.* In the background is up-beat music made formal by the sound of church bells. The bookshelves and the blackboard on the stage suggest the library of a learned person. The library door opens and a voice announces, "Ladies and gentlemen, his excellency Bishop Fulton J. Sheen." The bishop, garbed in a princely cape, sweeps solemnly onto the stage of the Adelphi Theatre in New York. In front of an enthusiastic but unseen audience, his program is being broadcast live around the country.

Pausing before the statue of the Madonna and Child, one of the few explicitly religious symbols in evidence, the bishop bows, nods toward the TV camera, and moves center stage to address listeners with the greeting "Friends." He begins with some icebreakers—usually anecdotes about young children—and then speaks extemporaneously for a half hour on a topic such as the dangers of communism, the values of family love, the duties of patriotism, or the need to examine one's conscience.

Sheen's persuasive presence and message focus on the distinction between right and wrong. He never leaves any of his own rhetorical questions unanswered; his task is to inform the audience of timeless values. All his statements are in declarative sentences, with little offered in the way of proof. He identifies his authoritative statements as the source for answers to the questions of day-to-day living.

Sheen speaks with an intensity emphasized by the many close-ups of his penetrating eyes, underlit to make them seem like burning coals. Although he is little more than five feet, eight inches tall, his expansive gestures with his cape make him appear larger than life. The TV camera follows his every move, encouraging the viewer to do the same. Sheen controls his blinking, and even when walking away from the camera he turns his head to keep his gaze fixed on the viewers, inviting them to laugh at his jokes, learn about life from his blackboard diagrams, and change their values after listening to his dramatic examination of conscience.

The one interruption in the telecast—an advertisement for Admiral Corporation, the program's sponsor—comes in the final moments, after Sheen's major address. Sheen returns to the screen for a final comment, reinforcing the program's theme. With outstretched arms that appear to embrace each viewer, he concludes, "Bye now, and God love you!"

Bishop Sheen, one of the first preachers to use the medium of television, is a significant figure in American popular culture and in the history of American Catholicism. More than forty years after *Life Is Worth Living* first aired, and twenty years after Sheen's death, he is still popular among certain audiences. Yet little research has been done on Sheen as a figure of popular culture or as a TV personality. No one has studied his program in its social and cultural context.

American Catholicism in the fifties has often been overshadowed by the events surrounding Vatican II. But the fifties were also a time of tension between the Catholic subculture and the wider culture of an America heavily influenced by Protestantism. This book looks at the phenomenon of Fulton Sheen to examine how he constructed his television message to alleviate those tensions.

American Catholicism was under the domination of Rome, and other American denominations found this offensive. Catholic Canon Law of 1918, the official policy of the church, forbade Catholic clergy involvement with Protestants in religious services. In 1947 the Vatican affirmed that no Catholic priest could participate in a civil ceremony if non-Catholics were present. Catholicism was not only distancing itself from Protestants but was also taking an elite posture.

Sheen spoke at a time when Paul Blanshard wanted American bishops to be declared foreign ambassadors because they pledged obedience to the Roman Pope. In his 1951 book, *Communism, Democracy and Catholic Power*, he equated Catholicism with the oppression of Soviet Communism. His criticism of Catholic authoritarianism received much support in the academic and religious community.[1] Bishop G. Bromley Oxnam (1891-1963), whose Methodist denomination was Protestantism's largest, argued, "We want neither the Vatican political line nor the Moscow political line in America."[2] Oxnam and other Protestants suspicious of Catholicism formed Protestants and Other Americans United for Separation of Church and State. Some feared that a Catholic president would be subordinate to church dogma; they were therefore leery of the candidacy of Al Smith when he ran for president as a Democrat in 1928. The issue came up again when Kennedy was a candidate in 1960. Blanshard was not alone in his memories of the anti-Semitism of Father Charles Coughlin in the 1930s.

Protestants feared Catholicism's embracing of fascism. Some Catholics saw the fascism of Franco and Mussolini as the lesser of evils and were embittered by America's silence over the persecution of priests and nuns in the Mexican Revolution. The Catholic press referred to Franco as the George Washington of Spain, though the laity were less supportive. A 1953 concordat signed by the Vatican and Spain to prohibit public exercise of non-Catholic worship in Spain aroused additional suspicions among American Protestants. Vatican support of Franco and his fascist government in Spain led some to fear that Rome would destroy the very principle of religious freedom that was a cornerstone of the United States.

Anti-Catholicism was intensified when Catholic bishops lobbied for public support of religious instruction in the parochial school system. Cardinal Francis Joseph Spellman (1889-1967) called those who did not support public busing of parochial school children "unhooded clansmen." When Eleanor Roosevelt came out in her newspaper column, "My Day," in support of the movement against aid to parochial school, Spellman accused her of "discrimination that was unworthy of an American mother." Bishop Oxnam described Spellman as inept and ignorant, a "little man with big ideas." Spellman and Roosevelt reconciled when Spellman clarified that the church was seeking support not for religious instruction but for auxiliary services.[3]

The tension between Protestants and Catholics escalated over controversies of sexual morality and family values. When *The Miracle* won the 1951 New York Film Critics award for best foreign film, Spellman—who had not seen the movie—condemned it as Communistic in a letter read from the pulpit of four hundred New York parishes. The fire commissioner, under Spellman's influence, issued violations against the theater, and the New York police raided it several times, claiming bomb scares. Protestants feared that the rights of the individual were being threatened by the force of Catholic moral teaching. That teaching, and strict regulations on intermarriage, led several Protestant denominations to warn congregations against marriage to Catholics.

Father Leonard Feeney, chaplain at Harvard University in the late forties, wanted to keep Roman Catholicism distinct from other denominations and free from compromise with American ideology and its tolerance of diverse denominations. The Boston archdiocese had been building a positive relationship with Protestant society when Feeney's militant Catholicism began criticizing Harvard's agnosticism and the atheism of the professors. The final straw was Feeney's declaration that there "was no salvation outside the Church." Feeney even called on Eisenhower and all members of Congress to convert to escape damnation. This enraged leaders of other denominations; the church moved quickly to silence Feeney in 1949 and finally excommunicated him in 1953.

A Vatican statement helped clarify Catholic teaching that one did not have to be a Catholic to be saved, though it said nothing about the possibility of salvation through other churches. But the fires of anti-Catholicism had been fanned by Feeney's statements, and the Vatican's response did not put them out. The Church of Rome and America's value of church and state separation were in opposition. Cardinal Alfredo Ottavani was the newly named secretary of the Holy Office in 1953. Ottavani's position was that in a country where the majority of the population was Catholic, the state should offer exclusive protection to the church; where Catholics were in a minority, they had the right to tolerance. Protestant hegemony had been on a decline since the mid–nineteenth century, and Catholicism was now the nation's largest religious body. Protestant ideology still dominated newspaper and textbook publishing, higher education, and government. However, Protestants lacked a doctrinal identity that would bond them together. Opposition to Catholic authoritarianism was the one solidifying force.

Tensions were tempered by the fact that Catholics were being assimilated into mainstream society. The move to the suburbs took them away from the tight control of the ethnic family system that reinforced Catholic traditions. The G.I. Bill provided opportunities for veterans to attend secular universities. There were few Catholics to challenge institutional authority until the late fifties because, although Catholics had the largest number of children compared to other religious groups, they were the least likely to be college-educated. They listened to the priest for answers; he was the educated member of their community.

Catholics began to become self-critical in the late fifties. Father John Tracy Ellis, a prominent Catholic historian, was one of the first to admit in a public forum the limitations and mediocrity of Catholic ideology. He reminded listeners of Cardinal Richard James Cushing's statement that every American bishop was the son of the working class. The solution was to overcome the self-imposed "ghetto mentality." Catholic scholars tried to improve the quality of Catholic education. Other critics within Catholicism challenged the idea in Catholic teaching that "there is no question which cannot be answered: the result is the illusion of a neat universe in which nothing eludes the conceptions of a searching mind."[4]

At the same time it must be remembered that this was an age of anxiety. Americans moving to the suburbs wanted peace of mind as they escaped the problems of the cities and rapidly changing technology. Society was changing too, and people lived in fear of a new war with nuclear weapons. At home the civil rights movement was forming as blacks moved into Northern cities, and the feminist movement grew as new possibilities opened for women. Elvis's gyrating hips helped create a new youth culture.

In the midst of these major changes, doctrines of a particular church became less important. Because Americans "liked their religion diluted,"[5] there was more tolerance of religious pluralism.

Americans turned to religiosity to ease their fears and reinforce an American identity as a self-righteous nation. Americans ranked religious leaders as more influential than government or business leaders in 1947. Over the next decade the proportion of Americans who considered clergy the "most useful"[6] leaders increased from about 32 percent to more than 46 percent. Booksellers in 1953 reported that one out of every ten books vended was religious. In 1954 nine out of ten Americans said they believed in the divinity of Christ.[7]

The movement to the churches represented not so much "religious belief as belief in the value of religion."[8] No European nation had such piety. America had experienced periods of religious revival before, but never in such an inclusive wave that captivated all denominations and sects, ethnic groups and social classes, young and old. This movement set the stage for Bishop Sheen.

Arguments between Protestants and Catholics gave way to coping with a common enemy: Communism. Americans and especially all Christians found a rallying cry for unity by fighting against Communism's evils. Affirming the "American way of life,"[9] as opposed to the sinful ways of Communism offered a way to new confidence at a time of great social unrest.

Billy Graham, the prophet of America's ideology, was concerned not with an individual's religious affiliation or religious doctrine, but with the importance of religiosity. He combined this with his own evangelical message that a person must turn to Jesus and be converted from sin, as well as with a message of American patriotism and fierce anti-Communism. Over a nine-year period he did not fail to touch on Communism in Sunday sermons or in revival meetings, declaring that it was "inspired, directed and motivated by the Devil, himself."[10] Christianity was equated with capitalism and military strength. The ideal of America's special destiny was heightened by appealing to the polarity between the Communist and the American ways of life.

Media contributed to this Cold War propaganda. Television programs pictured the world outside the United States as "wretched and unsettled."[11] Even programming for children played into this theme. Fans of the program *Captain Video* (1949-57) became honorary rangers by taking an oath to uphold the ranger code of freedom, truth, and justice in the world against the enemy.

Politics was not exempt from the religious fervor sweeping the nation in the fifties. In his 1949 inaugural President Truman noted that all were equal and created in the image of God and must fight Communism. Edward Martin, a Republican senator from Pennsylvania, argued on the Senate floor in 1950 for a peacetime draft, proclaiming, "America must move forward with the atomic bomb in one hand and the cross in the other." A dozen states barred atheists and agnostics from serving as notary publics; elsewhere, agnostic couples were not allowed to adopt. An "American atheist" became an oxymoron.[12]

President Eisenhower summed up the era's stress on the value of religion rather than on a specific doctrine when he described himself as "the most intensely religious man I know. Nobody goes through six years of war without faith. That does not mean that I adhere to any sect." At the Republican National Convention Eisenhower was referred to as "the spiritual leader of our times." A month later the candidate asserted, "We are now at a moment in history when, under God, this nation of ours has become the mightiest temporal power and the mightiest spiritual force on earth." When the cabinet convened on January 12, 1953, Eisenhower asked that the session begin with a prayer, and the practice of silent prayer persisted throughout his administration. He called the nation to cooperation against the common enemy of "godless" Communism, continuing Truman's rhetoric. America was fighting a holy crusade. In a prayer at his inauguration Eisenhower asked the Almighty to watch over the nation, bonding citizens together in faith and cooperation.[13]

Historical studies of Catholicism are often criticized for tending to focus on the clergy and religious women. This book is about a bishop, but it is a rhetorical study that places him in the context of the wider culture. In writing this book I had access to forty-two tapes of Sheen's programs that until recently had been lost or inaccessible (stored on kinescopes). Contrary to Sheen's own claim in the printed version of his programs, the video texts were edited when transcribed for book form. A rhetorical analysis of the tapes also makes it possible to discuss the nondiscursive elements of Sheen's presentation that were such an important part of his persuasiveness.

Bishop Fulton Sheen was a Catholic bishop who used the medium of TV before the age of televangelism. *Life Is Worth Living* aired nationally (first on DuMont, then on ABC) from 1952 to 1957. Sheen was so successful that his picture appeared on the covers of *Time* and *Cue* magazines in the 1950s. *Look* did a feature article on his life and gave him an award for excellence in television for three consecutive years. He received an Emmy in 1952; he is also remembered for his role in the conversion of such prominent Americans as the editor Clare Booth Luce and the Communist Louis Budenz.

Life Is Worth Living was the only religious program ever to be commercially sponsored and to compete for ratings.[14] Hadden and Swann's study of the history of televangelism claims that "Sheen's success in television probably was the single most important factor in persuading evangelicals that television—far more than radio—was the medium best suited for their purposes."[15] A 1955 survey in New Haven, Connecticut, showed that Sheen's program was as popular as the next six most popular religious television programs combined and as popular as the top ten religious radio programs combined. Although his audience was 75.5 percent Catholic, according to the researchers, he had appeal among Protestants (13.4% of the audience), among those of mixed backgrounds (7.9%), and even among some Jews (2.2%).[16]

Milton Berle, whose ratings were declining during the time his show competed with Sheen's, said, "If I'm going to be eased off TV by anyone, it's better that I lose to the one for Whom Bishop Sheen is speaking."[17] When Sheen finished his television season in the summer of 1953, he had a near-perfect Nielsen rating of 19.0, and the Videodex Report showed his audience pushing the 10 million mark.[18] While achieving this success, he was also writing two nationally syndicated newspaper columns.

Tapes of Sheen's television lectures are still in demand today among traditional Catholics. Supplements in Sunday newspapers, such as *Parade* and *U.S.A. Weekend,* run full-page ads for selected videotapes from the programs. In addition, as of 1993, the program was being shown in Detroit and in Rochester, New York, and over Catholic network programming in Scranton, Pennsylvania, and Orlando, Florida.

To understand Sheen's message we must examine the impact of television on Sheen's presentation. The personality of the television celebrity is important in television's flow. According to Fiske and Hartley,[19] just as the traditional bard rendered in verse the concerns of the day, appealing to mainstream society in order to win the approval of the majority, television—the cultural bard of contemporary society—presents the myths and stories that are valued within a particular community. Television thus serves a ritual purpose as it mirrors the communal experience of mainstream society, shaping stories and myths with which the audience can identify. Through the repetition of particular plot themes and characters, television helps the society represent itself to itself.

The technology of television encourages the style of direct address because the place of viewing is the home rather than the theater. As David Marc explains, "Television offers itself to the viewer as a hospitable friend: 'welcome to the wonderful world of Disney,' 'good evening folks,' 'we'll be right back,' 'see you next week,' 'Y'all come back now.'"[20]

The introduction of television into American society was postponed by the decades of the Depression and war. But it emerged in the postwar era as a surprising success. By the mid-1950s America had more TV sets than bathtubs in its homes.

Funding for early television was limited, and programs were often filmed in New York theaters before live audiences. Camera angles were restricted because of portability problems, the difficulty of concealing microphones, poor lighting, and fear of blocking the performers. The camera could get only a narrow picture, sometimes went out of focus, and could not photograph the panoramic settings that were common to film. As a result, the camera favored the close-up shot that complemented the mode of direct address. The close-up encouraged the viewer to analyze not the action of the unfolding plot but the reactions and emotions of the performer's personality. In mirroring the proxemics of interpersonal interactions, the close-up enhanced the idea of direct address between the television personality and the audience.

The fact that television favored direct address with the viewers stressed the importance of individual television personalities. The celebrity personality attempted to engage the listener in an unspoken dialogue; the listener, it was hoped, would tune in to the program week after week to continue the dialogue, thereby increasing the program's ratings. The audience came to perceive its relationship with the celebrity as an intimate one, based on (apparent) face-to-face encounters involving direct discourse. Whether the viewer liked or disliked the celebrity, the relationship kept the viewer attentive. The television celebrity promoted the familiar and the personal as he or she addressed the viewer in close-up. Naming television characters or programs after their stars—as in *I Love Lucy, Love That Bob, The Jack Benny Show, The Adventures of Ozzie and Harriet,* and *The Gracie Allen and George Burns Show*—complemented this process.

Each television genre was organized around someone who could become a familiar character: the evening news had the anchor person, the quiz show had a master of ceremonies, the talk show had a host, and even dramas were introduced by a host or narrator. These characters became so familiar that newscasters and actors were frequently approached by people who felt they had met them before. Actress Joanne Woodward, asked about the difference between being a movie star and being a TV actress, replied: "When I was in the movies I heard people say, 'There goes Joanne Woodward.' Now they say, 'There goes somebody I think I know.'"[21]

These factors contributed to a construction of celebrity persona that was different for the TV star than for the film star. Psychologists Horton and Wohl described it as a parasocial relationship, because it developed with the help of direct address and close-up. Thus, the barriers of the proscenium were erased. The television celebrity's persona encouraged the viewer to relate as an intimate, and the celebrity made regular weekly appearances that over time became integrated into the viewer's routine. The persona represented values that the viewer could identify with, and in time the viewer—or fan—came to believe that he or she knew the celebrity in a personal way.

The idea of the parasocial relationship between TV celebrity and viewer ties in well with the historical situation that gave birth to television. The postwar era was transforming film stars from gods and goddesses into realistic characters. As Americans became more sophisticated film viewers and as the technology became more realistic, they were more captivated by realism and the psychology of character. Audiences wanted to know about actors' personal lives; popular magazines and fan clubs sought to uncover that information.

The fifties was also a time when lines of class distinction were being erased. Wartime propaganda had stressed patriotism and equality through images such as G.I. Joe and Rosie the Riveter. The move of many couples to the suburbs and the upward mobility of many ethnic groups into the middle class made it natural that "visual representations of TV stars as ordinary individuals—frustrated butchers and homely aunts—. . . counteract[ed] the celebrity status as . . . upper class."[22] The House Un-American Activities Committee hearings, broadcast live on television in the fifties, may also have contributed to the decline in the star system and television's new emphasis on the ordinary person. That committee focused much energy on debunking Hollywood celebrities as idols by accusations of false patriotism or Communist involvement.

Nevertheless, it is important to note that television did have ways to distance the personality from the audience—by creating hierarchies of discourse. For example, the talk show host, who often was "ordinary," acted as an intermediary between the exotic personality he or she interviewed and the viewer. The personality, such as the Hollywood celebrity, could maintain a distance from the viewer by talking to the host. Yet the viewer could feel vicariously present by identification with the host, whose dialogue was a hierarchical bridge. Sheen dealt with the need for distance by balancing two roles. He could be the exotic presenter by posing as an aloof aristocrat from a past era, or he could be the intimate neighbor by telling corny jokes.

Over five years Sheen broadcast approximately 125 episodes of *Life Is Worth Living*. Many of the original kinescopes have been destroyed, but about sixty still exist. I analyzed forty-two of these programs, selecting randomly but including tapes from each year in order to note how Sheen adapted to the medium over time. Only four out of a possible twenty-six tapes are available for the 1955-56 television season; I was able to obtain three of these.

I viewed tapes that I purchased from Sheen Productions, Inc., Victor, NY 14564. From the 1952-53 television season, I analyzed "For Better or Worse," "How Mothers Are Made," "Pain and Suffering," "Reparation," "Something Higher," "The Philosophy of Communism," "The Psychology of the Irish," "The Role of Communism and the Role of America," and "War as the Judgment of God"; from the 1953-54 season, "Children: Burdens or Joy," "Inferiority Complex," "How Traitors Are Made," "Nurses and Doctors," "The Liberation of Sex," "The Philosophy of Communism," "Three Degrees of Intimacy," "Three Times in a Nation's History," "Why Some Become Communists," and "Women Who Do Not Fail"; from the 1954-55 season, "How to Be Unpopular," "Human Passions," "Juvenile Delinquency," "Macbeth," "My Four Writers," "The Greatest Trial in History," "The Glory of the Soldier," and "The Psychological Effects of the Hydrogen Bomb"; from the 1955-56 season, "East Meets West," "Meet a Perfect Stranger: Yourself," and "Message to Youth"; and from the 1956-57 season, "Abraham Lincoln," "A Dreamer in the Streets of London," "Fig Leaves and Fashions," "Should Parents Obey Children?" "Some Nice People Live in Alleys," "Something the Princess Could Never Forget," "The Best Town in Which to Be Broke," "The Desert Calls a Playboy," "The Life and Character of Lenin," "The Man Who Knew Communism Best—Dostoyevsky," "The Stones of Notre Dame Cry Out," and "How to Psychoanalyze Yourself."

The commercials are missing from the tapes, and, depending on the editing, some tapes do not show opening or closing credits. On all tapes, however, Sheen's presentation is intact and unedited. Quotations in this book from the programs are verbatim, with only punctuation added.

Sheen most commonly used a lecture format, playing the role of a teacher at the blackboard. During the 1956-57 season he altered the format, posing as a storyteller who narrated famous biographies or tales of international cities.

The analysis is grounded in rhetorical principles that shed light on how Bishop Sheen shaped and formed his messages—not just what Sheen said, but also how he said it.

The basic principle that grounds rhetorical research is that the world we perceive around us is constructed through symbolic interaction. We use symbols to create myths, stories, dramas, and fantasy visions that provide meaning and help maintain our social order; chains of symbols are reified over time as a natural reality that claims to be the truth rather than historic constructs of a symbol-using community. In this way, according to Burke, rhetoric becomes "equipment for living" because it helps us to "size up situations" that perpetuate various attitudes, values, and beliefs.[23]

The historical situation is central to any rhetorical study because the needs, constraints, and particular audiences are what influence the frame used to construct symbol systems. Audiences, or interpretive communities, are shaped by the differing symbol systems of a particular era that enable them to perceive the world in a particular way. Because people have diverse experiences, members of every audience have differing worldviews and symbol systems. Understanding the historical situation provides a key to unlocking the strategies a rhetor chooses in particular texts. At the same time, how the rhetor constructs a text and chooses a persuasive strategy provides insights into the historical situation and how he or she perceives it.

The rhetor who can help the listener identify with him or her can ease reception of the message. The rhetor may create a charismatic or heroic identification by embodying the needs and values of a particular audience at a particular time. A hero, cult, or crusade symbolically fills a gap, maintaining the social order or transforming the order to fulfill a need and reach goals. This action sustains communities so they can "celebrate and participate in a social communion."[24]

I use close textual analysis to examine how the structure and content of Sheen's message interact to create meaning and invite response. Textual analysis keeps in mind the theoretical perspective but asks questions of the text rather than imposing answers. The text, rather than the method, is the focus.

Historical situations affect the content of the rhetor's message and the form it takes. Each chapter analyzes Sheen's discourse in light of the general rhetorical situation and rich tradition of Catholicism.

Repeated viewings of the tapes of Sheen's programs revealed recurring themes, such as how Catholicism is described, tensions within American society, definitions of patriotism and of the individual, the role of Mary and women, and the fears of the Cold War. These particular themes were tracked by looking at the metaphors used to describe them. Patterns in the text suggested a particular perspective or root metaphors to give insights into Sheen's message construction and underlying motivation. For example, container metaphors describe what is contained by what while setting clear boundaries between concepts. Structural metaphors show how these containers are organized and shaped. By emphasizing a particular metaphoric configuration, the rhetor creates a perspective that excludes other possibilities while giving value to one perspective.

These metaphors were then clustered into subgroups by considering what was foregrounded and what placed in the background; what was opposed to what; what was related to what. Some terms were made sacred in the text and others portrayed as more negative or evil. The relationships between the subgroups were examined in light of ideologies that were sacred in society at large.

A rhetor's choice of metaphors tells us about the audience he or she is identifying with. A culturetype metaphor is significant for a particular culture. For example, in the United States a person who succeeds "hits a home run"; this baseball metaphor would be understood only in cultures that play the game. Archetypal metaphors, in contrast, are rooted in the experience of all people; they include concepts such as light and darkness. Archetypal metaphors are especially potent because they give the message a sense of stability; they usually have long histories and "are among the most powerful a speaker can summon, since they not only enhance the emotional impact of the speech, but identify the audience strongly with the speaker's purpose and align them against all that he opposes."[25] This analysis looks not only at the metaphoric clusters but also at significance in a particular metaphor type.

Another line of inquiry is how Sheen positioned himself in his television text. One way to uncover this is by using a theoretical framework that suggests that the rhetor constructs an implied auditor and an implied author within the text. This is not necessarily a real person, but images or personas that are constructed by the author to represent himself and the ideal audience that he tries to appeal to. The text was examined with special attention to how Sheen positioned himself, his peers, and the audience within the anecdotes he told. Also noted were his use of space to position himself physically in relation to the television camera, and how he related to his audience's laughter and applause.

The interaction between content and structure creates the persuasive message to which listeners respond. Structure is what the rhetor does to shape the message. In this study I look at questions of structure such as how the message was organized and what elements Sheen emphasized.

Each chapter examines how Sheen shaped his message for television by looking, in historical context, at a theme that emerged from the text. Chapter 1 provides a biographical overview of Sheen's life. Chapter 2 analyzes Bishop Sheen's response to the changes and tensions that Americans faced in the Cold War society of the fifties. Chapter 3 shows how Sheen implicitly supported a hegemonic place for Catholicism while explicitly trying to accommodate a plurality of religious belief on the part of others. Chapter 4 looks at how the role of Mary emerged in Catholicism and how it tied in with the role of women in fifties society; this model of womanhood is motivated by a need to sustain the authority of the church in a secular culture. Chapter 5 examines how Sheen responds to the expectations associated with the conflicting roles of ministry in American popular culture and in Catholicism, including expectations for his role as television celebrity. Sheen succeeded by balancing competing ideologies within his message through his appeals to the past and his reconstruction of a perfected medieval society as the solution to American tensions in the fifties. This argument is one that has been revived by traditional Catholics in the 1990s; a return to the theology of the fifties has become their solution to the problems of contemporary times. Other Catholics want to disown this part of their heritage as an embarrassment to free thought. The final chapter sums up Sheen's ideology and stresses the timeliness of his message as Catholics became assimilated into mainstream American society. It shows that current tensions within Catholicism are rooted in this era.

I
The Shaping of a Medieval Knight for a Modern World

Months before Bishop Fulton Sheen's death in 1979, Pope John Paul II, visiting Saint Patrick's Cathedral in New York, gave him a brotherly embrace that was broadcast, amid the drama of a papal visit, on national television. The pope whispered to Sheen, "You have been a loyal son of the Church."[1] These words and this image captured the core of Sheen's life. Sheen spent the last sixty of his eighty-four years as a priest, but his rootedness in the church went back far longer.

Sheen's life stressed his loyalty as heir to the tradition of Catholicism. His own autobiography, *Treasure in Clay,* says little about his family of birth and much about his mentors and superiors within the family of Catholicism. In this latter family Bishop John Spalding, the first bishop of Peoria, was an important progenitor. Spalding was descended from the English founders of the Catholic colony that became known as Maryland. He provided a lineage for Sheen, the grandson of Irish immigrants, into the tradition of American Catholicism. Spalding was a leader in the Irish Catholic Colonization Association, which encouraged Irish Catholics to move into the Midwest; perhaps this is what brought the Sheen family to El Paso, Illinois.

One day when the eight-year-old Sheen was serving Bishop Spalding's mass, he dropped a wine cruet, shattering the silence of Saint Mary's Cathedral. The boy was terrified of the possible consequences. However, after mass the bishop put his arm around Sheen and predicted that one day he would be a student at Louvain University in Belgium. His prediction proved accurate.

The two men's lives and interests connected in many ways. Spalding was a significant force in the establishment of a Catholic university in Washington, D.C.; Sheen became a student and later a professor in its graduate school of philosophy. Most importantly, both Sheen and

Spalding were spokespersons for the value of education and for the importance of Catholic education within the American system.

Spalding advocated separation of church and state to preserve the quality of American moral life and freedom. He urged the repeal of the Edwards Law, which advocated the rights of the public school board to intervene in parochial schools. The law was declared unconstitutional in 1892, three years before Sheen's birth. Spalding wanted a Catholic Church that was free of government control yet able to develop its own, uniquely American characteristics.

Sheen, in contrast, favored prayer in public schools as a way to instill religious morals in American school children. Asked by a congressional committee in 1964 what the school prayer would be, he responded, "In God We Trust." His support of school prayer stirred criticism from *Christian Century,* however, and he stopped short of supporting an amendment to the U.S. Constitution regarding this matter.

The contrast between Spalding's and Sheen's approaches shows how American Catholics had assimilated over the course of Sheen's life. Spalding had to speak out against government policies that sought to impose rule on the church, whereas Sheen was respected for his input into the American political process.

Spalding lived and ministered in New York City and came to the corn belt diocese only as its bishop. Sheen, in contrast, was a farmer's son who became a sophisticated New Yorker after being consecrated auxiliary bishop of New York in 1951. Indeed, Sheen lived the American dream: a little boy from small-town America who strikes it rich through the electronic media of radio and TV. As he notes in his autobiography, "I was born in the electronic age."[2]

In 1895 in rural Illinois, Edison's electric light was defined as progress. Henry Ford had just produced his first car, and Marconi was continuing his experiments with wireless radio. The United States had forty-four states; Grover Cleveland was president. Billy Sunday gave up his career in baseball to become a revival preacher advocating the assimilation of the massive wave of immigrants into American society. Booker T. Washington spoke at the Atlanta Exposition encouraging blacks—who had been freed from slavery less than fifty years earlier by another famous son of Illinois—to enter mainstream society as tradesmen and craftsmen. America was in a period of progress in the midst of isolationism.

Few places were more isolated than El Paso, Illinois, a community of 1,800 people that was 180 miles south of Chicago. Main Street, where this farming community could gather supplies, was filled with horse-drawn carriages that were only gradually replaced by automobiles. Sheen was born here on May 8, 1895, in the apartment above the hardware store owned by his father and his uncle. El Paso was so rural that even in the 1950s, when TV was becoming a nationwide phenomenon, few citizens of El Paso had sets; those who did had to endure snowy reception as they invited neighbors to join with them and 10 million other viewers to watch their favorite son on *Life Is Worth Living*.

Sheen rarely spoke publicly about El Paso or his early years, but we do know that when much of the El Paso business district was destroyed by fire, his family moved to a farm, once owned by his grandfather, outside Peoria. His father, Newton, prospered by renting land to tenant farmers. Newton never went beyond third grade in school; Sheen's mother, Delia Fulton, stopped at the eighth. Like Sheen, his three younger brothers all found success away from the farm: Joe as a lawyer in Chicago, Tom as a doctor in New York, and Al as an executive for Coca-Cola in New York. Sheen attributes the brothers' success to an ethic of hard work and discipline instilled in them by their parents.

The four Sheen children grew up in a devoutly Catholic environment; Delia led her family in the daily rosary, and parish priests were frequent visitors. In El Paso itself Catholics were in the minority—there were six Protestant churches and one Catholic one. Sheen's maternal grandparents were born in Ireland, as was his father's father; his paternal grandmother was born in Indiana. He was baptized Peter, after the grandfather whom he never knew, but spent so much time with his maternal grandparents that he became known as Fulton.

His autobiography suggests that his parents were firm disciplinarians. Sheen tells of being spanked when his father wrongly believed Sheen had failed to feed the horse that carried the family to church on Sunday. Once, having stolen a ten-cent geranium from the grocery store as a gift for his mother, Sheen was given a lecture on honesty and sent back to the store owner with fifty cents from his piggy bank as restitution. The generous store owner forgave him and gave him two plants. When Sheen complained to his mother that his father was slow to praise him, she explained, "He does not wish to spoil you, but he is telling all the neighbors."[3]

Sheen is quick to acknowledge that he never enjoyed life on the family farm; from his youth he was more fond of reading than farming. The bishop was a natural student, whose education began at Saint Mary's School. His high school was the Spalding Institute in Peoria (named after John Spalding's uncle, himself a bishop), where he was class valedictorian at his graduation in 1913. The Spalding Institute was one of the first central Catholic high schools established in this country. To make it as contemporary as the public school system, the innovative Bishop Spalding included athletics in the curriculum.

While in school Sheen stayed with his maternal grandparents and spent summers on his father's farm. He was never an athlete but learned to play handball, paving the way for his love of tennis as an adult. There is early evidence of his oratorical and dramatic skills. Sheen starred in the annual school play before he and his seven classmates graduated. Sheen describes the Brothers of Mary as "excellent teachers, given to discipline, yet much beloved."

In college at Saint Viators in Bourbonnais, Illinois, he continued to shine as a student, but he notes that it was not always easy for him. He became a debater, and one time the day before a debate Sheen's coach called him aside and said, "Sheen, you're absolutely the worst speaker I've ever heard." The shocked freshman was then ordered to repeat his prepared speech over and over. After an hour, the coach asked Sheen, "Have you any idea what's wrong with the way you're saying that paragraph?" Sheen thought a bit, then said, "I'm not natural." "That's right," the coach said, "you're not natural. Now keep on repeating that paragraph until you do feel natural." The next day Sheen's team won the debate. Critics would later marvel at how Sheen could appear so natural on camera and manage a half-hour presentation without a TelePrompTer.[4]

After graduation from college in 1917, Sheen acted on the desire he had had from early childhood and went to Saint Paul's Seminary in Minnesota to pursue his studies for the priesthood. He was ordained on September 20, 1919, at the age of twenty-four. Sheen was not destined for service in a parish but was immediately sent first to Catholic University in Washington, D.C., and then to Louvain University in Belgium, where he graduated with a doctorate in philosophy and the higher honor of Agrégé en Philosophie. He received the Cardinal Mercier Award, named after Louvain's founder and given about every ten years for excellence. While in Europe he was a frequent visitor to the shrine of Our Lady at Lourdes; over his lifetime he would make visits thirty times. In 1926, after receiving his degree, he became a noted preacher in the London suburb of Soho, where he served as assistant pastor for a year while teaching at Saint Edmund's College in Ware, England.

Although Sheen was offered teaching positions at both Oxford University and Columbia University, the local bishop ordered him back to Peoria. There he worked as a parish priest, serving at Saint Patrick's Church, which had been modeled after Saint Patrick's Cathedral in New York. When he had been at Saint Patrick's for nearly a year, the bishop called him in and said, "Three years ago I promised you to the faculty of Catholic University." Sheen asked, "Why did you not let me go there when I returned from Europe?" The bishop replied, "Because of the success you had on the other side, I just wanted to see if you would be obedient. So run along now; you have my blessing."[5]

Sheen retold this story often in his writing and speaking. It illustrates his obedient attitude toward the church and his belief that the church knew and could interpret the will of God. A second example illustrates this as well. Early in life Sheen learned a theology that taught him to deny himself in order to receive a greater reward. After college Sheen was offered a scholarship to go on for his doctorate, but on the advice of Father Bergen, his spiritual director at Saint Viators, he tore up the offer so that he could pursue his seminary training first. When he spoke of his graduate studies, he always suggested that God had provided him the greater opportunity to go to Louvain because of his obedience.

Sheen matured in both his biological and spiritual families as a gifted child who was not frequently praised but was encouraged to work harder to achieve success. This was consistent with the Scholastic ideology (sometimes called neoscholasticism) in which he became proficient at Louvain. That Scholasticism, originally espoused by followers of Saint Thomas Aquinas, promised that perfection was attainable through hard work and obedience to the greater will of designated authority, the church. This system was grounded in a belief in a natural, ahistorical order. Fixed forms in the universe were mirrored in nature, which reflected the truth. The church, in the spirit of Scholastic thought, believed itself to be the primary interpreter of God's laws as seen in nature. The papal encyclical of 1879, *Aeterni patris,* stressed the need to revive the teaching of Aquinas. Future popes encouraged that emphasis until Vatican II, after which the church focused less on Scholastic thought. The fact that Scholasticism claimed that the church was the ultimate interpreter of the truth worked well to legitimate papal authority. This was an age of upheaval within the universal church because of its changing political position in Europe at the end of the eighteenth century. The upheaval continued into the twentieth century, when the pope condemned modernism, which threatened church authority. The stress on Scholasticism provided a way of increasing centralization for the church, which was facing dissension in a changing society, while bonding American Catholicism to a European ideology from the Middle Ages. Louvain University became a center for the teaching of Scholasticism. Sheen's upbringing and personality thus made him the perfect candidate to popularize neoscholasticism, and he always grounded his ideals in that ideology—even when speaking against Marxism.

Sheen taught a graduate course in philosophy at Catholic University each semester (although his popularity as a preacher often took him away from the university during his career). Ironically, at the founding of Catholic University a generation earlier, Bishop Spalding had encouraged Catholic academics to embrace philosophies other than Scholasticism. This points to another key difference between Spalding and Sheen. The Church of Rome advocated neoscholasticism as a way to preserve its authority at the turn of the century; Spalding was thus demonstrating his independence from Rome. But Sheen would show his subservience to and respect for Rome by embracing the recommended philosophical system.

Early on his preaching got him involved in the medium of radio. Sheen was the first priest to preach on *The Catholic Hour* when it began on the National Broadcasting Company in 1930. But radio was not new to him. In 1928 the Paulist Fathers had invited him to give a series of talks on WLWL in New York. He also appeared on the first religious telecast in 1940 and was narrator of the March of Time film *The Story of the Vatican*.

Sheen was not the first Catholic priest to gain mass media celebrity. The experience of Father Charles Coughlin, the radio priest of the 1930s and 1940s, provides a context for understanding Sheen's celebrity on TV and his restraint in discussion of certain topics. Coughlin began his radio career in 1926 as he built his Church of the Little Flower in Royal Oak, Michigan; he found the medium a lucrative way to raise funds for his new suburban parish. Coughlin's lilting voice became a source of consolation and a confidence builder during the Depression, reaching a national audience that sometimes approached 40 million. As Coughlin became more popular, however, his messages became more controversial. He condemned Roosevelt and his New Deal programs, supported fascism against Communism, and upheld Mussolini, Franco, and Hitler as heroes. He became more and more vocal in his anti-Semitic condemnations of Jewish bankers. Coughlin became powerful enough to organize his own political party, and when the major radio networks dropped his broadcasts, he organized his own independent network of radio stations. He publicly criticized Cardinal William Henry O'Connell of Boston but could not be silenced by the church because Bishop Michael Gallagher of Detroit, his own superior, protected him. Only when the bishop died was the church able to intervene. When it was discovered that Coughlin had invested listeners' contributions in his secretary's name, Coughlin was finally silenced.

Perhaps because of Coughlin, Sheen was always hesitant to make any public political statements. Sheen grounded his television messages in what he described as ethical thought and steered away from controversy.[6] Unlike Cardinal Spellman, who was a key relative of Sheen's in the family of Catholicism, Sheen avoided explicitly discussing the tactics of Senator Joseph McCarthy and his House Un-American Activities Committee. Spellman openly supported McCarthy; Sheen chose to demonstrate his anti-Communism by addressing philosophical issues that kept him securely in the mind-set of mainstream America during the Cold War.[7]

On June 11, 1951, Sheen was ordained a bishop at the Church of Saints John and Paul in Rome. He confesses in his autobiography that he prayed throughout his seminary years to become a bishop. The Catholic historian Monsignor John Tracy Ellis had been living in Sheen's Washington home when word came in 1938 that Spellman had been appointed a bishop. Ellis writes that Sheen was so depressed he took to bed for several days; he had hoped for the position for himself.[8]

In 1950, the year before his ordination as bishop, Sheen had been appointed national director of the organization Propagation of the Faith, founded in the seventeenth century to spread Catholicism. Its offices were in New York under the authority of Cardinal Spellman.

Sheen was responsible for the support of church missionaries abroad. He was a very successful fund-raiser, raising over $200 million in his sixteen years in office—more than double the sum raised throughout the rest of the world.[9] Sheen contributed to the missions his stipend of twenty-six thousand dollars per season from his television program, making him a great American philanthropist at a time when the American Dream portrayed America as the world's savior. Through his organization, Sheen's fund-raising helped bolster this part of the American ideology and gave evidence to the claim that America was a benevolent nation.

It was during this time that Sheen had his falling out with Spellman, his one-time promoter. Sheen never spoke publicly about it, but he hints in his autobiography about problems with other clerics, saying, "I had to be brought through trials both inside and outside the Church before I could understand the full meaning of my life. It is not enough to be a priest; one had to become a victim." Sheen goes on to say that he does not want to pass judgment on others and that doing so would only divide the church.

Writer John Cooney, however, maintains that Spellman would often dip into Propagation funds to help his own pet charities and those of his friends. This irritated Sheen, who thought that money sent to Propagation should be spent solely by Propagation. The conflict exploded when Sheen appealed to the Vatican in 1957 over what came to be called the "Milk Fund Scandal." Spellman had entrusted Propogation to distribute surplus milk acquired from the government; Spellman wanted money from Propagation in turn. Sheen refused to pay for the milk, claiming Spellman had received it for free. In the end Pope Pius XII settled the matter in Sheen's favor.[10]

Sheen's silence in this matter is consistent with his loyalty to the church. He was very sensitive to issues of scandal, especially among clergy, whom he held to higher standards. He did not except himself; he was a workaholic who spent long hours reading his mail and preparing his talks. Ellis praises Sheen for his hard work and his generosity of character, noting that he was with Sheen one day when Sheen received a check for sixty-five thousand dollars from the estate of Genevieve Brady. Sheen immediately contributed the sum to the maternity hospital he had built for black women in Mobile, Alabama.[11]

At the same time Ellis notes that Sheen was not on a pedestal but struggled with his vanity. One can see this in his own writings. Sheen says he never counted his many converts because they did not belong to him but to God—but he does drop the names of his more famous converts, who included Henry Ford II, heir to the auto industry; Fritz Kreisler, noted musician; Heywood Broun, distinguished journalist; Louis Budenz, editor of the Communist paper *The Daily Worker;* Horace Mann, director of President Hoover's anti-Catholic 1928 campaign against Al Smith; Jo Mielziner, who designed Sheen's television production set; Virginia Mayo, screen star; and Clare Booth Luce, member of Congress, later ambassador to Italy, and wife of *Time* editor in chief Henry Luce. Sheen became so popular for his convert instructions that he taped them, allowing potential converts to listen to seven at a time and then join him for a session to raise questions. This method freed up Sheen for other tasks.

Sheen's name was not unfamiliar to Edwin Broderick, who, as a seminarian, remembered sitting in Studio 8H at Rockefeller Center watching Sheen broadcast on the radio. As a young priest Broderick, later the bishop of Albany, would help create and become the producer of Sheen's television's program.[12]

Broderick had been appointed the church's first director of radio and television by Cardinal Spellman. With the assignment in the early fifties to be a liaison between the church and public media, he sought to promote the positive dimensions of television as a teaching and entertainment tool. Many Catholics worked in early television and were so receptive to the input of the church that they formed a group called CARTA, the Catholic Association of Radio, Television and Advertising.

This was an age when television was experimenting with different genres of presentation. The Federal Communications Commission, fearing that television would erode public morality, insisted that the networks offer public service programming. That requirement benefited mainstream Protestant, Catholic, and Jewish groups because local networks gave them free access by producing their programs as a public service. Broderick had produced many programs that were broadcast locally in New York, including *Lamp Unto My Feet,* a program of questions and answers about the faith, as well as a Catholic news program.

Broderick recalls being approached by James Caddigan, program director for the DuMont network. They were looking for someone to fill a "graveyard" spot, a television spot that no sponsor would pay for because of the unbeatable competition—in this case, Milton Berle, who in the early fifties was nicknamed "Mr. Television." Thinking of Sheen, Broderick said, "I've got just the man for you." Caddigan volunteered that Sheen could do whatever he wanted during the half hour; DuMont would air the program as a public service to fulfill FCC requirements. Sheen thus made his way onto television in the same way as Smokey the Bear and public service health announcements.[13]

Bishop Sheen was enthusiastic about the idea of a television program. He was experienced in radio and was already a celebrity speaker. Sheen's idea was to broadcast his convert instructions in a different church each week and allow ten minutes for questions and answers from the future converts, who would be seated in the body of the church. DuMont had no problem with the idea of convert instruction but cautioned against questions and answers from the listeners because the bishop risked being put in an awkward situation on live television. DuMont also rejected the idea of using different churches because no Catholic church in New York was wired for television, and it would be a great expense to do a remote broadcast. DuMont wanted to spend as little as possible; after all, they thought nothing would come of the program. Much of early television was broadcast live from New York's theater district, and DuMont offered to construct a set of a bishop's study in a Broadway theater.

That was how Sheen came to speak from the stage of the Adelphi Theatre on West Fifty-Fourth Street off Broadway on Tuesday evenings. He started with three stations in New York, Washington, and Chicago on February 12, 1952. When NBC and CBS Trendex ratings dropped five points each, it was attributed to Sheen's success. DuMont was swamped with 250 letters of congratulations; within a week the network had received 3,000 fan letters.[14]

Sheen never did give convert instructions; on his own he decided to speak about topics of moral living that related to all religious groups. When criticized by fellow clergy for not being more explicit in his propagation of the Catholic faith, he said, "If the seed falls they have 52,000 branch offices of the Catholic Church where they can get instructions."[15] On the radio, in contrast, Sheen was sponsored by a religious group, so his message was firmly grounded in Catholic doctrine. Originally the TV program was to be called *Is Life Worth Living?* but Sheen decided to be more positive with the title *Life Is Worth Living.*

Broderick recalls that it was always difficult to get program titles from Sheen more than a week in advance, because Sheen planned the program week by week, meditating on his ideas during his daily holy hour in his private chapel. Throughout the week he would often test his ideas on office staff and friends. He made only a few written notes, scribbling them on scrap paper. By the day before the program he would be ready to practice his delivery, pacing in his office. Sometimes he would practice by giving his talk in Italian for the Convent of Franciscan Sisters on Forty-Fifth Street; often he would present it to a friend in French.

Broderick recalls that once Sheen was called to Rome for a meeting of the directors of Propagation of the Faith, as a result missing two broadcasts. Sheen came up with the idea of preparing three programs back to back with only minutes in between to bring in new audiences. One program would be broadcast live and the other two taped. Broderick was amazed at how Sheen could work so intensely and not even repeat a joke.

Sheen required few instructions from his stage director. He was keenly interested in the program's production and spent time each week watching other shows, "partly for relaxation, partly to learn." He believed that a television speaker should never sit down. He admired the good timing of Rochester, on *The Jack Benny Show;* some ideas, he recognized, required rapid speech and some long pauses.[16] Sheen skillfully employed these tactics. Jackie Gleason, who became Sheen's friend, would often sit in the production booth with Broderick and talk about Sheen's impressively natural timing. Sheen was proud of the fact that he could speak for twenty-eight minutes—without any cue cards—and end on cue. Edward Bunetta, the program director, wanted to give Sheen signals warning him that he had five minutes to speak. Sheen said, "No, just give me a thirty-second signal." His colleagues were amazed at his ability to end on the mark.[17]

Broderick feared that Sheen's religious garb of cape and cassock would distract viewers, who might "count the number of buttons on his cassock rather than listen to his message." He and other New York priests thought it would be better if Sheen appeared in a black suit. When Broderick gently broached this topic with the bishop, Sheen was firm that he would wear the cassock and cape.

Sheen even found his own theme music. Sometime after converting the noted musician Fritz Kreisler, Sheen asked him to write a theme for his program. Kreisler gave him several pieces to choose from. He

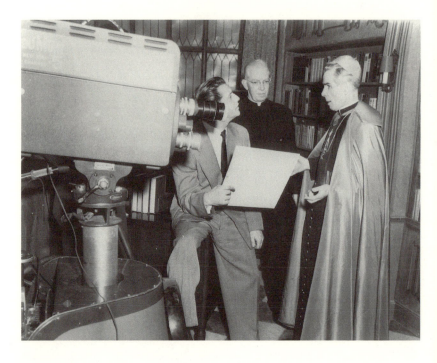

Bishop Sheen, director Edward Bunetta, and an assistant, Monsignor
McBride, discuss the next program in the television study at the Adelphi
Theatre. Courtesy of the Sheen Archives, Diocese of Rochester.

chose "Vienna March" but told Kriesler, "Fritz, this is the one I like,
but I can't march on the stage. Can you change it to waltz time?" At
first Kreisler said it could not be done, but at the urging of his wife he
transposed it for Sheen.[18]

After the success of the first programs, Ross Siragusa, a devout
Catholic and the owner of the Admiral Corporation, makers of televisions and electrical appliances, approached the archdiocese of New
York with the offer to sponsor the program, giving a commercial at
the beginning and one at the end. At first DuMont rejected the idea
because the program would then no longer fulfill the FCC public service requirement, but in time they gave way.

Sheen's chief critic during his television years in the fifties was the
liberal Christian publication *Christian Century*. It was "close to blas-
phemy," they claimed, for Sheen to equate television with the incarnation of Jesus. The editors claimed that television was a medium out

to provide commercial profit for its sponsors. However, even *Christian Century* noted somewhat cynically that Sheen was "Catholicism's most gifted performer."[19] Sheen was an innovator in bringing religion into prime-time television. (Billy Graham had had a short-lived television program in 1951 called *Hour of Decision,* but he soon decided to use his crusade format instead, buying blocks of time during certain periods.) Sheen was the first religious communicator to have a sponsor for a program in prime time.

Sheen's autobiography devotes only one chapter to his television career, perhaps because he wanted to highlight his role as a preacher rather than as a television celebrity. In fact Sheen titles the chapter "The Electronic Gospel." Perhaps downplaying his television celebrity status was a way to express the humility and self-deprecation that fills the pages of his book and was part of the spirituality of Catholicism in the tradition of Scholasticism. Nonetheless, Sheen's program became a national phenomenon. Jackie Gleason, who also started on DuMont, compared his show with Sheen's and remarked, "But I don't have your writers!" A young actor wrote to Sheen and asked if he could take his name as his stage name; he became Martin Sheen. Sheen does not mention in his autobiography that he received an Emmy as Most Outstanding Personality in 1952 (defeating Jimmy Durante, Arthur Godfrey, Lucille Ball, and Edward Murrow, and thanking his four writers, Matthew, Mark, Luke, and John).[20] Nor does he spend much time on his relationships with various celebrities, focusing instead on the popes he had met.

In 1955 the DuMont network was in financial trouble and fell apart. Sheen moved to ABC on Thursdays opposite *The Bob Cummings Show* and Groucho Marx's *You Bet Your Life.* (When asked why he changed, he replied, "I wanted to be able to watch Milton Berle," his competition in earlier seasons.)[21] In the 1956-57 season his program aired opposite *I Love Lucy,* the top-rated show, and NBC's *Medic.* By 1956 he was appearing on 123 television stations, and 300 radio stations carried the audio portion of his programs. The program terminated in 1957.

Sheen was back on TV in 1959 in a syndicated program called *The Bishop Sheen Program.* He did three short series in the 1960s: *The Life of Christ* in 1962, *Quo Vadis America?* in 1964, and *The Bishop Sheen Program* in 1966, which aired in color. He narrated the visit of Pope Paul VI to the United Nations in New York in the midst of Vatican II.

In the 1970s he did a series called *What Now, America?* In this series he spoke of a moral conflict within America itself.

At the conclusion of Vatican II, in 1966, Pope Paul VI appointed Sheen, then seventy-one years old, bishop of Rochester, New York. Sheen arrived in his new diocese with enthusiasm and new ideas raised by Vatican II, even though it was rumored by some that this was a demotion. Rochester was a small diocese in the shadow of Cardinal Spellman, who was telling New Yorkers that there would be no changes in his diocese after Vatican II.

Sheen's years in Rochester were the darkest in the life of a man accustomed to the limelight. The church was in a period of turmoil with the changes in Catholic liturgy from Latin to English and the transition to a more egalitarian, people-centered structure. The changing times brought an exodus of priests and nuns from their communities and a questioning of the order that had seemed so rock-solid. At the same time American society endured its own darkness with riots turning city streets into bloodbaths over civil rights and American involvement in Vietnam.

Sheen's first move as bishop was to rename the chancery office the Pastoral Center. He set up councils of priests and laity so they could have a voice in diocesan governance. He appointed an urban vicar to deal with the problems of poverty and homelessness in the inner city. He taxed parish communities that built new buildings and contributed the tax to funds for the poor. He radically reformed seminary education, requiring psychological testing for candidates. He set up a board of laity to have input into the acceptance of candidates to the priesthood. He affiliated his Saint Bernard's Seminary with the Protestant Colgate-Rochester Divinity School. He inaugurated courses in social work and ecumenism for the seminarians. He brought in professors from Europe and from other religious denominations to teach. He opened dialogue by speaking in Protestant and Jewish places of worship. For a Catholic to enter such spaces would have been unheard of a few years earlier.

Within his own diocese he was one of the first bishops to raise the age for reception of the sacrament of confirmation from sixth grade to high school. It was hoped that this would create a generation of Catholics more mature and educated in their faith. Sheen also got national press when, in a sermon at Sacred Heart Cathedral in 1967 on President Johnson's National Day of Prayer for Racial Peace in America, he called for the unilateral withdrawal of American troops from Vietnam. He used the principle of Saint Augustine, claiming that the moneys spent on munitions and the lives lost could better be used in American cities for the poor and racially outcast. This must have stirred the hawkish Spellman in New York, who had proclaimed his support of the troops with the words, "My country right or wrong." Sheen, the once ardent anti-Communist, could not now be easily labeled a conservative. He was the first American Catholic bishop to speak out as he did. Two years later, however, he withdrew his claim, stating that the situation in Vietnam had changed.

Sheen again made headlines that earned him many enemies in Rochester when he spoke out against hiring practices that discriminated against minorities at the Kodak Company and other leading Rochester businesses. But the darkest moment for Sheen came when he announced a secret deal to give Saint Brigid's school and inner-city parish to the government so it could build housing for the poor. The offer of the property, worth an estimated seven hundred thousand dollars, was commended by *Commonweal* and *Christian Century,* but *Ave Maria* noted that although Sheen's intentions were good, it had been "a public relations bruise." Sheen had not consulted advisers in the diocese, saying later that the government had asked him to keep negotiations secret. Nor had he consulted with the pastor and parishioners of Saint Brigid's, who were outraged by the failure of the great communicator to communicate. A petition against the action was signed by 130 priests, who argued that the parish was already serving the poor, and Sheen was forced to retract his offer. In a rare public discussion of the issue, on *The Dick Cavett Show* on January 30, 1970, Sheen described his failure in Rochester by saying, "I was intellectually too young for the old and psychologically too old for the young."

The incident at Saint Brigid's encapsulated Sheen's problems in Rochester. He had had little experience as a parish priest and in carrying out his ideas forgot the need for consultation, often choosing the dramatic over the practical. He did apologize for his mistakes on his premature departure from the diocese shortly after.

The incident left Sheen disillusioned, and he retired in 1969, just short of the mandatory retirement age of seventy-five. He returned to New York City, where he continued to speak and write until his death. In July 1977 he underwent open-heart surgery. The tireless worker notes in his autobiography: "The second year after the open-heart

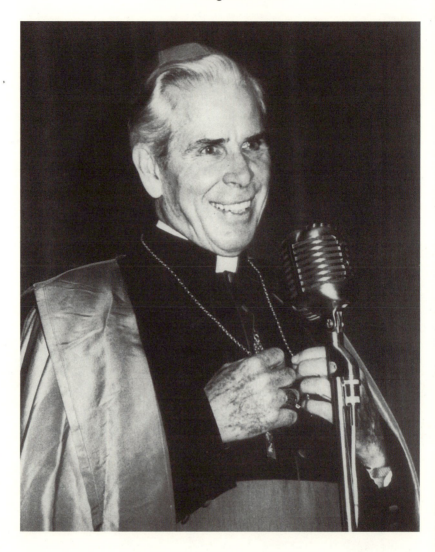

Even in his later years Sheen was known for his corny jokes, piercing eyes, and paternal warmth. Courtesy of the Sheen Archives, Diocese of Rochester.

surgery, because of overwork, I was confined to my bed again for many months. During that time I instructed four converts and validated two marriages. The horizontal apostolates may sometimes be just as effective as the vertical."

He died on December 9, 1979, the day after the feast of the Immaculate Conception, honoring the lady whose troubadour he had been. It had been his wish to die on or near a feast of the Madonna. He was buried beside his onetime friend and rival, Cardinal Spellman, in a crypt under the pulpit where he had so often preached.

Fulton Sheen had come along way from El Paso, Illinois. During his eighty-four years he wrote more than sixty books. He wrote a syndicated column in the Catholic press entitled "God Love You" and another in the secular press, "Bishop Sheen Writes." While at Propagation of Faith, supervising more than 130 local offices, he edited *Mission* magazine and *World Mission*. His *Life Is Worth Living* series is the edited compilation of his television talks. He was named titular archbishop to the See of Newport (Wales) on his retirement. A collection of his writings was republished, in *From the Angel's Blackboard*, on the centenary of his birth.

2
Quest for Stability in the Midst of Change

The Castle of Perseverance, a morality play dating from the early fifteenth century, enacts the struggle between the virtues and the vices for the soul of an individual journeying from birth toward death, en route to heaven or hell. The virtues are supported by a good angel; the vices—representing the seven deadly sins—by a bad angel.[1] The good angel advises, "Man, think of thine ending day when thou shalt be closed under clay! And if thou think of that array, certain, thou shalt not sin. Man consider the end! And in eternity you will not fail." But the bad angel urges the individual to enjoy the flesh and the world: "Thy flesh thou shalt foster and feed with lovely life's food. With the world thou mayest be bold till thou be sixty winters old. When thy nose waxes cold, then mayest thou draw to the good."[2]

The struggle concludes on judgment day when, despite having followed the bad angel, the individual is saved by the plea of Mercy to God. Mercy reminds God of the saving blood of Jesus' cross for sinners: "Lord, though that man hath done more wrong than good, if he die in very contrition, Lord, the least drop of thy blood for his sins maketh satisfaction. As you died, Lord, on the cross, grant me my petition! Let me, Mercy, be his food. And grant him thy salvation."

In sharp contrast to the world depicted in *Waiting for Godot,* which was being staged on Broadway a few blocks away from Sheen's telecast, the medieval morality play mapped out life with clear-cut boundaries that labeled the distance between good and evil by keeping in mind the end of life. It was a didactic play illustrating how the devil traps the individual and how one can attain divine grace by living a virtuous life. The morality play's emergence was heavily influenced by church doctrine. Unlike the miracle or mystery plays of the time, however, it was performed in the secular milieu, not connected to church liturgy or to a particular season.

The form of the medieval morality play is representative of the message of Bishop Sheen because he speaks on a Broadway stage using the secular medium of popular culture—television. But because he is a bishop, he speaks with the approval of the church. He uses television and popular vernacular, rather than Latin or the formal language of church ritual, to shape a message for the purposes of the church, even if not explicitly for conversion. This chapter explores Sheen's morality play and examines how he constructed clearly defined boundaries between good and evil by building on two archetypal root metaphors common to classical literature: drama and journey.[3] The structure of his message complemented his vision of an ordered hierarchical world where unity was an alternative to the tensions of the fifties.

Those tensions were created by shifting economic, social, and demographic patterns. In the postwar years two-thirds of the population moved into metropolitan areas; during the same period the structure of the family changed from extended to nuclear. Because of the emerging youth subculture that resulted, the Beatniks and rock 'n' roll were able to come of age. It was an age of mechanization in agriculture and new consumer appliances in the home. The civil rights movement was introduced: Rosa Parks's 1955 arrest for refusing to sit in the back of the bus in Montgomery, Alabama, led to a year-long bus boycott by Montgomery blacks. It was also the time when Catholics and Jews in record numbers left behind their immigrant roots.[4]

The Korean War complicated the picture. According to a Gallup poll, two out of three Americans felt that World War III had already begun. The Cold War between Communist nations and the United States, with its attendant propaganda, added fuel to the fears and anxiety. For example, McCarthy's claim in 1953 that he had a list of 205 Communists working in the State Department created a witch hunt. Books by Henry David Thoreau were burned: progressive education was questioned. Paranoia and fear became common. Americans turned to corporate conformity, the new consumer culture, or religiosity, the stress on religious practice, for relief.

In the corporate workplace an ethic of conformity to the structure and respect for authority emerged. By 1952 one-third of American corporations were using personality tests to determine whether a potential employee would fit.[5]

America's new prosperity and technology filtered down to the individual in the new consumer culture. New household gadgets, from dishwashers to food blenders, promised to make life more efficient and leisurely, calling into question the Calvinist work ethic. In this era of the credit card, anything could be bought on an installment plan. By the middle of the decade, 60 percent of all new automobiles were bought with as little as one hundred dollars down. The new consumerism that flowed from America's heightened status created new tensions for individual Americans, pressing them to conform to marketers' standards and to pay off the resulting monthly bills. Keeping up with the Joneses became the norm as "the nation of shoppers" came under the rule of slogans and advertising promises of a better future for the new "crowd culture."[6]

Television advertising was the voice of consumerism, dictating what each family should buy. Even children were targeted as potential customers.[7] Each program had a corporate sponsor selling its products. At the same time television was helping to shape a national consumer culture with cohesive symbols that modified the definitions of family, gender roles, and patriotism. Many Americans chose to conform to these new meanings.

Calvinist principles were being challenged as society changed. Protestantism itself was split over the question of involvement in the contemporary world. The fundamentalist groups wanted to maintain literal interpretations of the Bible, while the liberal branches wanted to adapt to changing times. The latter group preached a social consciousness rather than individual salvation. Only in their effort to battle the perceived threat of Catholicism, whose numbers and organizational structures were growing, did the denominations unite.

America's religious identity had always been closely tied to America's belief in itself. Thus, when mainstream Protestantism was suffering an identity crisis, it threatened the ideology of what America was all about. In this tense milieu, participation in religion became an act of patriotism, as well as of individual sanctity. Revivalists like Billy Graham offered one way for Protestants to preserve a religious identity. Graham stressed the power of individual conversion from sin and encouraged his listeners to attend the church of their choice. By labeling Communism the enemy of American piety, he created a clear distinction between good and evil. Graham emphasized that the Bible was the answer to all problems of alienation in an industrial age. He preached in mass rallies where individuals, no matter what their religious affiliation, could step forward and make a decision for Christ.

If this didn't work to reduce tension, psychology would step in .(as we will see later in this chapter) to help resolve the crisis of changing times.[8] Sheen embraced religiosity, the new consumerism, the corporate conformity as solutions to social tensions, but found psychology a threat to his ideology. His own message shared Graham's distinction between good and evil, but it took a different form.

Sheen presents a root metaphor that describes human life as a drama between good and evil, in the spirit of the morality play. It provides an outlet to reduce tension. Good and evil are clearly defined. By playing out the drama, persons can know where they stand amid the social tensions of the fifties and the fears of a nuclear age. Sheen extends the drama metaphor to describe a rehearsal whose characters—all of us who act—wear masks. "In a crisis," he says, "masks are torn off and people begin to assess themselves as they really are." He concludes, "Every crisis in history is a rehearsal for the last judgment. . . . So it is when our characters are put face to face with such a crisis as this; we begin to reveal everything that has gone into our lives. We will not be any different—we just merely unmask ourselves and show the depth of our character. We rehearse, actually rehearse for putting ourselves on the side of the sheep or of the goats. If it ever comes, we do not know yet precisely how we will act, but one thing is certain: goodness will not lose."[9] In the biblical narrative of the final judgment, God divides humanity into two groups, the sheep (the good) and the goats (the bad)—the protagonists and antagonists in the drama. By characterizing the fifties crisis as a rehearsal and placing it in the context of the greater drama, the last judgment, he gives meaning to the situation. Sheen's last sentence reminds listeners of the Scholastic ideal that good can never be eliminated because God constitutes perfect goodness. This gives reason for optimism in a changing world. Each individual is naturally drawn to this good but because of imperfect human knowledge can be misled to choose evil. Billy Graham, raised in the Calvinist tradition, would emphasize the sinful nature of the person, but like Sheen he would take a positive tone in that by choosing God there was hope that individuals could play a more active role in their salvation.

Sheen speaks of the drama in terms of "the great tragedy of our world . . . that most people have no one to love and forget the love of God." One reason for the tragedy is that "we surround ourselves with a good many masks. . . . we do not know ourselves." He expands on the tragedy, saying, "Our tragedy today is due basically to human will opposing Divine Will."[10] This polarity between good and evil, prominent in the medieval morality play, is also central to Sheen's text. God is forgotten and the individual is led away from good but (and here we see evidence of Scholastic theology) could look within to discover the natural law and, ultimately, God. The tragedy is that people are misled by the imperfection of sense perception; reality is masked, and the human becomes opposed to the divine.

The consequence is a drama that is dull because people are not orators, suited to the genre of drama, but are more passive: they are readers. Sheen's preference for orators indicates the traditional value of Roman Catholicism that the individual must play an active role in his or her salvation, speaking out in the drama of good and evil. Sheen says, "Our Western world lacks fire. . . . we are cold, dull and apathetic. That is one of the reasons why in our Western world there are no longer any orators. We have only readers in the world. Why readers? Simply because they don't have enough in their own hearts to speak out. . . . If we love God we ought to be able to talk about him."[11]

There is hope in this drama, because the actors have talent (which comes, as we will see, from God), giving them choice in overcoming tragedy. Whereas a mask disguises real character, talent is an internal or more spiritual quality. The masks and colorful staging of the morality play attracted listeners to the deeper message, but the church always valued most the more genuine message. Similarly, for Sheen talent was valued more highly because it came from within. In the same way, Scholasticism taught that virtue was learned by habit but in time became part of the person rather than remaining exterior. Sheen sums it up, saying, "Whatever talent we have we will use to the best of our ability. There are other talents we do not have, we will not be able to use." Referring to his own talent for being on television, Sheen notes, "I have a certain talent for it. . . . The good Lord has blessed me . . . but I'll also recognize my limitations. I'll never come out here and dance."[12]

Sheen extends the drama metaphor when he refers to the actor and the stage to illustrate the person who merely uses the exterior and has not internalized and used genuine talent in moral living: "The state of man is something like an actor. There are some people who never forget they were on stage." He continues by discussing an actor who played the role of Lincoln until he was retired; then "the glory of the theater was gone and he had to cover up the shame of the loss of that glory by parading in the costume of Abraham Lincoln." Sheen draws an analogy to the actor who needed the costume: "Those who go in for an excess of luxury in clothing are generally those who are poverty-stricken on the inside."[13] Something on the inside is closest to virtue in Sheen's ideology.

America's role in the drama, described in more detail later in this book, is a supporting one, like that of a stagehand or an assistant. Sheen says that America's "role is to roll up the curtain of the Eastern world"[14]—the Iron Curtain of the Cold War. Here Sheen's message parallels Graham's, although Sheen is less likely to embrace an un-questioning attitude of American righteousness.

God participates in this drama as provider of the light. This places God above the drama; Sheen notes that "under the glaring light of the perfect model, the Son of God, then we see our imperfections." But God is more than stage lighting for the drama. Sheen asks, "Should there not be audience contact with humanity?" and then answers his question: "If He is ever to convince man that He loves, He must tell man that He loves and God has spoken. He has spoken in many in-stances. All you need to do is turn over the pages of the Old Testament and you will find written there the speech of God. The Old Testament is something like radio, a speech without vision. . . . He must also be seen, and the New Testament is something like television, adding vi-sion to speech. And God was seen. Seen in the form of a babe first."[15] Sheen baptizes television and radio here by considering them as the media God has used to communicate. That is not surprising, since Scholastic theology recognized that the material was a container for the spiritual.

Sheen's drama has writers who benefit from the light as they write for the audiences. He jokingly refers to the biblical writers in much the same way a television personality would refer to the writers of the stage script: "Here are the names of my four writers . . . Matthew . . . Mark . . . Luke . . . John. . . . They wrote to different audiences and received different light."[16]

Sheen goes on to state that the message of his presentation is not fiction: "This year we thought maybe you'd be much more interested in hearing narratives and biographies. There's so many fictional and imaginative tales in the world, we thought possibly you'd like to hear some real stories of people who really and truly lived, and each week we will give you a different story." Elsewhere he says, "All the stories I tell on this program are true."[17] Once again we see a parallel with medieval drama and art, both heavily influenced by Scholasticism, which believed that the world around us mirrored God's kingdom and truth. Art and drama forms, in Sheen's case stories, mirrored for the laity the deeper truths of the spiritual realm. Sheen's program becomes a drama that can serve as a visible catechism in much the same way as medieval art and drama in the cathedral provided a visible outline of the truth.

Sheen uses the metaphor of a drama to describe the scenes of the salvation story as being replayed in modern society. When he discusses the trial of Christ, he says, "Remember the actors in this drama, as we told you in the beginning, are eternal. The scene could be the Chicago Loop, Times Square on Broadway, Peking, now in Moscow, now in Warsaw. It could be anywhere, and the people are you and me." Sheen talks about "the scene which the Roman soldier saw on Calvary."[18] Judas's betrayal in the biblical story of Christ's crucifixion and the current activity of American traitors are compared as stages of "the mask of patriotism." "When a citizen betrays his country and allies himself with . . . Communists, he wears a mask on the outside that he's patriotic, but on the inside he belongs to Russia. . . . If this mask is the characteristic note of traitors, well then, they are but sons of the man who used their mask; that was Judas."[19]

In another program he refers the strategies of Pilate, who sentenced Jesus to death, to describe contemporary Communist leaders, who are on the side of evil throughout the drama. Jesus came "before a Roman judge whose name was Pontius Pilate . . . who came into that particular land very much like the Soviets are in Poland today."[20] For Sheen, both the Roman invasion of Israel in biblical times and the Soviet invasion of Poland subverted the authority of local leaders and took power from the people.

He goes on to describe Pilate in terms of contemporary pragmatists who deny natural law, which is the basis of Scholasticism's belief in a clearly defined truth. In narrating Pilate's interrogation of Jesus, Sheen says, "Pilate, who had been reading James, Schiller, and Dewey and all the pragmatists . . . Pilate, who had been taught in the school of philosophy that there is no such thing as truth, there is only expediency and utility, sneered 'What is truth?' And he turned his back on it."[21] Pilate misses the fact that Jesus is the truth.

The fact that the characters are prefigured from generation to generation down to contemporary times ties in with Scholasticism's claim that certain forms are universal. In this view, nothing is uncertain—a very different perspective from the modern art and absurdist drama, such as *Waiting for Godot,* of the fifties. All the listener had to do was turn to the past, discern the formula, and follow it; success was guaranteed.

Indeed, Sheen always refers to the past as a solution, because the present has elements that are a replaying of the past. (Graham refers to the past, but not the medieval past. He refers to the Bible as having the answer.) With regard to the societal crisis of the nuclear bomb, Sheen says: "Read the history of the great calamities of the world, in plagues, in famines, in wars and revolutions and you will understand what we can expect of certain characters in the explosion of a hydrogen bomb. Just to explain that human nature has not changed, I will read two accounts taken from 430 B.C. and the other from our own time, 1917." Once again the characters are both good and evil individuals. "In a crisis the good become very good, and the evil become almost diabolical. Masks are torn off and people begin to assess themselves."[22] The characters of good and evil take the same form through history; what changes is the linear timeline of human existence that progresses from situation to situation. In other words, for Sheen history is a drama in which people play out recurring roles. The only thing that changes is the stage (situation) on which the drama is replayed.

Connected to the ideology that good and evil are fixed, unchanging forms throughout history is the place of the teacher in relation to the truth. Teachers have a significant role in the medieval drama because "teachers have one of the noblest vocations God has given to mankind. They are the carriers of the word." Although the drama could not take place without the word, or the script, already present and awaiting discovery, Sheen says that "those who instruct shall shine as stars for all eternity."[23]

Sheen exalts the profession yet subordinates it to the word of truth as found in tradition. He is critical of educators who step beyond the role of "custodians of the truth": "It is all too common in our Western world, particularly in the United States, for educators to go down to Communists masses not to give them the truth of which they are custodians but in order to enjoy the shock and thrill of mass revolutionary movements without intelligent and true direction."[24] The words *shock* and *thrill*—more suited as a response to an amusement or more risque entertainment—disassociate revolutionary movements from a positive role in the medieval drama.

Sheen's emphasis on tradition, as opposed to revolution, breaks with the fifties' emphasis on modernity. He quotes Horace, stating, "That which is past is best." His negative view of the modern world is strikingly contrasted with the glorification of tradition. For example, his objection to Communism is that "Communism is strong only when it borrows some of the moral indignation that has been inherited from the Hebraic-Christian traditions; Communism is weak when it departs from that tradition. Communism has bootlegged and smuggled into its system the decency and morality that have come from the great Hebraic-Christian tradition of the Western world and then uses it to pass judgment on the world."[25]

Sheen is critical of parents and educators who do not preserve tradition: "Youth today is protesting against the older generation. It is because the older generation has not given him that culture and those principles that youth needs and believes that it should have."[26] He repeats the theme, comparing contemporary times and their lack of the "wisdom of elders" to

> the ages where there was a great respect for maturity, for age, for the sagacity and wisdom of the elders. The fashions of the young imitated the fashions of the elders. The fashions of the young imitated the fashions of the old. Just like little girls, for example, want to put up their hair like their mother, put on long skirts and high heels. They have reverence for their mothers. In other ages where there is not that respect for the wisdom of elders, as for example, our own age, it is the aged who imitate the young. They all dress alike.[27]

Consistent with the medieval revival within fifties' Catholicism, Sheen singled out the thirteenth century as an exemplar for virtuous living.[28] There was a great movement of people in the late medieval era from the rural areas to the newly emerging and increasingly prosperous cultural centers of the cities. And like the Roman Catholic

Church and American corporate society in the fifties, the medieval era valued tradition and the authority of hierarchy. The two periods also were characterized by an alliance between state and religion. The paradigm was appealing to both common people and elites because Catholicism had been the dominant force in that era. The medieval paradigm drew on its own intellectual tradition and culture of popular devotions. The Catholic, "haunted by the notion that in being older, Europe is somehow truer to the Catholic tradition than the [individual Catholic] is," turned to European kings and saints as role models. As one observer put it, "The medieval pull operated in a number of ways. For the great majority, simple nostalgia was the key. While some were anxious to fossilize Catholic expression in Gothic stone, others were more concerned with defending the medieval heritage as one component of a general defense of western values. Underneath much of this medievalism, however, was the feeling that somehow the medieval knight and the optimistic American pioneer were cousins."[29]

In the early part of the twentieth century, Catholics were eager to dress up in something other than immigrant rags. The Middle Ages provided a memory of a golden age of Catholic influence and power and a source of pride that mitigated the ambivalence of their transition from poverty to cultural influence and wealth. Sheen was fond of sharing stories about nobility and European kings and queens.

Americans were captivated by images of nobility of ancient times, but with a contemporary twist. Disney succeeded in combining his Cinderella's castle with Main Street USA when his theme park opened in 1955. Many Americans tuned into the 1953 coronation of Elizabeth II of England, fascinated by the royal pageantry. The program *Queen for a Day* offered American housewives a release from the drudgery of everyday routine. Elvis would become the "king of rock 'n' roll." Gothic architecture and learning had been quite popular among sophisticated Protestants in the Victorian era, making the Catholic medieval revival all the more exciting. It gave Catholics, moving into the middle class, a sense of being part of something greater than themselves.

Sheen's emphasis on learning and the medieval professor as a model of truth helped promote the value of Catholic education. The late medieval period was often equated with great universities and learning. It also was a time of great prosperity for the Roman Church because of the reverence and awe of its authority. This reconstructed past was glorified because it suggested a source of truth, but at a price: it sentimentalized truth in a system of easy answers. Locating truth in this reconstruction of the past helped Sheen promote an idealized spirituality that promised security and direction in life. In the process it encouraged conformity to the status quo of social institutions, forcing individuals to look within themselves to solve their problems. Ultimately this opened the way for religion, more specifically the church, to be the authoritative guide in Sheen's moral drama. Sheen's idealized view of the medieval world became a way to live in turbulent times by looking to a past golden age of the church.

Sheen explains that the massive building projects in the late Middle Ages came about because of people's faith in God during that era:

> There was a kind of fever of building. There were fifty cathedrals, many of them almost about the size of Notre Dame in Rheims, Chartres, and Lyons that were built in France. . . . What was it that inspired people in those days to throw up great piles of stone in the air? Faith, certainly. As Ralph Adams Cram said, "We could not build cathedrals like that today simply because we do not have the faith." But in the natural order there was something else; men were always fond of building towers. Hence the Tower of Babel was a dedication to a humanism that was anti-God. The Greeks used to build their towers and monuments to honor philosophers and dramatists. The Greeks honor their generals, the Americans . . . honor their enterprise, but these towers and these great piles of stone were erected only for one purpose, namely to glorify God. . . . As one architect of the twentieth century said, "In those days they never made a mistake in their works of art." And then in addition to this inspiration there was the fact that many of them were coming back from the Crusades. They had seen the great architecture. . . . At any rate this became one of the great showplaces of the world, where 12,500 people could worship at one time.[30]

The cathedral is a showplace, a theater for the drama of good and evil. The exaltation of individuals—such as Greek dramatists—was contrary to the spirit of Scholasticism. Even the medieval drama, in the thirteenth and later centuries, was designed to glorify God and provide inspiration for audiences to do the same. The actor or the artist was not encouraged to seek glory, because to do so would be seen as an act of pride.

Sheen is careful to acknowledge the role of evil in medieval times— even good had potential for evil—but he clearly prefers the past to contemporary times. In differentiating these two opposites he claims: "In those days there were good men and there were bad men. One of the differences between those days and ours is that then the bad men knew they were bad [men]. You know, it's one thing to get off the road and another thing to throw away the map. Those people never threw away the map."[31]

As the plot of the morality play mirrored the way to heaven, so, too, Sheen's message mapped out the place of heaven and the world order as the individual journeyed through life. He idealizes the late or high medieval period because it had "the map"; it offered a sense of direction very much in keeping with Scholasticism's teaching that human beings were directed toward the end, which was God. This map—an extension of the root metaphor of journey—is one of church authority because all roads are measured to and from Notre Dame Cathedral, a symbol of the church hegemony in medieval society: "Within a radius of 150 miles of Paris . . . all distances . . . are measured not by the distance from the Arc de Triomphe or from the au courant. All distances in Paris are measured from Notre Dame and to Notre Dame."[32] Sheen here rules out the authority of country or of contemporary trends. This is no ordinary map or journey, not only because all roads lead to and from Notre Dame, but because the traveler is on a pilgrimage to and from the church.

A pilgrimage, a medieval practice of popular piety continued today in Catholicism, often involves penances along the way and focuses the believer on the transcendent or the spiritual kingdom that exists alongside the earthly kingdom. This idea is similar to Saint Augustine's doctrine of two cities. The monastery and the church represented the city of God on earth. Among other places, pilgrims travel to the Holy Land to walk in the steps of Christ and to Lourdes, the site of Marian apparitions in the last century. Pilgrimages often served the needs of particular church groups because in medieval times they were a source of income for a monastery and a way to bond people in solidarity behind an ideology.

The pilgrimage for the fifties as outlined by Sheen also served the needs of an authoritative church. Sheen's drama is a spiritual journey with a map telling how to get there. In the spiritual kingdom that Sheen maps out, hell is a place in the opposite direction from heaven, which is "above." Sheen structures a hierarchy of the spiritual world with heaven, earth, and hell. Each traveler has the choice of direction while on this earthly pilgrimage. Once again emphasis is placed on the idea from Scholasticism that the individual has the choice between good and evil, but now we also get a glimpse of Sheen's mystical theology that sees the spiritual realm interacting with the material:

> First of all, man has been living for centuries, and many still are—those who give a tone to life still are, living under this philosophy of life that man is living on the earth as a kind of novitiate, and above him is Heaven, which must be won. And below Hell, which is the place of voluntary failure. And during the earthly pilgrimage a man could say "aye" or "nay" to either one of these eternal destinies. . . . Many there are who still believe in that philosophy of life. I do, but then within the last two hundred years man is said to have no other existence than merely the horizontal plain of earth.[33]

Novitiate is a monastic term referring to the place of formation or transition for monks before they profess vows that lead to spiritual perfection. Sheen's use of this term suggests that the earth is a place of passage to the spiritual realm. Sheen even extends the pilgrimage metaphor to describe himself as a mendicant.[34] Mendicants were members of medieval religious communities, such as the Franciscans, who lived lives of simplicity, traveling the roads as popular preachers.

As God overshadowed the medieval play, so too God blesses the journey, because it is in Christ's path that the believer follows. Sheen quotes a poem from Francis Thompson in which he refers to the presence of Christ on the earth, noting that "all pathways by his feet are worn." He also quotes poet Joyce Kilmer, who writes, "Tread holy feet upon my heart." Sheen refers to the feet of Jesus as "sandaled harbingers of peace."[35]

As in the metaphor of the drama, Sheen's journey gives a prominent place to television. Once again his metaphor blesses television as a vehicle that carries the truth on the journey. Sheen says, "May I publicly thank Almighty God for all the opportunities he has given me to use the vehicle of light and television for the communication of the truth."[36]

Sheen's discourse creates a map that includes a vertically structured hierarchy with distinct polar boundaries on a horizontal plane, ensuring an ordered existence for those who believe in his ideology. The structure of the fifties is out of order, says Sheen, because people are emphasizing the wrong values. His clearly drawn map is defined by crossroads as he points to places between the finite and the infinite that are crossed, above and below, by faith or insanity:

> Man is trying to put the infinite into the finite. What we are trying to do with our soul and heart that was made for the infinite life and truth and love, we are attempting to pull this infinite down into the finite structure. It simply cannot be done. Rather what we should do to be happy in the midst of our prosperity is to take the finite nature and plunge it into the infinite. As Hans Virsel said, this line of human and the finite and reason must be crossed, and Virsel continuing said it is crossed above by faith and crossed below by insanity.[37]

Sheen maps out the hierarchy and boundaries on his chalkboard, often saying "over here" and "there," giving his map heightened reality by using both visual and verbal elements of discourse.[38] He underlines his main points in the same program, as if to give them a firmer foundation by this visual emphasis. These clear boundaries are designed to keep the contemporary listener from getting lost. The map on the chalkboard has a hierarchy capped by the authority of God as indicated by the letters *JMJ*, representing Jesus, Mary, and Joseph. Every Catholic schoolchild was taught to write this acronym at the top of composition papers; that put the child under the protection of this family from the spiritual realm.

On a horizontal level, which is the everyday or human realm, there was a clear distinction between good and evil. Sheen maps two poles on the blackboard: "know thyself," which became a synonym for "normal," and "psychology," which is related to "abnormal." The completed map looks like this:

Psychology	Know Thyself
No conscience	Conscience
Not responsible	Responsible
No need for amendment	Amendment needed

In his view the left-hand, "psychology" column takes away individual freedom because the person cannot think for himself or herself, or take responsibility for action, or seek to make amends for wrongs done. This schema of polarization is consistent with Scholasticism's tenet that the individual is always responsible for moral action—the condition Sheen defines as the normal state of an individual. Psychology, in contrast, asserts that an individual is dependent on societal conditioning for moral action. Sheen is careful to position his audience on the side of good, the right-hand side of his chart, when he walks toward the camera and jokingly says, "You are normal, aren't you? If not, you can turn off the TV. Tonight is for normal people."[39]

Although psychology was becoming a respected authority in the fifties, Sheen must debunk it because it threatens the traditional authority of the church. He often refers to it as the "new" or "modern" psychology, contrasting it with the valued tradition.[40] Psychology differs from Sheen's ideology because it values emotions and subjective experience rather than universal truths discovered by reason.

The horizontal plane of Sheen's map is joined by a hierarchical or vertical one, involving the levels of heaven, earth, and hell. Truth, for Sheen, is always bound to hierarchically determined laws that ultimately serve to direct the individual to and from God. God, at the top of the hierarchy, is perfection and pure love; the other levels of the hierarchy are imperfect by degrees in comparison. This Scholastic notion that all creation strives toward God's perfection becomes a rationale for the hierarchy. The idea ties in well with medieval society, which was very hierarchically organized; it must have had appeal for leaders of the new postwar corporations.

Sheen describes "the various hierarchies of the universe: chemical, plants, animals, man." He adds, "If man is to be elevated, God must come down to man."[41] Elsewhere he differentiates the animal and human orders by making reference to a person's soul: "It must be recalled that man is composed of body and soul. He is composed of matter and spirit, finite and the infinite. Inasmuch as he has a body, he is like an animal and has emotions. Inasmuch as he has a soul, he has some resemblance to God."[42] Once again we see the Scholastic rationale for hierarchy mapped out. The closer one is to God, the higher one is in the hierarchy.

Within the human being is another hierarchy. Sheen maps this vertical plane when he says, "In a human being passion is preceded by knowledge, by will, by reason, by some information about an object." Once again reason is closer to God. Sheen says, "Higher knowledge comes from faith and revelation." Reason has a higher place in the hierarchy and is therefore closer to God, because it is more abstract and is believed to be further removed from the material sense perception. For Sheen part of the medieval era's appeal is that its people had both reason and passion, but passion was always subordinate to reason: "The people who built [the cathedrals], they had a dual nature. First of all they were deeply sensitive, passionate, almost primitive, and on the other hand they were keenly intellectual. Reason reached a higher peak in those days than it did at any other time in history. . . . And when you get a combination of this deep passionate nature allied to a flashing intelligence you create a tension which can really beget cathedrals and other works of art."[43] It is especially noteworthy that Sheen's notion of hierarchy also involves a social class structure—surprising at a time when so many individuals were moving into the middle class. But for Sheen the class hierarchy mirrors the spiritual hierarchy while providing a rationale for a hierarchy of the spiritual over the material, the clerical over the laity, church over the state.

The state, according to Scholasticism, existed to lead individuals to happiness—that is, to the possession of the truth. This was a variation on Aristotle's teaching that the state was an end in itself. Although there were fixed hierarchies in the universal forms, even the humblest citizen had the potential to be raised to the highest power. At the same time no social life could exist without the authority of the state, to which all members owed obedience. The goal of the state was to build a Christian republic that would embrace all.

Sheen's message provides a motivating reason for Catholics in the lower classes to subscribe to the values of the American dream and aspire to climb the social ladder of American society. Sheen laughs at the notion that America could ever be without a social hierarchy:

> We all want to be more than we are. We all want to keep up with
> the Joneses. Of course, here in a democracy we boast that there
> are no classes, everyone is equal. We wouldn't have in America
> what they have in Europe: for example, trains with divisions of
> classes, first class, second class, third class. That's undemocratic.
> We have coaches and Pullmans [applause], and not only on the
> ground but in the air everyone is equal. No such distinctions, so we
> have sky tourists and first class. And then kings and queens . . .
> We're beyond those. We don't believe in kings and queens, but we
> have copper kings and we've got movie queens, rose bowl queen
> and cotton bowl queens and asparagus kings.[44]

Sheen provides one more reason for the hierarchy when he explains it as a directional signal, an indication of "which way to go" on the map: "Everyone is trying to be like everybody else. . . . Just like the automobile, we gotta have a new model every year. . . . And so the the Cadillac comes out right at the heap of automobiles. The little Chevrolet comes along and looks exactly like it. The little cars in between get ulcers because they don't know which way to go."[45]

Hierarchy and class are important in his ideology because they help to provide a sense of stability, whereas the horizontal plane is a place of tension where the individual struggles between polar opposites. Sheen acknowledges this when he says, "Tensions are like a tug-of-war. There is nothing wrong about them. They are native almost to human existence."[46] He repeats the theme when he states, "There are certain conflicts that are inevitable in human nature." He goes on to note, "The greatest cross in the world is to be without a cross."[47] We have seen several of these polar opposites on the horizontal plane so far: good versus evil, virtue versus vice, traditional versus modern, reason versus will, faith versus insanity, normal versus abnormal.

Constructing these poles helps Sheen to create clear categories and, ultimately, a clear distinction between good and evil. The map shows the way to goodness, leaving little room for gray areas at the boundaries. There is a certain tension between poles, because the individual is always striving toward perfection. Sheen says, "This is the normal goal of human beings. And perfect life and perfect truth and perfect love is the definition of God. In other words, in seeking happiness, you're seeking God." This prescription for happiness sets standards that the individual can never achieve, because it is defined by the ideal and sets as the goal finding God, who is perfection. Jesus is ideal, or as Sheen put it, "the standard" and "perfect life, perfect truth, perfect goodness."[48]

In other words, Sheen is telling the listener that if he or she does not achieve perfect happiness while living in a world of suffering, then there is need of repentance for sin. The consequence of this theology is that the individual believer is always trying to overcome his or her own sin and achieve a certain perfection in order to make the world a happier place with less suffering.

Of course, the individual could blame suffering on other, sinful persons. But a standard of perfection leaves room for a certain amount of guilt in each individual that could be relieved by reparation. One way to do this, according to Sheen, is "to ask the good Lord to take the pains that come to us in expiation, redress, atonement for all the wrong we have done." He goes on to note that "the balance of justice has been destroyed and the balance must be restored."[49] This places the individual in a state of constant reparation for the imperfections of the world because the ideal can never be reached.

The consolation is that the polar boundaries and the map itself remain consistent, offering meaning rather than anomie; all one needs is faith. A second consolation is that something can be done to overcome sin; a third is that this ideology, though leaving the individual susceptible to guilt, offers a way for him or her to feel more normal than others because he or she has the faith. This involves an unending striving for the goal, the key to which is through the church.

One way to pursue a more perfect way of living is in terms of distance on the map or closeness to God, who parallels the role of parents as a source of life in the heavenly realm that interacts with the human realm. Sheen puts it this way:

> There are many indeed in this world who would give their old
> bones to God. Of course, God takes their old bones. But it is
> much more beautiful to think of the young giving their life to
> God. After all, they are the ones who are always young, because
> how do we know when anyone is young? By closeness to the
> source of life. There is another source of life than parents, namely
> God. Therefore, the closer we get to God the younger we become,
> the more we live in union with Him. The more fresh we become
> till we reach our birthday, the day we are united with Love. No
> wonder our Lord said that no old people enter the kingdom of
> Heaven "unless you become as little children."[50]

Sheen elaborates on the polarity of young versus old in another program, noting that the key to the heavenly kingdom is always innocence. When speaking of Jesus, he says: "They saw him, for example, gather children to himself, press them to his heart, and bless them. They saw him too when the apostles were disputing among themselves as to who would be greatest. They saw him place a child in their midst and say, 'unless you become as one of these you cannot enter the kingdom of Heaven.' That is another way of saying that no old people ever enter Heaven; we all have to have something of that childlike simplicity of which He spoke."[51]

Sheen places much value on innocence and a "childlike" character in order to achieve salvation. Stressing the idea of innocence becomes a way to idealize the past. It creates the adult fantasy of a perfect past in which "social, sexual, economic, and political complexities fade into the background."[52] Sheen also emphasizes innocence because the Catholic Church believes that innocence lost by original sin is restored in baptism. This gives the church a significant place in the passage from the earthly into the heavenly. Baptism is the sacrament of initiation into the church. Grace is the presence of God in the innocent child's life; it restores something lost—another reference to the spiritual map—by Adam, the first adult. Here innocence is prized, and the church, which had tremendous importance in Sheen's ideology, has custody of the rites of innocence and grace: "In baptism a white garment is placed upon a child. To the child it is said, 'Wear this white garment without blame and mayest thou carry it before the judgment seat of our Lord and Savior, Jesus Christ.' In other words, when the child gets baptized, he's restored to something that was lost in Adam. He gets back the garment of beauty and of loveliness and of grace."[53] Sheen's ideology provides a rationale and an ordered way of explaining the world's problems and the individual's suffering. Religious faith is described in an extension of the root metaphor of a journey; the traveler is lost, and the polar opposite of being found is implicit. For example, Sheen speaks about a young woman from Holland who had "lost the faith." It was regained after he "stayed with her three days until she was at peace with herself and the good Lord."[54]

In the same program he speaks of Felix Leseur, "a rank unbeliever" who did not have to go through a process (journey) of questioning the faith. Through the prayer of his wife "he received the gift of faith. So total and complete was it that he had not to go through any process of juxtaposition and say, 'Now that I believe how will I answer this difficulty or that difficulty?' He saw all error in its naked stupidity."[55] Sheen's ideology promises a faith that can easily be grasped and in some cases even eliminate any doubt or error.

The way to faith is through denial of self and turning to the church. This quest to deny self led many sons and daughters of Catholic immigrants to enter monasteries and convents in the postwar years. Here, although the goodness of the material world was not denied, the higher status of the spiritual was promoted. Perhaps the most notable of this group was the Trappist monk Thomas Merton.

Sheen teaches that humility, prayer, penance, or asceticism is necessary for the salvation of the individual. Asceticism is not an end in itself; rather, it helps the individual to break the material bonds of the senses that lead toward evil and to strive toward the good, which is ultimately God. Sheen sees humility as a way to recognize the true— an alternative to the deceptive masks of the earthly drama: "Humility is a virtue by which we recognize ourselves as we really are . . . when we examine our consciences." He goes on to stress the values of sacrifice when he says, "One loves the nobler, so one sacrifices the lower."[56]

Sheen talks about the value of prayer and penance, telling the audience that he prayed for trouble—"some inconvenience, something very hard for me so that someone will be helped very much." He noted that these prayers are always answered. He compares doing something hard to "a mother who gives us bitter medicine for our own good." Once again the believer is positioned as a child receiving from a parent: "Sometimes, you know, when we're young, our mothers give us bitter medicine, and they say, 'Well, sometimes it's for your own good.' Sometimes bitter medicine can be for other people's good. And she [Mary] gives bitter medicine from time to time. I can remember over a couple years I seemed to get every hard cross always on her feast day."[57] This asceticism produces good results that Sheen claims bring one closer to God. His narratives often praise those who led ascetic and prayerful lives. One model is King Saint Louis, who "used to get up every midnight and go into the cathedral to pray. Four o'clock he was there again for matins and early mass. And every single night he used to have two hundred beggars at his table." In the same program he describes Lacordaire, the preacher, a great success because of his asceticism:

> In that cathedral too the great Lacordaire preached, and one understands how great preachers are made when you see how Lacordaire lived.
>
> Lacordaire had a little niche cut in the corner of his cell from which he could look out on the tabernacle below, from which to derive inspiration for his sermons. I've seen at the base of the Carmes in Paris. It is still there, the cross on which Lacordaire used to rope himself, the crown of thorns he used to put on his head on Good Friday morning in order to prepare himself by some kind of mortification for preaching the sermon on Good Friday afternoon in the cathedral of Notre Dame.[58]

The practices of Lacordaire and King Saint Louis of visiting the tabernacle and making frequent visits to the church sound very much like the medieval knight's practice of spending the night before a battle in a prayer vigil before the tabernacle, the most sacred place in Catholicism. This was a practice inherited from the tradition of the monks, who kept prayer vigils at all hours of the day.[59]

Sheen's emphasis on asceticism in working to achieve heavenly reward suggests a work ethic that accords with the Calvinist tradition of working to achieve worldly success as a sign of God's blessing. Catholics influenced by this asceticism were prepared to function under the new corporate work ethic. They were skilled at being unquestioning team players, always self-disciplined and subordinate to the needs of approved authority.[60] In the minds of many, Catholics seemed to specialize in occupations that valued obedience, discipline, and self-sacrifice. This discipline taught them to assimilate rather than to rebel against society. By hard work, perseverance, and self-abnegation, the individual could climb the hierarchical ladder of American society. King and peasant had equal potential to achieve greatness. It was not necessary to deny the material, only to see its potential through the more spiritual truths. The world was good; only a person's misuse of the world caused sin and evil. In contrast, the Calvinist tradition, in which much of mainstream Protestantism was rooted, saw the material world as evil and to be treated with suspicion. The Catholic belief in a more innocent world, where the natural order and hierarchy led to truth and goodness, preserved society's status quo while giving hope to the sons and daughters of immigrants.

The ideology allowed Catholics to embrace capitalist culture with a spirit of optimism because the material world was not inherently bad. In many ways even Catholic priests had been forced to become businessmen, embracing the material world, in order to financially maintain the many structures of Catholicism. Catholic ideology emphasized service to preserve the system; this fit well with the Rotary motto, "He profits best who serves best" or "service with a smile."[61] Catholics came to view their buildings as parish plants that turned out products, Catholics who fit easily into careers where they could serve with discipline and obedience.

Where medieval ideology and American capitalism met, Sheen added another Catholic dimension—one can also work to gain heavenly reward—that was contrary to Protestant theology, which valued salvation as pure grace from God rather than being based on individual merit.

Sheen encourages resignation in the face of problems, telling the listener to "see purpose in it, see it as a means, see it as a transparent opening onto something else." On the other hand, rebellion sees "no purpose in pain." Ultimately Sheen embraced the status quo of the structural authorities by criticizing groups that those authorities often scapegoated and by placing all responsibility on individuals. Sheen says, "Pain is expected to be exhausted here. There will come another world where tears will be wiped away. These sorrows of this life are not to be compared to the joys that are to come." Pleasure and joy are intended to continue in the next world; "Happiness is being saved for Heaven."[62] In fact, suffering should be embraced, because "suffering reveals character."[63] This must have been appealing to a Catholic audience that was working on the difficult climb to middle-class success. Sheen's ideology helped them to live hopefully within the class structure.

Sheen offers a very different solution to the world's tensions than that offered by Norman Vincent Peale and his followers, who promised success by ignoring suffering and choosing instead to contemplate the positive. Peale, pastor at the Marble Collegiate Church in New York, was named to the "List of the Twelve Best U.S. Salesmen" because of his persuasiveness in "selling" the Christian message. Peale's preaching and his best-selling books made him the high priest of the "cult of reassurance" or "peace of mind movement," as a 1955 article in *Life* magazine described it.

The cult of reassurance was the religious approach to tension that claimed an alliance with the science of psychology to gain credibility and fight pessimism. Peale and his followers believed that the mind could control reality and that by a process of positive thinking one could achieve success and reduce any tension. Sin was due not to events in the world but rather to internal confusion. Much like the popular religious literature of the period, Peale claimed that religion was a source of health, both physical and emotional. Prayer was a "prescription" to be repeated to put one in an optimistic framework; God was benign but not needed in day-to-day life because the individual could work out his or her own salvation by adopting a positive attitude. Peale and preachers of this ideology stressed salvation in this life, rather than in the afterlife.

For Sheen the solution is in the church as the place to do penance, to practice asceticism, and to look to the perfection of Jesus. Sheen's message contrasted sharply with Peale's and the new emphasis on leisure, which was used to avoid tension in the fifties. The leisure culture was created when Americans had more free time on their hands with improved technological efficiency and more money in their pockets so that they could afford leisure-time.[64]

But Sheen's message did not deny the leisure culture and its material pleasures. Sheen's message is one of optimism because of its Scholastic spirit that recognized good in the material world, even as one struggled to avoid vice and strove for the perfection of virtue. Ultimately that message offers security in an anxiety-filled era of change. His solution is to listen to the voices of traditional authority, which ultimately point in the direction of the Roman Catholic Church. This is in sharp contrast to the youthful Elvis, who got the nation's attention with his gyrating hips, his clothing, and his new musical style, which questioned tradition, or the movie celebrity James Dean, who encouraged rebellion. Elvis was so controversial that at first Ed Sullivan refused to invite him to be on his show.

We have already seen how the structure of the medieval drama completed its message by encouraging the avoidance of vice. Through the morality play the church found a form, outside of its own liturgy and ritual, that could promote its teachings while entertaining the listeners. In Sheen's discourse structure and content combine similarly to create a sense of stability that complements his use of the metaphor of the medieval morality play and its map. Elements of the structure that helped to shape the message include the use of the television camera, anecdotal humor, generalized example, and extended narrative.

The camera follows Sheen around the stage in one long take without any editing for the entire twenty-eight-minute presentation; there are no commercial breaks. This means that Sheen is the uninterrupted focus of attention. His penetrating eyes, often in a close-up, focus on the home viewer in a captivating way. The unbroken flow of the narrative text, and the almost hypnotic delivery, give no opportunity to reflect on what is being said. The absurdist drama, in contrast to the morality play, forces the viewer to evaluate its truth rather than offering a representational meaning of truth itself in a closed system.[65]

Audiences are especially ill equipped to evaluate visual messages because they lack the emotional distance and the tools necessary to critique and test the highly persuasive visual assertions of a text.[66] If this is the case today, as television reaches middle age, it was all the more true in television's infancy in the fifties.

In addition to camera angle and delivery, humor shapes the structure of Sheen's presentation. Whenever Sheen digresses from the content of his speech, it is to make humorous asides that distract the audience from analyzing the message and point instead to Sheen's rhetorical persona.[67] For example, Sheen is generalizing when he argues below that if society has chaos or no order it will become Communist; it is not true that communism is directly correlated with chaos. An audience caught up with his charisma and the value of anti-Communism, however, will miss this critical insight. In this case Sheen draws their attention to his humor rather than his reasoning. His discourse develops as follows: "Under this false theory of liberty—that is to say license—everyone seeks his own. So one individual goes one particular way to satisfy his own egotism. Another goes this way. Another individual goes this way. Another goes this way. Another goes this way. The result is, since [there is] no common goal or purpose, society becomes chaotic. Now society cannot endure when everyone seeks its own. It therefore becomes necessary to impose some order by compulsion on society. Along comes communism and dictatorship, and there you have the face of a Communist. [Laughter and applause.]"[68] The audience laughs because Sheen has been drawing arrows to represent persons going in different directions. These arrows are arranged so that when he draws a circle around them they become a face. The laughter distracts from the message and makes the audience less attentive to the logic of his argument.

Examples add color to discourse. But more importantly, the more concrete or specific the example, the more authentic the persuasive point appears for an audience. Specific examples also create emotion and draw the listener into the discourse. Interestingly, Sheen rarely uses specific examples. He chooses instead to generalize about parents and children, doctors, husbands and wives, men and women, teachers, Communists. This form of example ultimately distances his audience from the complexity of the issues and reduces emotional involvement with his illustrations, constructing a world where everything fits into neat categories. For example, the generalized mother whose child ends up in court is always in the wrong. Sheen says, "How many a mother there is in the court, a court where perhaps her son is a juvenile delinquent, who will say 'I could never do anything with him. There is no love on the part of the child.' She never did anything for him."[69]

Sheen is fond of telling stories, and his characters meet nice, neat endings in which—as in the morality play—good always triumphs. The characters live in a kind of bubble where they have no need to deal with the messiness of moral decision making or emotion. By remaining distant from the emotion of the character, the listener is preserved from the messiness or emotion of the story.

One example is Sheen's tale of the beautiful princess Lily, who as a child loses her religious medal of the Madonna over a cliff into the sea. The young woman "prayed that someday she would find it." However, even "divers could not find it." In France a king proposes to Lily, cautioning her, "[I] cannot assure you of much happiness. These are war days; there could be sorrow and trial and captivity—there could even be imprisonment. Would you want to share a lot like that? It is not a happy prospect for a princess." Lily responds, "I have lost something very precious too." Lily's equating of the loss of her medal to the death and destruction of war illustrates Sheen's sentimental reality. Lily continues to pray over the years for her medal, even when she and her husband become prisoners of the Nazis. Finally, Sheen concludes, "The doctors said she was dying of a blood clot" and "needed a miracle." The princess explains, "'There is one miracle that can save me, the miracle of finding the image of the Lady I love.' At that very moment there came a knock on the door and in ordinary post there came a medal that said 'Lillian, November 28, 1917.' And she lived!"[70]

Sheen's stories promise a world of innocence where things go wrong but the answer will be found if one has faith or if, in one's own confusion and despair, there is a consolation that answers exist. The structure of Sheen's text, interaction of visual and verbal text, long takes and close-ups, interspersed humor, and the message of a return to the past with clear directions and answers presents the listener with a sentimental rhetoric, one with no room for argument. It encourages a "passivity of deference" from the audience toward the rhetor.[71] This rhetoric emerges at times of social insecurity in order to show clear-cut distinctions between good and bad.

The final outcome for Catholics in the fifties was that they had a unique identity that helped to preserve the boundaries of traditional society during a time of great social change. They had a sense of tradition because tradition preserved the truth. At the same time their tradition encouraged an other-directed orientation to life that fit in well with the tone of fifties' society, which emphasized role over individual personality. Thus, they learned to conform and to respect authority.

Catholic medievalism was an alternative to the traditional social structure—now in crisis—because it appreciated the American respect for the individual and suspicion of too much state authority. On the other hand, the individual was subordinate to the hierarchical order of the church, giving a means of internal authority for the functioning of Catholicism as an institution. Misfortune was explained as resulting from too much emphasis on the material at the expense of the higher, spiritual order. For Catholicism, the stress on Scholasticism and a revival of the high medieval spirit became a way to present itself as a noble way of life, with an emphasis on order and unity as opposed to the upheaval of social change that the early twentieth century had witnessed. At the same time it complemented the Cold War rhetoric of boundaries between godliness and evil. Both gave a certain freedom to the individual, but always in subordination to the institution.

The medieval morality play became less popular in medieval times with the development of the Reformation, when Protestants came to believe that religion was a matter of personal responsibility for each individual. Protestantism saw the dogmatic intervention of the church as a distortion of Christianity. The fact that the morality play would emerge on television through the popular words of Bishop Sheen helps to confirm the fact that in the fifties individuals were seeking an alternative to secular culture, the expertise of psychology, and traditional Protestantism, which encouraged a subjective individualism. Sheen's acting out the drama with a clearly defined moral map shows an alternative response to the anxiety of the fifties.

The tensions of the fifties set the stage for an era of new anxiety. The years after Woodstock, War in Vietnam, Watergate have been ones in which cynicism runs high and some people worry that individual freedom of expression has harmed the core of American culture. Tradition has been abandoned for the sake of change. In the fifties we see the formative stages of what James Hunter describes as a "culture war" in American society. He sees culture as the source of worldview or vision.[72] In the fifties a person's religious affiliation determined one's worldview and solidified one's identity. This is no longer the case as many Americans, including Catholics, have chosen to express their religiosity through personal spiritualities rather than institutional allegiance. In the process society has become polarized by two divisions that cut across and divide all religious groupings. The media has helped to polarize these groups by emphasizing their extremes. The one pole favors unchanging standards; the other values human experience and diversity. At the end of the twentieth century the cultures shaped in the fifties are in an all-out war over the boundaries of morality, boundaries that help shape a person's identity.

Sheen's morality play, acted out in the fifties, forms the basis for the first group. It represents people who long for an ordered world. Today they seek this world by an emphasis on traditional devotionalism and unquestioning obedience to their interpretations of papal teaching. Yet this can be a sentimental world if we forget that Sheen's morality play was surrounded by tensions of its own, as was the medieval era that he idealized. It is sentimental if we forget that Sheen's morality play is only one era's interpretation of Catholicism.

Vatican II, which Bishop Sheen actively supported, encouraged dialogue with society. Most Catholics acknowledge the need for Vatican II; disagreement is over how the documents of Vatican II are to be interpreted. Catholics are now divided as to how much dialogue is acceptable. The culture war has escalated in Catholicism to the point where even bishops and theologians are in disagreement over the boundaries and meaning of Catholic authority. The basis of the argument is, How much can one question Catholic authority and still be a Catholic or a moral person? The deeper question is, Who is the authority?

The final act of this drama needs to be acted out. Meanwhile, Catholics find identity not just by affiliation with a golden past, but by being opposed to each other in disagreement over the past that they share.

3

The Medieval City and the
Crusade for the American Ideal

Imagine your sense of anticipation after a long journey over land or sea, having weathered storm, sickness, and danger. Now you catch your first glimpse of the journey's end—the city on a hill. This was the experience of Puritan leader John Winthrop in 1603 as he gazed at the new colony of Boston. Winthrop declared that the new colony would be "as a city on a hill" and that "the eyes of all people are upon us."[1] America was to be a new Jerusalem, a nation chosen with a sacred destiny to bring about God's reign. That vision would form the basis for the American ideology. Colonists fought the American Revolution with the belief that they were leaving behind corruption, violence, and injustice for a new nation united in covenant with God. Every community develops its own ideologies or mythos as a source of identification and bonding among its members. The Puritan ideology became secularized and passed down from generation to generation. America saw itself as innocent in the face of a world of evil.

Bishop Sheen has a similar vision, but his is not of a Puritan colony as a shining city on a hill. His vision is of a medieval city—Rheims, Paris, Canterbury, or Cologne—whose center is a majestic cathedral, with towers that reach to the heavens as two arms in supplication. For the medieval traveler the cathedral was the refuge against physical danger or a well of spiritual renewal. Whole cities were built up in its shadows. The monastery and guilds, connected to the cathedral, helped to create a center of commerce and education. Sinners and beggars could find mercy under its arches. The cathedral connected the heavens and the earth and became a meeting place for king and bishop, providing legitimacy to civic life.

This chapter analyzes the relationship of the American ideology to Bishop Sheen's message, which implicitly claims that the spirit of

America is, at root, Roman Catholic. For Sheen, the relationship of the Catholic Church to the state parallels that of the Catholic cathedral to the medieval city. He never seeks explicit political hegemony for the church in America as an institution, because to do so would have stirred Protestant-Catholic tensions that were brewing in the fifties. As in the "city on a hill," religious tolerance is valued in Sheen's city. But the spirit of Catholicism is made primary. Catholics are heirs to the American mythos, which is described as inherently Catholic. Sheen's schema spiritualizes the place of the Catholic Church rather than vesting it with political power. His medieval cathedral is a principle that emphasizes the values of freedom and fellowship.

Sheen defines America, metaphorically, as the land on which the medieval cathedral dwells, where the medieval morality play is acted out. God is the king, with both human and divine qualities. Individuals are invited to become children of God and share in God's divine qualities as "heirs" in the kingdom, protected by the city walls that are allegorical images of natural law. The cathedral is where the individual bridges the gap between earth and heaven. Sheen's message is that America needs the church because the church is the source of patriotic ideals. Mary, the spiritual protectress of the church, much like a medieval lady, invites America to take the role of the noble champion in the battle of good and evil. Sheen preaches an American jeremiad that calls America to live up to its destiny and fight the inner war against secularism.[2]

Sheen lays the groundwork for the centrality of the Catholic Church in society by interpreting life in terms of a polarity between two great principles. The *pyramid* is related to death (and Communism); the *cathedral* represents the pole of life that is good and, for Sheen, defines what America should be:

> The pyramid is constructed stone on stone, one imposing itself upon the other, with a kind of absolute equality in which there is no differentiation by function. Finally at the peak, the keystone arch . . . rests upon them all and almost thrusts its weight on all. That keystone of the structure can be either a Khrushchev or a Bulganin. It makes no difference which. At the base is death: a tomb, whether it be a Lenin or Stalin. There is no belief in any other kind of life in the pyramid principle. In a cathedral the stones are related one to another as regards their function. The great arches have a foot on the earth, their heads in the heavens.

The cement is the charity that holds the stone, symbolic of
persons, above all else in freedom with fellowship because the
cathedral makes room for air, makes room for light, makes room
for truth and love.[3]

Although Sheen never explicitly defines the cathedral principle as
Catholicism, his metaphor is connected to the ideology of Catholicism rather than Protestantism. The cathedral itself—Sheen's container
for the cathedral principle of good—is the center of a diocese in Catholicism, which gives it a higher distinction in Catholic religious architecture. The word comes from the Latin *ex cathedra,* which refers
to the authority of the bishop. The embodiment of his cathedral principle is Notre Dame—"Our Lady," or Mary—built over the ruins of a
pagan church.

The stones in Sheen's structure have functions or roles that show
an ordered, hierarchical society—quite different from the equality
stressed in the Protestant congregation. In Sheen's construction, as in
the Scholastic theology of Catholicism, the cathedral connects two
distinct realms—the material and the spiritual, earth and heaven. In
contrast, mainstream Protestantism since the Reformation had embraced the secular culture and did not see the spiritual as a separate
realm requiring church mediation.[4] Similarly, much popular religious
writing in the fifties stressed the spirituality in the secular world as
the only genuine spiritual realm.

Sheen's description of Notre Dame ends with an explicit statement of the role of Mary in Catholicism:

It was dedicated, yes dedicated to a woman. Do not think because
it was dedicated to a woman that she is adored. She is not adored.
She is not a goddess. She is human. Why then is so much veneration and respect paid in a cathedral; why is it dedicated to her?
Because she is the rampart; she is the outpost. She is the human
door by which divinity came into this earth. That's why to regard
her as someone who is to be revered. So long as the ramparts are
safe, then the city will be safe. So long as the mother is secure,
then the Son will be proclaimed as divine. That's the reason of
veneration for her. So in that stone, and all of us are summoned to
her to make us warriors, warriors of the faith that she may make
the assault upon omnipotence.[5]

Mary is the protector who makes an "assault" and requires us to become "warriors of the faith"; as we will see, the oppressor is secularism. The text's message also stresses that the "city is safe" behind its ramparts. This implies, again in opposition to Protestantism, a hierarchical relation between the secular and the spiritual, with the spiritual having the higher protective status.

Sheen emphasizes that America needs the cathedral because it serves as the bridge between the earth and the heavens. It has light and air, two elements of modern architecture that suggest an open spaciousness lacking in the closed pyramid. The cathedral principle thus is made relevant in contemporary times. The emphasis on light in the Gothic cathedral always references the presence of God shining in from above.

Although in describing the pyramid and the cathedral Sheen talks about the different functions within the cathedral's plan, he does not name particular church functionaries, perhaps to avoid controversy about Catholic loyalty to the hierarchical Church and its pope.[6] But he does discuss the role of the Pope under the guise of historical fact, telling how Pope Pius VII, centuries earlier in this cathedral, refused to crown Napoleon as head of state. Recognizing "no power but his own, not even God's, [Napoleon] snatched the crown from the hands of Pius VII and put it on his own head."[7] While testifying to the authority of the pope, unjustly usurped by Napoleon, Sheen softens the emphasis by embedding the pope's role in the narrative and by using a historic instance that offers the listener a distance from any current controversy. At the same time he can make an implicit claim that the church is superior to the state. This is the medieval conception of society against which popular American ideology rebelled.

The idea of the church as a container is evident when Sheen quotes a conversation between Douglas Hyde and his wife, both former Communists who converted to Catholicism. Sheen describes how Hyde became aware of his wife's conversion. He says (speaking the part of Douglas Hyde), "'You are beginning to talk as if you might go into the Church.' She said, 'I am.' He said, 'Shake, so am I.'"[8] The words "into the Church" imply both a container and a particular church. The container metaphor separates the world into inner and outer spheres; the Hydes are now part of the former. Popular American civil religion would not give special status to the spiritual over the secular. But for Sheen there are only two principles of life, two choices—Communism and the cathedral of Catholicism. Communism was the enemy of both Catholicism and the United States; the cathedral is a place of freedom and fellowship, two virtues of popular American ideology. These virtues are now found within the church, and in the spirit of earlier American bishops, Sheen is implying that the spirit of America is inherently Catholic.[9]

Tolerance of plurality has always been a cardinal virtue of the American ideology. Enlightenment thinking, which helped shape the American spirit, valued the autonomy of the individual over the interests of the state. Sheen's rhetoric is inclusive of the three major religious groups, Protestant, Jewish and Catholic, in a spirit similar to that of John Courtney Murray rather than that of Leonard Feeney, who wanted to exclude non-Catholics from salvation and the kingdom of God.[10] However, other religious groups are never described as churches in Sheen's medieval church-state relationship—implying that they are less than the Catholic Church. Sheen walks a tightrope between Feeney's excessive lack of toleration and Murray's emphasis that the real enemies of the church were not different denominations but technological secularists who wanted to forget God. Murray found much support from both conservatives and liberals in America but was criticized by conservative Catholic theologians. His toleration was censured by Rome in 1955. Sheen's medieval cathedral stopped short of embracing Murray's controversial position equating all churches.

The opening frames of the program suggest a certain amount of tolerance for diversity. When the announcer introduces the telecast and notes that it "deals with the everyday problems of all of us," he goes on to say that it is for all "races, religions, colors, and creeds." Sheen himself says, "Last year we helped sixty-five million people: aged, sick, and orphans, 95 percent non-Christian."[11] His work is described as interreligious, but his stress on the Catholic philosophy of Scholasticism does not give an equal voice to other religions, and his tolerance has limits.

On the other hand, Sheen's rhetoric avoids terminology that would disrupt inclusiveness. For example, the organization he represents is known in Catholic circles as The Propagation of the Faith. This has connotations of a particular belief system and could be disruptive on TV if the viewers felt he was proselytizing. Instead Sheen's organization is referred to as the "World Mission Aid Society." This name's philanthropic connotations tied in well with the American ideal that voluntarily supporting one's neighbor was a sign of America's salvific world destiny.

Sheen's rhetoric of inclusion is also embedded in his narrative text. For example, he tells viewers that at the trial of Jesus all humanity was present: "All our martyrs who are dying in China, all the Protestant missionaries, the sons of Maccabees. All humanity that ever bore the divine image and suffered for it." Although his vision of religion includes Protestant, Catholic, and Jew, Catholics are of higher status because they are described as "martyrs"—in the Christian tradition, heroes of the faith.[12]

In this recounting of the biblical trial that led to the crucifixion of Jesus, the Jews are never portrayed as responsible for Christ's death or as having less faith than Christians. The rhetoric connects Herod, the Jewish leader, with Rome rather than with Judaism. Sheen refers to him as "a Roman representative" and says that the "Romans led by Pilate came into the land like the Soviets came into Poland." Herod is in town for "the feast"; Sheen does not name the Jewish feast of Passover. He goes out of his way to describe the historical roots of Roman control, portraying the Jews as victims of Roman oppression much as the contemporary people of Poland are oppressed by the Soviets. He places blame for Jesus' death squarely on Roman heads when he concludes, "And from that day to this we say in the creed, 'And He suffered under Pontius Pilate.'"

In referring to the "great Hebraic-Christian tradition," he again places Judaism in a positive light and suggests that it is inclusive of Protestants.[13] Like John Carroll, America's first Catholic bishop (1735-1815), who used the term "Catholic Christians" to recognize a common heritage with the Protestant majority and not stir controversy, Sheen's phrase suggests that Catholics are not separate from other religious groups, yet an implicit separation embedded in the text gives superiority to Catholicism.

Every Catholic Church had a pulpit, but in the fifties Catholic liturgical tradition gave the pulpit a less central place in the physical space of the church.[14] Prominence went to the altar and the tabernacle.[15] Thus, a subordination is implied when Sheen describes other religious groups as having pulpits—never churches. When he calls for a day of prayer, fasting, and penance in America, he says, "We can all do it. The Jews have their feasts and fasts that they keep; Christians have their own. Let Jews, Catholics, and Protestants from their pulpits, as men and women of God, all of us, make America free, make America at peace."[16]

In fact, in all of Sheen's anecdotes about being in church, that church clearly is Catholic. For example: "We received a letter recently from a family in Detroit with three children, and [one is a] little boy, Ralphie, aged five, who is sometimes a little bad. He will say, 'Mother, will you give me another chance.' This particular Saturday she came out of the confessional box and knelt down next to little Ralph. He asks, 'Did God give you another chance?'" [Audience laughter.][17]

Sheen's rhetoric of tolerance is constrained by his need to appease the Roman influence that would eventually silence John Courtney Murray for suggesting that the church should be civil to other religious bodies. By implicitly claiming special status for the church, Sheen could present himself as tolerant while satisfying the demands of Rome. Though not compromising Catholic beliefs, he avoids having his program labeled as a Catholic one.

For Sheen, America is inherently Catholic. He goes on to show that although America has a great role in the drama of good and evil, it does not have the status of the cathedral that spans the earth and the heavens. America is the land upon which the cathedral dwells.[18]

In the metaphor of the land, an extension of the root metaphor of the medieval city, the land represents the political nation. For example, Sheen describes Ireland as "a land of farming and fishing," "a land where people are poor," and "a land where there are labor leaders and capitalists";[19] he also refers to "Ireland's soil." He is critical of "Americans who have betrayed their land" by becoming Communist. He allies American patriotism and God, noting that "divinity and fatherland are always sold out of proportion to their true worth."[20] He describes God as "the father of all lands." Lands still have oppressors. He singles out Communism when he says that "the Romans were in the land of the Jews very much like the Soviets are in China or Poland."[21]

Sheen's rhetoric, reminiscent of the American ideological creed, often constructs America as a nation chosen by God with a special destiny to the world. His metaphorical terms—*destiny, freedom, mission, chosen*—resonate with traditional civil religion in suggesting the millennial mission of America. At the same time he adds his own dimension when he challenges America, not so much in ideology (because that ideology is inherently Catholic) but as a nation of individuals who have abused the ideals of America and turned from God.

Sheen never compromises his Catholic theology, but through the use of metaphors he converts notions of traditional American ideology into Catholic ideas. One root metaphor gives America a Christic or salvific role. The emphasis on America's saving mission fits in with the American value of the millennial responsibility. Americans had come to believe that "they had a manifest destiny" to fight against sin or wrongdoing.[22] By doing so they would bring about peace and prosperity in the land. This provided a rationale for the westward expansion and for the suppression of the American Indian as a satanic obstacle to God's plan. In more recent times that millennial responsibility became the validating force for the American success ethic. America's Christic role, for Sheen, has several extensions: America as child, as shepherd, and as Simon of Cyrene.

First, Sheen refers to the prediction from the Hebrew book of Isaiah, "a child shall lead them," which is often applied by Christians to Christ as Messiah. Sheen explains that America is "one of the young countries of the world. If young, then a child. Then in peace a child shall lead."[23] This approach ties in with America's sense of innocence, which is also valued by the American mythic system.

The second metaphor defines America as a shepherd. Both Hebrew and Christian Scriptures use this image for the Messiah. Sheen says, "We are destined to be shepherds to those sheep" that are lost by Communism. America has the unique role of bringing to life in a moment of resurrection, which describes another Christic event. He adds, "We will resurrect the Eastern world."[24]

America has a "beautiful destiny," Sheen continues, and he likens America to Simon of Cyrene, a stranger who was commissioned to take up the cross of Jesus.[25] Carrying this cross is a "noble" task. Again the salvific image of America is supported, but now in the role of helping Christ while sharing in his own roles of savior, child, shepherd, and glorified Christ in the resurrection.

Sheen qualifies America's salvific role by making it a secondary cause of salvation. In the following quotation, God as "Providence" gets priority in a way suggestive of a hierarchy in which Sheen implicitly preserves a place for the Catholic Church. This is different from the God of the Founding Fathers, who, because they were influenced by Enlightenment deism, believed that God creates the law and distances himself from creation or any particular church:

We have a magnificent role. We are destined, under Providence, to be the secondary cause for the restoration of the freedom and liberties of the peoples of the world. We are the secondary cause: God is the primary cause. To fulfill that role, we shall have to make ourselves worthy of it. Our country has always had a great role. In the beginning we were a sanctuary for the oppressed. In our times we became the arsenal for democracy. In the last few years we have been the pantry for the starving world. Every American has given five dollars to Africa. That is the mark of beneficence and goodness. In the near future we may be called upon to roll up the curtain of the Eastern world, that is to give to the East the prosperity, peace, and fraternity with the other nations of earth. Our great country was hidden from the eyes of men for centuries behind a veil. The ships of Columbus pierced that veil and brought this vast continent into view. Now, it is the destiny of America to pierce another veil, the veil of the Eastern peoples of the world, in whom we are so interested in our mission lands. Our role is to restore these people to some decency of living. At present, two-thirds of the people of the world go to bed hungry every night. To fill their stomachs with our abundance and to fill their souls with the truth of God is our task and our mission.[26]

The metaphors of sanctuary, arsenal, and pantry limit America in relation to the structure of a cathedral. They are only parts of a structure; the principle of the cathedral and of the pyramid are complete structures. This again argues that the church will ultimately be superior to the nation. Sheen subordinates America by noting, "America builds towers to honor American enterprise. This tower [the cathedral] is to honor the glory of God."[27] The tower of enterprise has overtones of the biblical tower of Babel, a monument to individualism in contrast to the "ivory tower" that is Mary's spiritual love for humanity.

The image of being hidden suggests the purity of a virgin bride who wears a veil and is pierced. The veil further suggests the biblical image of the inner part of the temple, the Holy of Holies, which is so sacred that only the appointed ministers can enter. This imagery gives a Catholic spin to the image of American innocence, a central ingredient in the millennial hopes of the traditional American mythos. When America had to deal with its flaws, its mission of innocence was called into question. American Protestantism, which had shaped the American ideology, was in conflict over its own identity. America learned through the Korean War that it had not ended the spread of Communism. The American way was being questioned. For example, when the Rosenbergs were executed as spies in 1953, Pius XII and other world leaders wrote to President Eisenhower urging him to rescind the death sentence. John-Paul Sartre called the Rosenberg executions "a legal lynching that has covered the whole nation in blood."[28]

Sheen's rhetoric helps preserve America's self-righteous role as innocent savior to the world. The mission of America is now one of filling Eastern "souls with the truth." But given that America must "pierce" another "veil," American innocence is not unique. Sheen continues to discuss America's role: "to change these symbols so that one day the hammers carried aloft will look like crosses as they parade in the name of God; and the sickle will look like the moon under the feet of the Lady to whom these telecasts are dedicated. May they help bring us to God and make Americans love one another for the betterment of the world and the peace of the human soul."[29]

Sheen brings a new dimension to traditional views of American destiny: "the Lady" who has a role in helping America reach its destiny. For Sheen, the lady is the mediator and America a medieval knight who battles for her and then lays the trophy of victory at her feet. "In order to do this, we in America must make ourselves worthy."[30] Making oneself worthy suggests some medieval purification rite for the knight before doing battle. This is no ordinary war, as it is fought in "the name of God." The enemy is both the swastika of Hitler's Nazism and the hammer and sickle of Communism, but Sheen is also shaping a spiritual battle: "So let America trust in its stars and stripes but also realize America will conquer by other stars and stripes, namely the stars and stripes of Christ." He continues using metaphorical extensions of America as the knight with shield, sword, and breastplate, who fights as an army under the protection of the woman already defined as Mary. The battle weapons are spiritual: justice, spirit, faith, and "a woman." Here we are far from ideas of traditional American ideology: "Let us put on the breastplate of justice, the shield of faith. Carrying the sword in the spirit, marching with courage under the great God who is the Lord of Hosts and under the protection of a woman who is as invincible as an army in drawn up battle array, [we will] preserve our country."[31] This reference to a warrior God, "the Lord of Hosts," is reminiscent of the Scriptures, where God leads the angelic hosts into apocalyptic battle against Satan. Sheen's rhetorical descriptions of God blend well with the images of God in traditional American ideology, which emphasized the transcendence of God. Ultimately, however, Sheen's God is the God of Catholic Scholasticism, both transcendent and immanent. Like the medieval warrior king who inspires his subjects to action against evil, this God wants his people to earn salvation by acting against evil and working for virtue.

America's founders believed that God distanced himself once he had set in motion the law, leaving the individual to act freely in the world. Similarly, Sheen says, "God implanted certain laws in the universe by which things attain their proper perfection. God did not make man like the sun, which can only rise and set. Having made man free, He gave him a higher law than natural law, namely moral law." This does not mean that God has no place in the universe, because he is custodian of the law as well as enforcer. Sheen quotes from two heroes of the American mythos in describing the warrior God. Quoting Penn, he says, "The blessings of peace are so great that when God chooses to punish us severely for our sins, it is always with wrath of war he chastises us." He supports that claim by quoting Lincoln: "It may very well be the civil war is a punishment of God for our sins."[32] Sheen describes the hydrogen bomb as part of God's punishment: "nothing but fire, and in this [it] is like any other crisis, for a crisis is God's fire."[33] Although this side of God is to be feared, even here God is not a cruel God because He is only acting as directed by the law. Such a predictable God would be quite consoling in times of rapid social change.

Sheen goes on to note that God is subject to the law in the same way an aviator is to laws of engineering: "The Jews did not mean that God punished them in the same way, for example, a father picks up a rod to spank a child. Rather, God made the world in a certain way. And when we disobey his natural law and moral laws, certain consequences follow. For example, if an aviator disobeys the laws of engineering or the laws of gravity, his plane falls. That's a judgment. God made the world in such a way that if the rational laws of engineering are ignored, there will be a consequence and the fatal cause result from it."[34] This is a very different image of God from that portrayed in popular thinking at the time, as espoused by Norman Vincent Peale and his followers, who believed that God offers rewards rather than judgment.

According to Sheen's definition, God participates in the struggle of humanity. He always has authority but can be both immanent and transcendent; as in Scholastic ideology, which also valued both, the spiritual world is emphasized over the material. Closely connected to Sheen's idea of God's immanence in the world is God as a model for moral action. The immanence is illustrated in the image of God as the earthly lord, connected to the material world by his birth and suffering, yet with transcendent qualities that inspire people to action against evil.

The immanence is further balanced by a God who is always in authority as the lord, much as a medieval king was. Sheen often highlights the transcendence of this king by noting he is "our blessed Lord"[35]—"blessed" elevating God above the earthly lord. On the other hand, Sheen's God is much more active in creation than the God of the American mythos. Sheen's emphasis on the birth and suffering of Jesus parallels the Catholic focus on the humanity of Jesus that emerged in the medieval miracle plays of the fourteenth and fifteenth centuries. For example, Sheen says, "At the Incarnation of the Son of God in the Person of Jesus Christ, God was seen—seen in the form of a babe in fulfillment of the prophecy seven hundred years ago that his name would be called Emmanuel: 'God with us.'"[36] This God shares the human struggle and by His presence blesses it; the implied worldview is very different from that of some Protestants, who often saw the world as corrupt and struggle as evil. The incarnational emphasis of Catholicism blesses the world of struggle because God is involved, leading persons to find the spiritual in the material world.

Sheen's God is always in control. Sheen chooses to emphasize the biblical title "Son of God," which focuses on divinity, rather than "Son of Man."[37] However, he is quick to point out that Jesus is not just the "poor babe of Bethlehem"; God "takes on" the poverty of human nature, "but we miss the picture if we think this is a poor child like the poor child in an alley in Louvain. Do not think this babe of Bethlehem was just a poor babe. Something very different: He who was rich became poor, became poor, so that through his poverty we might be rich. . . . Here is God who takes human nature upon himself."[38]

At the same time Sheen's baby has few childlike qualities because he is described as a "captain of salvation." Jesus, a God with much authority, always maintains his power while bringing "omnipotence and wisdom to the earth." His role as a baby is described as a "self-imposed limitation on his divinity."[39] God is in authority even in allowing for the limitation of humanity. Transcendence triumphs over immanence.

We see this triumph in Sheen's Christ, who is always an authority even in suffering, when he is described as a king: "The thief on the side of Christ turning to the divine savior . . . said, 'Remember me when thou shall come into thy kingdom.' Kingdom. The thief looked at the crown of thorns and saw a royal diadem. The nail was to him a scepter of power and royal authority. The crucifixion was his installation. His blood was his royal purple. It was the foundation of democracy, the worth of a single soul."[40] Note that the cross on which Jesus' royalty rests now becomes the "foundation of democracy." Sheen is using Catholic theology but shaping God into an American patriot by his death on the cross. Suffering and oppression become patriotic virtues, not necessarily for the sake of suffering but in order to recognize the true worth in the kingdom: the single soul.

The light that fills the rooms of Sheen's cathedral principle is now identified as Jesus, who models the law and its perfection, toward which the believer is expected to strive. Sheen describes God as "perfect love" but lays out the implications when he uses another metaphorical extension of the God of authority: "The perfect example . . . is our blessed Lord: perfect life, perfect truth, and perfect love. In that light we see ourselves as we really are. . . . Under that glaring light of the perfect model, the Son of God, then we see imperfections. He who is the light by which we truly know ourselves and the standard by which we judge ourselves is also our physician. He's the one who heals our wounds. If I have a wound and the physician comes to the door, I do not concentrate on the wounds but on the curative power of the physician."[41] The emphasis on Jesus as a perfect model of life, love, and truth is specifically Catholic because it calls the believer to individual moral action as part of salvation.[42]

Sheen's vision of God offers to take our minds off our problems or "wounds" and let us see "imperfections"—our inner qualities. By turning us toward an inner world where we can choose to strive toward perfection, this ideology embraces the status quo, because it does not call for social change.

God is in a battle caused not by an unjust social order but related to inner evils that are "armored" in "might" and "power," causing suffering. These evils are the principles of death or the pyramid. We hear, though, that Jesus has opened the tomb and conquered death.

When he was sent to the cross, this was the worst thing that evil could do. The worst thing evil can do is not to bomb cities, or kill children, or open concentration camps. The worst thing evil can do is to kill goodness. And having killed goodness on that day, evil was panoplied in the greatest might and armored in the greatest power, and yet it was defeated three days later by the glorious resurrection when He gave to the earth the only serious wound that it ever received, the wound of a gaping tomb, the scar of an open sepulchre as He rose as God in the form of a glorified human nature. . . . Other religions will do when there is sunshine and when there are fine bank accounts, but we need a religion born in defeat in these days of crisis and catastrophe that we have today. We need a religion born out of crisis. We need a religion born in defeat. Good Friday was a prelude to Easter Sunday; so long as we bear innocently the divine image in the face of evil in the world we shall never perish. Why? We have already won, only the news has not leaked out![43]

Sheen's downplaying of atrocities fits in well with the traditional principles of Catholic charity that believed suffering could not be overcome in this world but must be endured.

In the above quotation Jesus again takes the passive role, much like God the creator did in reference to natural law. On the cross Jesus accepts his destiny as the one "sent" to the cross by the more active "evil." Evil causes suffering, yet suffering is a part of life. Sheen adds, "Conflict is inevitable in life. The greatest cross is to be without a cross."[44]

Sheen's neat package for the world's problems must have been consoling in an age of social change. There is always a source of evil and suffering; yet the individual is never alone because God understands and values suffering, which will one day be overcome. With its emphasis on suffering to overcome defeat, the Roman Catholic Church is implicitly the preferred religion, because it values the oppressed while offering a promise of glory on Easter Sunday. Defeat becomes a sacred term. This theology is quite different from the success-oriented theology of Norman Vincent Peale and the popular religious publications of the time that emphasized this world.

Sheen explicitly notes that Jesus' kingdom is otherworldly and defines Jesus' mission as apolitical. In Sheen's narrative of the trial before Pilate, Jesus says, "I am not challenging the power of Stalin, Tito, or Mao Tse Tung, or Caesar. I have come to give testimony to the truth." Jesus' kingdom is spiritual; "I rule hearts and souls," he says.[45] In another place, Sheen claims that Judas was disappointed in Jesus because he "refused to become a king; now He is too much interested in the soul."[46]

Even though Sheen's God is apolitical, He is also a participant in the economic system—both capitalist and laborer. Sheen recounts his conversation with people who wanted to establish a feast of Christ the worker: "You're influenced by the Marxist division of classes into capitalist and labor. And you want to put the Son of God into one of these classes. Suppose you put him in the class of the worker. Who is going to save the capitalist? The capitalist needs saving just as much as the worker does. . . . He was a capitalist who became a proletariat. Therefore, the only one in all the world of whom capital and labor, rich and poor, wise and simple can say, 'He came from our ranks. He is one of our own.'"[47] That God is from "the ranks" serves as a promise of advancement in the ranks, while not being in "a class" places God in his position of transcendence.

Sheen goes on to describe heaven as a place that can be "purchased": "Our Lord never asked us to give up anything; He asked us to exchange: 'What exchange shall a man give for his soul?' When someone is in love with God, he finds that there are some things he can get along without, such as physical pleasures, and something else that he cannot get along without, namely the peace of soul that comes from obeying God's will. So he exchanges the one for the other, he surrenders the lesser good to gain a kingdom. He makes a series of such profitable exchanges every day he lives."[48] Salvation is a process of bartering or exchange to get the good.[49]

Sheen is baptizing the economic system by including God in it, but we will see that this baptism is not without the need for repentance by its participants. The church will be the conscience of this economic order. In keeping with the medieval theory of redemption advocated by Saint Anselm, God is very much like the feudal lord who protects his loyal subjects and purchases them back from slavery. Sheen's baptism sets up an ideal economic system that complements Catholic theology.

Earlier chapters noted that individual freedom was one of the foundational virtues in the American ideology. Natural law as interpreted by Aquinas also focused on the individual, but more in terms of individual salvation within the norms of institutional authority, rather than the American focus on subjectivity and freedom from the institution. This focus on decreased institutional authority over the individual was also foundational in the writings of Catholic convert and priest Isaac Hecker (1819-88). At the time of Hecker's writing, the Vatican was fighting for its life amid anticlericalism that threatened the authority of the European Catholic Church. One of the consequences of this was that thinking such as that of Hecker's was condemned by the Vatican at the turn of the century as the heresy of "Americanism." Sheen uses the philosophy of the American mythos regarding the rights and freedom of the individual but again adds an implicit, uniquely Catholic dimension: For the Catholic, the material is enriched or disciplined by ascetic virtue that leads the individual to the higher, spiritual realm.

Sheen promotes his Catholic view of the individual by haloing it in the patriotic image of the American flag. His purpose is to convey a message that reflects the Scholastic claim of a spiritual and a material realm. As the cathedral connects the two realms, the individual is divided between the material and the spiritual:

> Depriving people of personal liberation and privacy is not American. [Applause.] I believe that man has exactly the same qualities as our flag. A man has a body and soul, matter and spirit. And our flag also has something material and spiritual. Materially it is only a piece of cloth: red, white, and blue. Spiritually it has significance as a symbol of our country and traditions and its institutions. I know that there are some in our land that would say the flag is just material and that life itself is only materialistic, and they will demand the right to put the flag under our feet. I beg you, as Americans, to defend the flag and to defend man. To say that just as there is something above the body of man, there is something above the cloth of the flag. And we should keep it there [applause grows stronger] because it has spirit and meaning.[50]

Once again Sheen uses the metaphor of the land to describe the nation in which the individual is situated, with both material and spiritual qualities. To the metaphor of the land he adds the metaphor of a house to describe the individual. As a separate unit, the house provides a rationale for individual freedom. Yet at the same time the house is part of Sheen's Catholic medieval city because it is subordinate to the higher levels that connect one to God.

For example, he describes a house with three levels. The individual can ascend from one level of the house to the next. Some live in the cellar, but these people are like "animals because they only want pleasure." The second floor is the place for those who value art, science, philosophy, and reason. The third floor is the ideal place—a "diviner world where great happiness, and peace of souls surpassing everything" can be found. It is a "world of faith, joy, inner peace, and happiness." Sheen has not explicitly named religion as one of the floors, but in a comment moments earlier he used the authoritative "we," noting that "we climb four flights of stairs three times a day" in a house much like this. This leaves the subtle impression that Sheen can move between the levels and can even go higher, to a fourth level. In light of his bishop's robes, a connection is suggested between church authority and the levels of the house. The higher level of the house has spiritual qualities—faith, peace, happiness—similar to those found in the cathedral principle of life.[51]

Extensions of the house metaphor focus on the door and the key. Sheen's development of these metaphors fits well with the American ideology of privacy. He says, "Each and every one of us has a key to our own front door and our own home." Rationality is connected with the higher levels, while emotion not controlled by reason is as "a screen door in the summertime; children play with it and the screen is tugged . . . so that the screen door will not close."[52]

The highest level of the house is the virtue of love. Sheen uses the metaphor of the bird's nest as an entailment of the root metaphor of the house. In it he notes that the bird can rest in the house or the nest but is intended to soar to the heights above the nest: "Love is like a bird. You know sometimes the bird is in the nest. When the bird is in the nest, its wings are confined and limited by the nest. At other times the bird in the wing has infinite horizons for its view. Sometimes the heart just rests in the nest of another creature. At other times it is dissatisfied. It seeks some infinite love."[53] He refers to the better dwelling for the person as "living under the cover of the divine wings above the senses, above reason, in a world of faith and joy and inner peace and happiness." These qualities are very similar to those of the cathedral principle. He continues by calling people not merely to live in the house but "to die to lower self and you can live in my kingdom."[54] The notion of the kingdom also endorses the medieval city, which could itself be described as a kingdom.

Sheen's subordination of the individual to the higher realm would normally clash with American ideology, but in the fifties there was an emphasis on the corporate structure and the subordination of the individual. At the same time his ideology would have appeal in the political mood of McCarthyism. Sheen states that it is not a violation of one's rights to be called to testify before a government committee without the protection of the Fifth Amendment. Sheen makes this civil right subordinate to the higher need of the state, and his audience applauds in enthusiastic support: "Many educators are betraying the great American tradition and vocation of teaching. There is no danger whatever to academic freedom when a professor is asked if he is or is not a member—absolutely not—a member of the Communist party, but there is a danger to academic freedom when a professor hides behind the Fifth Amendment and uses America's liberty in order to destroy it and deliver us over to Moscow."[55] Although here Sheen is talking about educators, his comments represent his broader view of preferring limits to the freedom of the individual, a freedom that is valued in the tenets of the American ideology. The individual is entitled to rights and privacy in this rhetoric but always within the context of the hierarchy, whether it be the spiritual over the material or the institution over the individual. This rhetoric of the subordinate individual is balanced and structured in a hierarchy by Sheen's message that the individual has a choice of house in this medieval city: "If we are inns, we are filled. We are filled with our own ego, our own self-importance, our mind is filled with all that we think is knowable. Our will is filled with our own tiny view of what we think is good. Our passions are filled with every kind of satiety. There is no room in the inn." In contrast to the inn is the stable, with its connotations of the stable of Bethlehem where the Savior was born: "This stable, this cave, proud men cannot enter it. Because in order to enter a cave you have to stoop. You almost have to get down on your knees. . . . proud men will not humble themselves."[56]

Still using a structural metaphor, Sheen claims that "man today is locked up. Man is imprisoned within himself. He is almost his own jailer. Modern man is imprisoned in a mind without windows, without doors."[57] This statement suggests that it is wrong to be self-enclosed. The prison is very much like the pyramid in contrast to the cathedral. Like the pyramid, the prison has no windows or doors, suggesting a lack of the life and air that are contained in the cathedral.

The individual can choose to live in either principle, the cathedral or the pyramid, with the cathedral preferred.

In Sheen's ideology an individual must have something more than himself on the inside in order to break free from the prison. This is the difference between a creature and a child of God. The inner action of being a child of God puts the person on a higher stage in the hierarchy and involves a change in one's human nature. The individual functions in a parallel way to the cathedral with its possibility of bridging two realms. The difference between the house and the cathedral is that the individual is subordinate to the superior institution:

> Now if a man, by nature, who is only a creature, becomes a child of God, begins to share the Divine Nature, this does not belong to his nature any more than blooming belongs to a stone or sensitivity to a rose or speech belongs to a dog. . . . We are made a child of God . . . when we have this life inside us; then we're not just creatures made by God. We become something else. Then we are really begotten. That's the way we go up. That's the way we're lifted out of the natural order of ours. There are not many who wish to go up that high.[58]

Using this ideology of the child of God, Sheen makes implicit application to Catholic baptism, by which a child is believed to become a child of God. He adds, "We are begotten as children of God, made partakers of His divine nature and heirs of the kingdom of Heaven."[59] The inference can only be that the individual needs the cathedral, the bridge between the two realms. The cathedral, the place of baptism, reminds the children that they are not just individuals but "heirs" like medieval royalty; the kingdom is now spiritual.

Here the individual, like God, is described in terms of an economic system. However, in this case the individual is not only a participant in the financial system but a product of it. Sheen tells us that an economic system of grace is needed because "there is a price tag on every single soul." He continues, "Some souls are very expensive, some are not." When a person is not open to grace, "the grace must be purchased for them by others." We have already discussed Felix Leseur, an atheist whose wife purchased salvation for her husband by means of her sufferings. Sheen continues the story: "In her last will and testament, she revealed that she had asked Almighty God to send her sufficient suffering 'to purchase his soul.' She added: 'On the day that

I die, I will have paid the price; you will have been bought and paid for.'" Sheen notes that the man converted and became a priest after his wife's death.[60] The problem with society is that "not many men want to die to their lower selves; it costs so much."[61]

The economic order is blessed here because it is made part of the process of salvation. However, the economic system is not capitalism but feudalism. The overlord, in this case God or those who are spiritually rich, protects those who have less. At the same time the individual gains purchasing power by achieving spiritual virtue.

This system ties in well with the traditional view of Catholicism that one can achieve salvation by actions and charity. As Sheen reminds listeners, "We have no crusades, no action. I think that is why there is not much action in political life against traitors, for example, against juvenile delinquents and against any kind of evil." He continues, using his metaphor of the house: "Hence, for the restoration of peace . . . it is possible for every human being to lock some of these passions and to enthrone reason here. To open the door and to have reason, the moral law and faith decide what emotion will possess them and to what extent." The goal is emphasized through the illustration of Mary Magdalene, who came "out of an emotional cellar such as this and became a saint. . . . So it is possible for anyone who may live in these cavernous depths to arouse his reason, his faith."[62]

We have seen that the individual is always subordinate to the higher order—becoming a child of God through the Catholic sacrament of baptism and the moral law of which the church is a custodian. The higher order allows one to have citizenship in another city, the heavenly kingdom, rather than just the earthly city, as God's saint. Sheen says, "The greatest royalty of all comes at baptism, when one is incorporated into the Kingdom of Heaven."[63] This indicates that the medieval city is only a stopping-off point, and the Catholic cathedral, as the place of baptism, becomes the way to the greatest royalty, which is heaven.

So far the medieval city is shaped by houses that represent individuals. God is the lord over the city, while the nation is the land on which the city is built. At the same time the nation is conceived of in a chivalrous way. The cathedral is the center of this city because it provides the way to the kingdom of God and the means to royal membership in that kingdom.

No medieval cathedral would be complete without the gargoyle

figures that look out from the cathedral arches. These figures, representing demons and monsters, were constructed as a reminder that
evil forces always sought to possess the individual, who had to be ever
vigilant in the choice of good over evil. Sheen refers to them as "hor-
rid little demons" that remind us that "even in Church there are temptations."[64] As we will see, temptations and evil come from secularism.

The gargoyles in Sheen's city are "winged creatures," "vultures,"
"winged monsters," that live in the "rocky" heights:

> Wherever the carcass is, there shall come the vultures. . . . out of
> the mountain fastnesses, the rocky crags, the vultures of the sky
> come down to this glittering rottenness in order to devour it.
> These winged creatures are a kind of avenger and a punisher.
> They are a judgment upon death and corruption. Just as soon as
> corruption sets in, these winged monsters appear shrieking and
> croaking and winging their way to death itself. . . . Whenever a
> civilization begins to die morally or spiritually, then there begin to
> appear vultures. That is the mission of Communism in the world.
> Communism is the scavenger of a decaying civilization.[65]

Communism is a gargoyle or scavenger of death. It has taken on an
animal type of existence that is beneath the dignity, as claimed by
Scholasticism, of the individual. Sheen, unlike Billy Graham, does not
totally condemn Communism; rather, he notes that the principle of
communism is rooted in the Western world and the Hebraic-Christian tradition: "Communism is strong when it borrows some of the
moral indignation that has been inherited from the Hebraic-Christian
traditions; Communism is weak when it departs from that tradition.
Communism has bootlegged and smuggled into its system the decency and morality of the Western world."[66] When Sheen roots Communism in the West, he is in keeping with his principle of natural law
that recognizes both good and evil within nature. Even the scavengers
of Communism can be redeemed. But Sheen never downplays the evil
of Communism: "Communism came out of our Western civilization;
it was produced out of what was putrid, foul, and rotten in the atheism and materialism of the nineteenth century."[67]

If Communism is the scavenger of death, who or what is dying?
Sheen points out that the scavengers appear when a "civilization begins to die morally or spiritually."[68] The principle of death is more
than Communism. It is secularism that has turned people away from

God; Communism enters the picture to take advantage of what is already dying.

For Sheen, the dying victim is like the sick world: a "world is sick, not just one part of the world. When a human organism is poisoned, one cannot amputate an arm or a leg. . . . We have all sinned, and all stand in need of the mercy of God." Sheen's metaphor of sickness implies the root metaphor of the world as a body, one that is "being crucified by Communism."[69] He uses extensions of the metaphor of the body that describe death as "cold, dull, apathetic." The problem is, he says, that "our Western world lacks fire. . . . We are cold, dull, apathetic." He also observes that "the whole world is suffering from hunger" and describes two kinds: "The hunger of body is Eastern. . . . The hunger of soul is Western." The West is the head of the body and the East its center. Although the head has traditionally been seen as superior in Catholicism because it is the place of God and the authority of the church, Sheen does not make this distinction, which would have stirred controversy.[70]

The ultimate goal of the body is to "die to self in order to be incorporated into divinity."[71] The word *incorporated* has as its root the Latin word *corpus,* or body. Sheen's metaphor is very much in the spirit of Pope Pius XII, whose encyclicals *Mystici corpris* (1943) and *Humani generis* (1950) declared that the Body of Christ and the church are one. Sheen is not so explicit as to say baldly that the church is the body of Christ, but that is implied by his principle of the cathedral.

His claim that the whole world is a body means that countries have a responsibility for one another. This provides a new rationale for American philanthropy to the world. America no longer is the chosen nation, fighting a millennial battle against evil outside forces, but rather is leading the rest of the world in a shared battle.

Sheen goes on to label America's sickness as blindness: "We had our moment of blindness, our national blindness. . . . in World War II there were three wicked, evil philosophies in the world: Communism, Nazism, and fascism. The only difference between the three was the difference of murder, killing, and taking of life. In our moment of blindness we said only two of these are evil. One is good. We called it a democracy. Woe to those who go down to Russia for help." Here Sheen is referring to America's alliance with atheist Russia in World War II, which the Catholic hierarchy criticized. Picking up on the themes of death and blindness, he adds that those who live in lower levels of existence are "just like the deaf. The deaf are dead to the great environment of harmony. The blind are dead to the environment of beauty, and so are these people deity-blind, and they refuse to recognize that there is something higher."[72]

Sheen notes that the problem in the world of sickness and death is not so much physical as spiritual. Communism is a "judgment of God on those countries that have lost their faith in God and morals." He picks up the theme of loss when he attributes the death agony of the Western world to a crisis in faith: "Something died in our Western world, namely the strong faith in the God who made them."[73]

He claims that "our Western world is losing its great spiritual foundations, something like the prodigal son that left his father's house and is living on husks." He adds, "Our hunger is a hunger of the soul as our Western world is losing its Christian foundation. The Western world is becoming mental patients because we're undernourished spiritually."[74] This time the illness of the world is described as "mental." The prodigal son left his father's house of his own free will, suggesting that we have brought this sickness on ourselves. The use of structural metaphors—foundation, base—suggests that, consistent with natural law, there are basic, inherent principles of life.

In the spirit of the jeremiad, Sheen offers not just a problem but a return to God: "Godlessness causes war; therefore let us be Godly."[75] Sheen's critique of America is softened by the fact that the victim is the whole Western world, not just America. His rhetoric invites people to health and a wider "environment," suggesting not just the metaphor of country as the land but light, air, and the other elements of the cathedral principle. Sheen uses the container metaphor again to describe the individual in relation to the environment. He compares individuals to a chick emerging from an egg, claiming that "the chick inside must have the instinct to realize that there is a bigger and broader environment than the confines of a shell." There is remedy for this container of death in the egg: "Once it [the chick] knows the greater environment and tries to establish a relationship with it, then it uses its own efforts to escape the shell, and that is the remedy we're going to offer."[76]

Elsewhere he refers to America as the dying patient in need of recovery:

We need the kind of revolution in the United States and the rest of the world that purges out of a man's heart pride, and covetousness, and lust, and anger, and envy, and gluttony, and sloth. In other words, then, the battle against Communism begins within the hearts of every single American. It means the recovery of our own great traditions, of our belief in God, of an affirmation in politics, and in economic life and among our politicians, of the things that are right and true before God. Then we need not fear Communism, for if God is with us who can be against us?[77]

The battle Sheen describes is a millennial battle of life or death for the human race. There is an element of urgency to this battle because the patient is already sick and the vultures are gathering, even in America. But there is hope: "Traitors will stop in America when Americans recover their faith."[78]

Sheen's jeremiad is in the spirit of the Puritan call for America to be the "city on a hill." However, Sheen is pleading for Americans to do battle not only with external forces but with mystical forces of good and evil within each person. Sheen elaborates, saying that a treaty of peace must not just be on "paper but in the hearts of men." He goes on to note, "What good does it do to abolish the external conditions of war, if the internal conditions of selfishness, hatred of neighbor, bigotry and intolerance and forgetfulness of God continue to exist?" He continues, "When you get enough men and women in the world with civil wars—the kind of wars that produces psychosis, neurosis, and mental disturbances—when you get enough of those in a man and multiply them into the mathematical infinity, then you have a world war."[79]

Sheen further modifies the jeremiad tradition by stressing that mere sorrow or conversion with the lips is not enough.[80] He also calls for action that moves beyond the recognition of Jesus as Savior. This contrasts with the popular religion as preached by Billy Graham, who taught that conversion alone was enough because the individual could not do anything to earn salvation.

Sheen wants more. The problem is that "we have no crusades, no action."[81] Action is significant:

There is a great difference between sorrow and reparation, making up for sorrow. . . . Suppose every time we did wrong we were told to drive a nail in a board, and every time we were forgiven we were told to pull a nail out. There would still be holes in the board. That's the record of how we disturb the order of justice. People think all they have to do when they do wrong individually, socially, before God and man is just merely be forgiven. No, they have to make up for it. Equilibrium and the balance of justice must be restored.[82]

He goes on to use the analogy of the physician restoring a patient: "Doctors will graft skin if we burn our face from our back to our face to restore our pristine elegance. If a person is suffering from anemia, the doctor will transfer blood from the healthy member to the anemic member in order to cure a person of that condition. If it is possible to graft skin, don't you think it is possible to graft some reparation, some sacrifices?"[83]

Once again Sheen's jeremiad adds a uniquely Catholic element to the American mythos:[84] that salvation can be earned and death in the medieval city overcome by individual actions and sacrifices. The action is a philanthropy that is rooted in the individual, not to better society, but as a means to self-purification to earn the love of God. Sheen goes on to elaborate the Catholic belief in acts as a means of salvation when he asks the viewer, "Will you make a sacrifice? I do not say a gift. Because a gift is something you can hand off to anyone. A sacrifice is not something hard but a gift done with love. . . . Would you make a sacrifice . . . send me a dime . . . and send it to me with love . . . say 'I give this for the love of God.'"[85]

The collective acts of individuals can change the world—but not just for the sake of change or as a social gospel that tries to transform society. Societal change is an *indirect* outcome of individual action. Sheen is calling Americans to acts of "prayer, penance and fasting" when he adds, "this is why we asked you to write our president to ask him for a day of reparation, of prayer, penance, fasting for the peace of the world." When Sheen began his broadcasts, America was in the midst of a war that had not ended evil in the world, as had been promised by earlier war rhetoric. President Truman's policy of containing the Cold War by stopping the spread of Communism suggested that America had failed in its millennial destiny. Truman and General Douglas MacArthur, in a very public debate, argued whether Communism should be contained or eliminated. Containment rather than elimination made Americans question their role as victors in the millennial battle. The 1950 trial of Alger Hiss, the 1953 execution of Julius and Ethel Rosenberg, and the televised denouncing of America by American POWs during the Korean War challenged Americans in how they saw themselves. In addition Protestantism had been in crisis since the turn of the century with the formation of fundamentalist branches at war with more liberal branches. Against this background, Sheen's jeremiad offers a solution to the crisis of American ideology. He claims that the millennium has not come about because the individual has failed to fight an inner war against the self. In this way Sheen is able to preserve the spiritual values inherent in the American mythos.

Sheen's jeremiad notes that America is a chosen nation whose guiding principles are inherently Catholic. These Catholic principles rest on a belief of individual freedom, but always within the boundaries of moral or natural law as interpreted by the church. The nation suffers because individuals have forgotten God, who is found in the cathedral principle of the medieval city.

Sheen's presentation does not reject American culture but offers to change it to make a place for Catholic ideology. At the same time he recognizes and respects American traditions. He even blesses America's new role as an economic leader; Scholasticism, unlike Calvinism, saw spiritual value in the material. Sheen seeks to modify rather than overthrow the system by showing that the medieval city is the dwelling place of God. American abundance and prosperity through new technology and capitalism added legitimacy to his claim. America's true destiny is more than the "city on the hill" of traditional American ideology. It is found in this medieval city of Catholicism, the place of truth and the genuine charity that flows from true patriotism.

Sheen is a religious figure speaking about religious practice in an age when the American ideology was often defined as the expression of religiosity. However, his message goes further than that. He wants viewers to act with reparation and charity for the sake of their own salvation. Unlike Billy Graham, who uses the jeremiad to call the sinner to conversion and unqualified acceptance of America, Sheen never fully embraces the American mythos or Graham's popular evangelicalism without adding the elements that are specifically Catholic. At the same time he qualifies the traditional goodness of American culture, not by criticizing the social order but by criticizing individual abuse of it that leads to secularism and forgetfulness of God.

According to Sheen, God has chosen both the citizen of the medieval city and the American citizen, but for both of them, mere words of conversion are not enough for salvation. Merely being American is not enough because God chooses individuals rather than nations as he calls us to the moral action that gives life rather than the death of the pyramid principle. As members of a world community, all individuals must work to become part of the heavenly city by embracing the cathedral principle. That principle provided a rationale for America as it became a world leader; it also became an implicit argument for Catholic legitimacy and authority in a diverse society.

Since Vatican II Catholicism has been more tolerant of other religious traditions. John Courtney Murray, silenced in the fifties by the Roman Church, was acknowledged as pivotal at Vatican II. The desire of America's first bishop, John Carroll, to have Catholic liturgies in English became a reality. The church has become Americanized. Pope John Paul II was welcomed at the White House in 1993. When the National Conference of Catholic Bishops spoke out on issues of war and peace and the American economic system in the 1980s, they saw themselves not in a defensive mode but as participants in a dialogue about America on issues of war and economy.

The Catholic laity have become more independent in their thinking; they more freely dissent against teachings of Rome and institutional authorities. Catholic laity, conservative and liberal, lobby for their positions with Rome. Individual bishops have encouraged Rome to be more tolerant in its dealings with the American situation. The group Call to Action, a grassroots organization of Catholics advocating a more democratic church, holds national conventions each year supported by some members of the American hierarchy. At the same time Catholic leaders have found themselves forming alliances with conservative Protestant groups over issues of abortion and homosexuality. These issues put them at odds with their more liberal Catholic brethren. This is another example of James Hunter's "culture war," where fewer people are identifying with institutional religion but choosing to form alliances with people who share their worldview.

Bishop Sheen's cathedral metaphor stressed the church as structure. Some Catholics still want these structures. Other Catholics in the nineties have moved beyond that to a metaphor of the church as the people of God, which was popularized through the rhetoric of Vatican II. In France one bishop has chosen to dissent from Roman structures. He has been removed from his diocese since 1995, but Bishop Jacques David Gaillot has chosen to create a "virtual diocese" on the Internet. His experience is one example of the church as people rather than the cathedral principle.

One thing that the opposed sides have in common is that everyone wants to be heard. Laity from all sides claim a place in the debate. It is no longer only the leaders who have a voice. At least one bishop has tried to bring the sides together. Before his death in 1996, Cardinal Joseph Bernardin of Chicago formed Common Ground, a group to promote dialogue among opposed sides. Only time will tell whether or not this movement is as successful in uniting Catholics as Bishop Sheen was in bridging the gap between Catholics and members of diverse American denominations.

4

A Television Troubador Sings
His Medieval Lady's Praise

"As you noticed, this year we have a new Madonna. This is Our Lady of Television. . . . As you know, television is a projection [of] the human word. Every human word is nothing but a broken syllable of the word Divine. Now inasmuch as the Mother of the Lord projected the Divine Word to the world, we name her the Lady of Television. She may project our world, draw mankind together in love and peace and unity, the spirit of fraternity, neighbor, above all worship of God."[1]

With these words Sheen acknowledges the statue of Our Lady of Television, positioned prominently on stage. The Madonna stands on a pedestal, tall and noble, her Child sitting on her shoulder; they hold above their heads the globe, with the cross planted in it. The femininity of her body is de-emphasized by broad shoulders; her features suggest impersonal distance or stoicism. The asexuality, a lack of intimacy, is softened only by the presence of the Child. Yet the Child is not held tenderly but rather is lifted high. The Madonna's eyes look above and beyond the viewer, suggesting a determination at her task: the projection of "the Divine Word" through the medium of television to a fifties audience. Although Sheen describes her as a mother who is to draw mankind together, she represents a stoic idealism rather than tenderness.

This statue is not Our Lady of Lourdes, the Blessed Virgin, Mother of God, Queen of Rosary, or *Theotokos*—all traditional titles for Mary in Roman Catholicism—but Our Lady of Television. This new title suggests a modification of tradition and an adaptation to the needs of a new rhetorical situation. The statue of the Madonna is a metaphor for Sheen's ideology of womanhood in America. Sheen goes on to say, "To her I dedicate America and pray to her. Let not America be inhabited by God only in ruins."[2] (Secularization was one reason that Sheen

Television audiences often saw Sheen with outstretched arms and Our Lady of Television over his shoulder. Courtesy of the Sheen Archives, Diocese of Rochester.

feared America would be "in ruins.") It was amazing that a Catholic bishop would talk about Mary, and dedicate America to her, through the mass medium of television when Protestantism was in open conflict with Roman Catholicism over the theology of Mary.

In his 1953 encyclical, *Fulgens corona,* Pope Pius XII proclaimed a Holy Year, a year of special prayer and devotion, in honor of Mary. The pope connected the doctrine of the Assumption—Mary's bodily ascension into heaven after her death—to Jesus' redemption when he said, "Mary shared his glorious triumph over sin." This letter made Mary an active participant in the redemptive process and gave her qualities that transcended ordinary human life. Mainstream Protestantism was outraged by this new official doctrine, as seen in a 1950 editorial in *Christian Century:* "By promulgating the doctrine of the Assumption of the Virgin as a dogma, the Roman Catholic Church will . . . give the term "faith" a content which would place Christian discipleship beyond the possible allegiance of millions with the best mental training our times afford. It will provide new ammunition for those in the Kremlin and outside, who attack religion as the last citadel and source of superstition. . . . it becomes more than ever apparent that the spiritual welfare of contemporary man requires the Protestant witness."[3]

The Protestant Reformation had put many of the basic beliefs of Catholicism on the defensive, and this was especially true of the doctrine of Mary. Reformers did not deny that Mary was the mother of God, but they were critical of the emphasis on Mary as an intercessor, rejected titles that honored Mary as a queen, and denied that she played more than a passive role in the redemptive process. Holding the married state to be virtuous, they also criticized Catholic emphasis on Mary's virginity. The current statement by Pius XII opened old wounds about papal authoritarianism, claims to infallibility, and the Catholic focus on devotionalism over scriptural accuracy. This reaction created a rhetorical problem for Sheen. His background would demand he support Pius XII's Marian devotion, but if he used the Marian discourse of the Catholic tradition, he placed himself at odds with the Protestant culture.

This chapter looks at how Sheen constructed Mary within his discourse in light of the tensions inherent in speaking to a mixed audience. It explores Mary's role in the discourse and what Sheen's use of Mary suggests about the role of women in 1950s society. Finally, we will look at how, without compromising his Roman Catholic beliefs in Mary or the traditional definitions of women, Sheen's rhetoric presents Mary in a way that does not alienate his mixed audience.

Sheen presents himself much like the medieval troubadour responding to his lady. This was an image of the relationship the church had to Mary with roots deep in tradition. In the eleventh century the troubadour sang love poems of praise and service to an idealized lady of higher status and practiced chivalrous discipline at her service. This spiritual image of ascetic love came to counter the twelfth century's notion of erotic love. Using this trend to its advantage, the church referred to Mary as a lady who as queen deserved honor as a mother and a model of virginity. Cathedrals were built to her under the title of "Notre Dame" or "Our Lady." As royal lady she became intercessor for the needs of the devoted. The church used Mary to assert its authority, now over carnal love.

Mary was central in Sheen's own life; his dedication to her was unconditional: "Those who accept the background of Lourdes, then, they have two mothers, just as I have two mothers. I have a mother in the flesh, then I have her as a spiritual mother because Our Blessed Lord gave her to us all on the cross when he said, 'Behold thy mother.' I read Mass once a week to her. When I was a little baby my mother placed me on the altar of the Blessed Mother and dedicated me to her. So I've dedicated all my books to her, everything that has been written in my whole life."[4]

For the rhetorical critic, beginnings and endings suggest a theme or a frame for the entire text.[5] The program itself begins with Sheen standing in front of the statue of Mary and Child and concludes from the same place. This nonverbal dedication to the woman he describes as spiritual mother complements the discourse and stresses Mary's importance.

Her role as a spiritual mother suggests two worlds—one of the flesh and one of the spirit—that Mary bridges. She is the biological mother of Jesus and our spiritual mother. As spiritual mother she is described in sublimated terms; her sexuality is something mystical. Sheen notes this mysticism, saying, "Then when he took on human flesh and became a Babe, we can understand why He climbed up her body as an ivory tower, to kiss upon her lips a Mystic Rose."[6] The image of a tower suggests a distance; an ivory tower and a mystic rose imply sexual purity. This fits well with the structure of the statue of the Madonna. Her strength and nobility are emphasized rather than her sexuality.

Sheen is able to make such an overtly sexual description for two reasons. First, the image of a mystic rose has deep roots in Christian spirituality, which stressed the spiritual rather than the erotic quality of love. The rosary comes from a Latin word meaning rose garden. The rose was believed to be the queen of all flowers; in early pre-Christian mythologies it described Venus and the voluptuousness of a prostitute's love. The biblical Book of Sirach (24:14) speaks of a rose blooming in the desert and the Song of Songs of a lover in the garden. These passages were Christianized and often said to refer to Mary as the mystical bride of Christ and the church. The mystical rose became an especially popular title for Mary in the twelfth to fifteenth centuries. Saint Bernard popularized this image of Mary, as well as the image of a tower of strength. Pope Leo XIII, at the end of the nineteenth century, added the title "Mystical Rose" to the traditional Litany of Loretto, which honored Mary.

Second, the priest was described in the fifties as asexual. His asceticism and virtue were supposed to keep him innocent as he sublimated his desires. Sheen, for example, often associated himself with the innocence of children and of an imaginary angel that wiped the chalkboard for him. Thus, for Sheen the mystic rose was not explicitly sexual but spiritualized.

Significantly, the role of spiritual mother, which Sheen obviously values, is downplayed by the infrequent mention of Mary. Even in the titles of the program, Sheen does not explicitly name his spiritual mother, although sometimes the discourse is implicitly about her. For example, the town in "The Best Town in Which to Be Broke" is in fact Lourdes, site of the Marian apparition in France. Sheen explains that he has visited the shrine twenty-six times, seeking favors that are spiritual, emotional, and material.

In the program on Lourdes, Sheen argues the validity of the Marian devotion that takes place there.[7] This is one of the few times when Sheen prefaces his message by presenting arguments for the theme. He takes care to identify Lourdes with images of secular culture that are persuasive in the 1950s. This implies that he knows he has to accommodate an audience wider than Catholics.

Sheen shapes his pro-Marian message by associating Mary with values of contemporary society to make his message more appealing to a mixed audience. He argues for the validity of Lourdes by identifying it with credible authorities of the fifties. These credible authorities are rational men, such as doctors and scientists, theological standards, and skeptics. Another way he gains credibility is by placing ideas in the context of modernity and the medium of movies.

Sheen begins building credibility for Lourdes by association with the popular medium of movies. He describes Lourdes as "a city in France . . . You've heard about it; it was in a movie, *The Song of Bernadette*, the city of Lourdes." He goes on to place the happenings at Lourdes in the context of the modern world—one of the few times when modernity is not described in negative terms:

In that particular city in the year 1858, which was very important because, oh, six months in either direction of that year our modern world to some extent was born. Darwin wrote his *Origin of Species;* Mill wrote his essay *On Liberty;* Karl Marx, the founder of Communism, wrote *The Introduction to the Critique of Political Economy;* and then another world broke onto this and there appeared to a little girl by the name of Bernadette, the Blessed Virgin of Lourdes. Well, obviously there has to be some verification, because if there is none, then what is to prevent any psychotic or dreamer from coming along to say God or an angel appeared to me. So they investigated Bernadette; she was found to be very humble. That's one of the conditions. I know one investigation that stopped very quickly when this person claimed that God had appeared to her. And the investigating committee said, "Are you the saint?" "Yes I am the saint." That ended it.[8]

These final sentences suggest another attempt to build rapport around the controversial discussion over Lourdes by showing the audience that there are limits to the possibility of miracles and visionaries. By distancing himself from fanatics who claim to be saints, Sheen makes his own claims about the miracles of Lourdes appear more rational. He sets his discussion within the context of objective science by the use of words like *investigated* and *verification* and by applying the clinical label of psychology, "psychotic," to the fanatics. What is being investigated in Sheen's description is the girl Bernadette and her humility, yet another proof for the authenticity of Lourdes in Sheen's eyes. Humility was both a sacred term in Sheen's ideology and a traditional female character trait valued in religious circles.

Sheen goes on to argue more explicitly for miracles, again using the credibility of science and the objectivity of the medical profession: "And then in addition to that there had to be other tests made that were scientifically verifiable, such as miracles. And there is established at Lourdes the International Medical Association, which is made up of some of the very best doctors of the world. I am not going to give you any verifications tonight, just simply state that in 1902 Dr. Alexis Carrel went there, and he said he went there as a skeptic, and after studying the miracles he was absolutely convinced that they took place."[9]

The conclusion of the program gives all the more credibility to Mary's presence in Lourdes because it is framed in the testimony of Dr. Leseur, an extreme skeptic who comes to believe by the prayer of a devout woman: "Elizabeth Arrighi married Felix Leseur, a French doctor, who promised to respect the faith of his wife but spent about as much time propagating atheism and anticlericalism as he did medicine. As a matter of fact he was the editor of one of the anticlerical newspapers of Paris. Forgot his promise and tried to break down her faith."[10]

Sheen hammers home his picture of the skeptic again when he notes that after his wife's death Leseur heard an inner voice saying, "Go to Lourdes," but "he was a rank unbeliever. He had already proven it a fraud, a superstition." The voice became so compelling that Leseur eventually did go to Lourdes, where "he received the gift of faith, so total and complete . . . that he had not to go through any process of juxtaposition." Leseur's conversion was so complete that he became a Dominican priest. To emphasize Leseur's earlier lack of faith, Sheen says that, upon hearing Leseur's request to be a priest, even the "Holy Father" initially said, "I forbid you; you must remain in the world and repair the harm which you have done."[11]

Sheen made his retreat with Doctor—now Father—Leseur, concluding, "It is not often one can make a retreat under a priest who every now and then says, 'As my dear wife, Elizabeth, said.'" That he had been married gives him all the more credibility because he had lived in both worlds, the earthly and the mystical, the world of men and the spiritual world of Mary. He had lived in the world of skepticism but found belief.

In preparing to discuss the controversial topic of Lourdes, Sheen uses another form of identification, his own identification with men and manly traits. In an icebreaker he jokes about a telephone survey in Boston: "We telephoned one thousand men and asked the question, 'What are you listening to?' Nine hundred ninety-four answered 'My wife.' [Applause.]" He continues by jokingly describing the "beerdrex method" of testing ratings: counting how many men in a bar in Wilkes Barre, Pennsylvania, bought drinks while his program was being telecast in the bar. He notes that among fifty men watching, no drinks were sold.

Sheen thus illustrates his popularity by stressing that his viewers include men in bars—men so captivated by his message that they do not drink while his program is on the air. This will help him in his discussion of Mary because it implies that men—associated in this period with rationality—agree with his message. Sheen's message is implied to be more than mere emotionalism because men in the very earthy bar atmosphere prefer his program.

Usually Sheen makes bald declarative statements without prefacing his remarks. He needs to lay a groundwork in this controversial program because of skepticism regarding Catholic belief in Mary and in miracles. Sheen's discussion of Mary is potentially explosive for a mixed audience; otherwise he would not have to preface it to such an extent. His rhetorical strategy is not to start with an explicitly religious declaration about Mary but to conclude his presentation there. This ties in well with persuasion theory, which suggests that if an audience might be hostile to an argument, the rhetor should place his or her most controversial arguments last.[12]

A second program illustrates another strategy that Sheen uses to support his discussion of Catholic belief. Here Sheen begins by discussing the use of writers for the medium of television; his own writers, he claims, are the four evangelists. This claim would have credibility among Protestants who valued the Scripture as authority. Sheen makes his point by using the testimony and the authority of the evangelist Luke to speak in favor of the virginity of Mary. Because the focus on Mary and the suggestion of a superhuman Mariology would have been controversial for a mixed audience, once again Sheen uses the credibility of science and the profession of medicine to give legitimacy to his claim. But even more interesting is Sheen's use of deliberate pauses; he waits for the audience's applause to validate his statements:

> It is particularly interesting [pause] it is indeed impressive [pause] that Saint Luke, who was a physician, who therefore was skilled in obstetrics, who knew all the facts of life and death, that he who might be the only one of all the evangelists who might be expected to deny one of the fundamental facts of Christianity, yet is one man who affirms it above all others, namely the virgin birth. [Sheen's arm is raised with his hand in a fist, and his voice loud. He looks at the camera and waits four seconds, a long pause, for the audience to applaud. They applaud enthusiastically.][13]

Sheen again uses the strategy of placing the values of Catholicism at the end of the presentation when he describes the building of the Cathedral of Notre Dame. He shares stories of history and legend about the cathedral—Napoleon's coronation, descriptions of the glass windows—but concludes with a dramatic declaration of the role of Mary in the church. Defending another Catholic teaching that was controversial at the time, he makes it clear that she is not to be worshiped and that she is human:

> It was dedicated, yes dedicated to a woman. Do not think because it was dedicated to a woman that she is adored. She is not adored. She is not a goddess. She is human. Why then is so much venera-tion and respect paid in a cathedral; why is it dedicated to her? Because she is the rampart; she is the outpost. She is the human door by which divinity came into this earth. That's why to regard her as someone who is to be revered. So long as ramparts are safe, then the city will be safe. So long as the mother is secure, then the Son will be proclaimed as divine. That's the reason of veneration for her. So in that stone, and all of us summoned to her to make us warriors, warriors of the faith that she may make the assault upon omnipotence.[14]

Sheen describes Mary's role in terms of a holy war that provides safe passage between two worlds. Earlier we noted Sheen's use of mar-tial imagery to evoke the battle against secularism and spirituality. (Whereas, in Marian traditions, such as devotion to Our Lady of Fatima, Mary was defined as leader in the Catholic anti-Communist movement, for Sheen the war is much bigger; it is against secular-ism.) This text makes Mary a significant influence in that war, placing her in a very masculine role as a general who trains her troops to become "warriors." At the same time her assault is waged not only against the enemy but also against God, who is described as "Om-nipotence," not as a friend or a brother as in more immanent Protes-tant images. This helps explain Mary's role as protectress because this image of God distances him from the viewer, who then needs an inter-mediary.

But Mary's role as intercessor is described rather than baldly stated. Sheen needed to accommodate a mixed audience that was skeptical of the need for a mediator other than Christ. The closest he gets to frankly describing Mary as intercessor is his statement that Mary would "in-tercede for a miracle for us, just as she did at Cana."[15] He is careful once again to make an association with the acceptable argument of authority through Scripture.

In the same program he implies that Mary is an intercessor by saying, "Mothers give us bitter medicine. They say, 'Well, it's for your own good.' Sometimes the bitter medicine can be for other people's good. And she gives bitter medicine from time to time. I can remember over a period of a couple years I seemed to get every hard cross always on her feast day." This implies that Mary grants favors, although not always for our benefit. He concludes the same program by once more affirming his belief in Mary as intercessor, hoping that at the final judgment he would hear God say, "I often heard my mother speak of you."[16]

Again, less baldly, he refers to the Catholic belief in Mary's intercessor role when he says, "Over the main altar stood a statue of Our Lady of Equity, listening as it were to the disputes, but with mercy and kindness and tenderness symbolized by holding the baby in her arms as she was reconciling conflicting parties."[17] The title Our Lady of Equity would not be identified immediately with the more explicit, controversial label of intercessor.

Another way that Sheen presents potentially controversial information about Mary is by narrating scriptural events. The fact that he uses the Bible gives him legitimacy with a wide audience, but his paraphrases give a particularly Catholic twist to the stories.

For example, in the birth narratives the role of Joseph is de-emphasized in the plan of salvation, in order to give Mary more status. Sheen shows the audience a drawing of the nativity that the camera captures in a tight frame. This is a sign of things to come because, as in Sheen's narrative retelling, the camera's framing of a picture of the nativity cuts Joseph out of it. The camera focuses on Mary and the Child.[18]

More significant, Sheen changes the scriptural narrative to give Joseph less importance and Mary and the Child more. The scriptural birth narrative of Luke recounts the census of Caesar, noting that Joseph "went from the town of Nazareth in Galilee to Judea, to David's town of Bethlehem because he was of the house and lineage of David— to register with Mary, his espoused wife" (New American Bible, Luke 2:1-6). Sheen changes a small but significant detail: "Everyone is to be enrolled in his own city, the city of his birth. Finally, the order is posted up in a tree in an outpost of the Roman Empire in a little village called Nazareth. A woman with child read it; that meant she would have to make a four-day journey on a donkey all the way to her city, her native city, the city of Bethlehem."[19] Not only is Joseph left out of this version of the journey narrative, but Bethlehem now becomes Mary's homeland, rather than Joseph's. Sheen describes Joseph as a foster father of the child.[20] His description of the "virgin" Mary downplays Joseph's role in the process of conception all the more, while enhancing Mary's role. At another place Sheen brushes Joseph aside, saying, "We have a feast of Joseph the worker, because that's all he ever was."

Sheen's telling of the birth narrative eliminates the biological process of birth and preserves the belief in the virginal birth, through mystical imagery using extensions of the root metaphor of the bird's egg: "There was a flash of light. He who was born without a mother in Heaven is now born without a father on earth. He who made his mother is born of his mother. The eternal world is dumb; the one who built the nest of the earth is hatched. Therein the Word became flesh and dwelt among us. Poor, yes. But we miss the picture . . . if we think he was physically poor."[21] The nest is a temporary dwelling, suggesting a more spiritual home. Also, by talking about the birth of Christ in terms of an egg that is hatched, Sheen is able to speak of a virginal conception without having to explain it or deal directly with controversy.

Once again, in an account that spiritualizes the birth of Christ, Joseph gets eliminated from the birth narrative. Once again the two worlds are emphasized; this enhances Mary's role as intercessor because she is the bridge between them. In the quotation above, Sheen adds yet another element to the biblical narrative by noting that although Jesus was born into a poor family, his heavenly origin made him quite rich. This is significant because it preserves the fantasy theme of the American dream by implying that the poor of this world can be raised to riches. Sheen makes this possibility clear when he says, "God took human nature from Mary, and He would like to also take ours and to lift it up to be divinized, like His own by grace."[22]

The message emphasizes the value of humility. Society's problem, according to Sheen, is that people are not humble, as Mary is: "We are inns or stables. If inns, we're filled, with our own egos and self-importance. . . . But this stable, this cave . . . proud men cannot enter it because in order to enter a cave you must bend, you must get down on your knees . . . but the humble people, they bend and then discover they are not in a stable at all but another world where there was a woman holding a Child and the Child has poised the earth on His fingertips."[23]

Parallel to this image of motherhood was the idea of nobility of a woman. The key to entrance into this heavenly kingdom is humility, humility in the sense of submission. As we will see later, submission is primarily a feminine quality, according to Sheen; we have already seen that humility was a test of Bernadette's credibility. Sheen is preaching a gospel that works to maintains the established order rather than one that threatens it.

Humility is a key element in Sheen's description of Mary. Time and time again, Sheen notes that Mary submitted and was kneeling, that she was not a "daughter of the great kings" but a "woman kneeling in prayer." This reminder that even the lowly can find a place of achievement was a reality for many upwardly mobile families in the fifties, making Mary all the more relevant as a symbol. This religious narrative of the American dream is seen when Sheen says:

> There was a mother once who conceived because she submitted to the love of God. One day from the great white throne of light there came an angel of light descended over the great plains of Israel, passing over the daughters of the great kings of the East, . . . to a woman kneeling in prayer and saizd, "Hail! Full of grace!" These were not words. They were the Word. The Word was made flesh. She as a mother became a living ciborium bearing within herself the guest who was really the host of the world. This was the greatest love the world ever knew. The love that came down into an woman and ended in an incarnation.[24]

In this account Mary has a passive role in the history of salvation. This would have appealed to Protestant theology, which did not appreciate the emphasis on Mary's active role in salvation; it would also have appealed to the views of women in the fifties, which stressed woman's subordinate role in worldly matters. But at other times, Sheen also prizes the fact that a woman took an active role in the incarnation by freely giving consent: "He will not come into the order of humanity without first asking man if he freely will receive Him. God sent an angel to consult a woman as a representative of humanity. The question was, 'Will you freely give me a human nature?' God did come down to earth in the person of Jesus Christ through the free act of a woman. . . . He willed to lift man to Himself."[25] This implies a certain freedom that would appeal to Americans who valued the freedom inherent in the American way of life. It has special appeal also because of the rhetoric focused during that era on the lack of freedom in Communism.

Sheen does make references to Mary as "Queen of Heaven" and "Virgin."[26] But more often he avoids controversial terms, choosing to refer to her as "mother," a word that had positive connotations to a fifties audience and is also rooted in the biblical text, the doctrine of the *Theotokos,* and agreed upon by Protestant theology when it did not give glory to Mary alone.

In the postwar years the image of the American woman changed from the war image of Rosie the Riveter, representative of female presence on the labor market in the war years, taking on a renewed emphasis on marriage and motherhood. Statistics bear this out. The median age of marriage for women in 1940 was 21.5 years but fell to a low of 20.1 in 1956. Whereas two children had been mothers' goal in earlier generations, by the 1950s they aspired to three or even four. The divorce rate in the United States, as opposed to that in Europe, experienced a temporary decline through the 1950s.

Women dropped out of college to become homemakers, while the G.I. Bill enabled veterans to go to college so men could take on the role of family breadwinner. By 1947 veterans constituted nearly half of all college enrollments. Women who stayed in college were advised to follow courses that would make them ideal mothers and housewives. The college curriculum adapted to the needs of the fifties homemaker. By 1956 one-fourth of all urban, white, college women married while still in school. Women were twice as likely to enter college as their mothers, but much less likely to finish their degrees.[27] An educated wife, with tools for good conversation, was seen as a plus for her mate, the up-and-coming businessman.

Men and women who had survived the Depression, the war, the tensions of a new and prosperous economy, and now the pressure of the Cold War wanted security. Cold War ideology advocated marriage and motherhood as a fortress against the pressures of the nuclear world. Even the ranch-style suburban house, with its low roof and attached carport, seemed to evoke protection and privacy in the nuclear age. With security as a common thread, the domestic revival and Cold War ideology reinforced each other. It was believed that men in sexually fulfilling marriages would not be victims of loose women and prostitutes, pornography, or homosexuality. Children provided tangible results of a successful marriage and family life; they gave evidence of responsibility, patriotism, and achievement. They would, presumably, tame the wayward tendencies of men and fulfill the sexual energies of women. Even when child rearing led to stress and exhaustion, parents still pointed to their offspring with a sense of accomplishment.

Togetherness became the buzzword, with mother and father acting as partners while raising children. Consumption for personal needs was rare; consumption for the needs of the family became a priority. Television and consumer advertising promoted ways for the woman to become a better mother and wife and a more effective homemaker.

The media glorified motherhood; celebrity women were pictured as contented mothers. The magazines *Seventeen* and *Mademoiselle,* as well as Mary McGee Williams and Irene Kane's book *On Becoming a Woman,* which went through seventeen printings, were only a few examples of the journalism advocating the ideal for any woman as marriage and motherhood. Happy and smiling families became the norm in the new medium of television, with shows such as *Leave It to Beaver, Father Knows Best, The Donna Reed Show, The Adventures of Ozzie and Harriet,* and *The Danny Thomas Show.* The episode of *I Love Lucy* in which Lucy gave birth had twice as many viewers as the Eisenhower inauguration the next morning. Normalcy and freedom from problems were key to those sitcoms. Conformity to the norm of togetherness was central. If there were problems, it was the husband's job to straighten things out.

Experts on the family were emerging at that time. In his 1953 best-seller *Child Care and the Growth of Love,* Dr. John Bowlby stressed the importance of a mother's being at home with her child in the first five years of life. Dr. Benjamin Spock, in *The Common Sense Book of Baby and Child Care,* first published in 1946, concurred. This made the woman dependent on the man to support the family unit.

Motherhood and Mary, in Sheen's discourse, become the paradigm for all women, even women who do not have children. The life of the nun was the alternative to motherhood for the Catholic woman, but even here she served as a spiritual mother, educating and caring for children. The number of Catholic nuns increased by more than eleven thousand in the five years before 1950 and by over twenty-one thousand during the following decade. Even as the numbers increased, Catholics were in desperate need of more nuns to educate their children, a rapidly growing population. The emphasis on the sacredness of that vocation helped increase the numbers of religious women during this era and preserve the structure of American Catholicism. Sheen's rhetoric includes them in his stereotype for women.

Motherhood is the natural state of women; *feminine* and *maternal* are treated as synonyms. Sheen describes this as "keeping normal," defining normal with reference to natural law. Normal is wanting to be a mother. Being a mother, as we will see below, has a biological and a spiritual sense, very much in keeping with papal teaching of the fifties; but in an interesting adaptation Sheen allows room for the possibility of women working:

> It is not true that professional life hardens women. Every woman in the world was made to be a mother, either physically or spiritually. Here we are not speaking of physical motherhood. We are speaking of spiritual motherhood. A woman in professional life is happy when she has an occasion to be feminine. A man is the guardian of nature, but a woman is the custodian of life. Therefore, in whatever she does she has to have some occasion to be kind and merciful to others. She cannot look at a limping dog or she cannot look at any flower that has a broken stem without her heart and her mind and her hands going out to these things, as if to bear witness that she was appointed by God as the very guardian and custodian of life. If a woman does not have an opportunity in the working hours between nine and five to manifest those feminine qualities of tenderness, meekness, and gentleness, then she will have to find an occasion afterwards, that is to say from five o'clock on. Then she keeps normal, then she keeps feminine, then she keeps happy.[28]

Why does Sheen allow for the possibility of a woman working? Perhaps he is aware that at this time a great number of women were back in the workforce. Cracks were emerging in the ideology of the woman as mother and homemaker. By 1960 ten million wives were employed—triple the number of women employed in the war years—but less than half worked full time. Professional jobs were limited for women, and when they held jobs comparable to those held by men, they were paid much less. This was important because women were beginning to see themselves as more than mothers.

Sheen's own organization, Propagation of the Faith, had many women employees. But Sheen's statement is less liberal than it appears because it is qualified by his description of stereotypical women's jobs in his organization: typing, mailing letters, receiving letters—in other words, secretarial. He claims that these women are happy because they are doing feminine work that will help the poor and needy.

Sheen is stereotypical in his definition of the feminine as maternal. Womanhood is connected with the emotions and caring, especially the need to care for a child. He says, "A mother sits up all night with her sick child. To the neighbors it is agony; to the mother it is love." The image of women is contrasted with the image of men:

> We noticed very often at Baptism how awkward men are when they hold the baby. . . . They never know what to do with the baby. A man's hands were never meant to hold a child. Somehow or other a man's hands are like cranes always in transit. A child is always in transit; pick a child up here, and they wonder where they can put the child down. Some hold children like cocktail shakers. To have and to hold. And then there are others who hold children like footballs, always looking for an opening to get rid of the ball. Then there are others who regard this little bundle as a kind of mystery; they never know which end to hold. Where is it? There was something in here when it was given to me.[29]

In the same program he discusses another stereotype of gender roles, masculine strength versus feminine beauty. He remarks that when a "boy is born, the father begins to revive in his strength. . . . As daughters are born, the wife begins to revive in all her beauty. The chalice of father and mother is so overflowing now."[30]

Sheen often connects women with fashion consumerism through the stereotype of beauty. It is a popular topic of his humor. He says, "Maybe you heard about the man who said of his wife that he married an angel: she is constantly flitting about and never has anything to wear."[31] Another time he says, "A woman went to buy a hat. 'How much is it?' she asked the salesperson. 'Seventy-five dollars.' 'But there is nothing on it!' 'Madam, you're paying for the restraint.'" He talks about a woman's need to weigh herself privately: "Woman likes to weigh herself by herself."[32] Women, according to this stereotype, are very body-conscious, which could be related to a concern for fashion and consumerism. One of woman's problems, according to Sheen, is that she becomes a "spendthrift."[33]

Over and over, the body and concerns about it are spoken of as inferior, in comparison to the mind and thinking. (This same thinking influenced Ed Sullivan to censor Elvis's gyrating hips, which implied sexuality, when he appeared on Sullivan's show in the fifties.) Sheen says, "Whenever we think of fashions, we always think of women, but after all, there are fashions for men too. Fashions for men are in the realm of thought, for women in the realm of clothes. We could just as well laugh at fashions of thought as clothes."[34] Sheen locks both sexes into specific roles—men are the custodians of thought, women the custodians of emotion—but men have the worldly power in Sheen's schema because in his ideology, rooted in Scholasticism, reason and thought are always the superior qualities.

This support of male power is developed in other ways. Sheen says, "Woman cooperates with God; she is the bearer of the gifts of God." Her role is to "submit to God and man."[35] In the same program Sheen goes on to describe man as not merely cooperating but as "a refraction of the Divine Paternity." The earthly father is a reflection of God. This association with God makes male the preferred gender. In addition, men are able to reject their role as they mature, whereas a mother stays bound to her role: "Another thing every man must do for himself is blow his own nose. When we are children, mothers get hold of our noses and say, 'Blow hard!' But a day finally comes in the life of every boy when he resents it. [Laughter.] That day he can say, 'Today I am a man!' He resents the intrusion of his privacy when he finally comes to the recognition that he is a personality and he ought to be left alone, and there ought not to be any meddling."[36]

Ultimately, mothers have less power in this world where reason is superior. A woman's source of power comes in the intercessor role of "bearer." Her power is connected to a different world, the spiritual world. This gives women hope for the future, but in the present world mothers are given tremendous responsibility in acting out their roles. Sheen illustrates by saying, "Every mother is the bearer of God's gifts to man. She adds a new dimension to the love of husband and wife. She does most in the production of what is actually the mutual incarnation of the love of the husband and wife, namely a child."[37] Once again the word "incarnation" mirrors the sacred in giving birth to the Christ Child; giving birth becomes a sacred act. Most of the responsibility is given to the woman, who "does most in the production" of children. But she is a "bearer" in this world rather than a "reflection of God."

A woman's place always centers in the family. The anagram JMJ, which is on the chalkboard every time Sheen writes there, refers to Jesus, Mary, and Joseph, who together form the model of sanctity for families in the fifties. It is interesting that the fifties produced this new trinity with emphasis on the family. "The father and mother cooperate to make the body; God cooperates with them to make a soul." At another time Sheen says, "The secret of home is for the parents to say to the children 'You must obey me because I am responsible to

God for you. He gave you to me as so much clay; I must mold you in his image.' Then . . . the child will say in his own heart, 'I must obey because in the home the parents take the place of God.'"[38] The focus on the authority of parents gives weight to age rather than youth. We have seen in an earlier chapter that this is significant for Sheen's ideology, especially given an emerging subculture of teenagers.

The purpose of sexuality is always for the family, but only a family divinized by the woman's role as bearer of God's gifts. Sheen claims, "Sex is replaceable, but love is not."[39] Sheen's theology of sexuality speaks of sexuality as having two levels: first, "love in the form of sex," which is more sublime and proper, and second, "sex," which is more animalistic or instinctual and equated with "slobbering": "There are those in our contemporary world, for example, who would say, speaking of the emotion of love in the form of sex, there's nothing wrong with sex. There's nothing to be ashamed of it. Certainly not if you mean it as a gift of God for the propagation of the human species. In that sense we would say there is nothing wrong with eating. Why be ashamed at that? Is there something wrong with slobbering at the table, though we have the instinct to eat?"[40]

Sheen is critical of this instinctual sexuality because it leaves out God. He blames it for problems of juvenile delinquency, "the breakdown of public morals," and "flaunting the laws of God."[41] The goal of sexuality is stated when Sheen says, "Husband and wife in love for one another find they are creating something greater than themselves, which is a family."[42] Together husband and wife are responsible for the family, but ultimately the woman plays the role as intercessor between the worlds.

With the role of intercessor comes responsibility for the well-being of the family because women are expected to teach obedience through "mothercraft," learned through "passive observance of the laws of nature." Connected to the woman's role of teaching obedience to the law is the role of equity, the ability to show compassion and read between the black and white lines of the law. Once again, this reflects the discourse of Mary, more specifically her role as Our Lady of Equity, which women mirror. Equity distances women from the male role of law-enforcer; the distinction parallels that between God as the omnipotent lawgiver and enforcer and the more tender image of Mary. Sheen says, "Woman who does not fail in professional life is the woman, therefore, who manifests this feminine quality of what we will call equity. There is a world of difference between law and equity. Law is concerned with rules, exactness with justice, and is not concerned with circumstances. Equity finds a reason not to be strict."[43]

In Sheen's presentation children are not responsible for wrongdoing, and although men play a role in the production of children, the ultimate responsibility rests with the mother. Sheen mentions this awesome responsibility several times. It is a patriotic responsibility because "mothers who do not fail will raise great citizens for a great America of tomorrow." But Sheen warns women of the primacy of their otherworldly responsibility when he says, "What a tremendous responsibility devolves on a mother, for the child that is given to her is as so much clay. She has to mold it in order that it may be fashioned as a child of God. For when a child was born here, there was a crown that was made in Heaven. Woe to that mother if the crown is ever empty."[44]

Sheen further underlines the duty of a mother: "How many a mother there is in the court, a court where perhaps her son is a juvenile delinquent, who will say 'I could never do anything with him. There is no love on the part of the child.' She never did anything for him." In the same program he goes on to emphasize the wrongs of a woman who fails to live up to the caring responsibility of motherhood: "John Ruskin, the English writer, said once to his mother after he had arrived at some prestige, 'Why is it there is not the affection between us there ought to be? [The] mother-son relationship among others is deeper than our own.' Ruskin's mother said to him, 'Because I was too self-indulgent.'"[45]

Sheen idealizes motherhood by claiming that it is a terrible thing for a woman to refuse to give birth to a child:

> There is no woman that ever goes into a garden and just as soon as the buds appear in the spring cuts off the bud. Love by its very nature wants to bear fruit. . . . Those who deliberately frustrate it have been written about by the poet Davidson, who wrote, "Your cruelest pain is when you think of all the honey treasure of your body spent and no new life to show. It is then you understand how people lift their hands against themselves. . . . You lie awake and you see the pale, sad faces of the little ones who should have been your children as they pressed their cheeks against your window pane looking in with piteous wonder. Homeless. Famished babes denied your womb and bosom."[46]

Women play a key role in the production of the family, but they are also idealized—not as sexual images such as Marilyn Monroe, but placed on a pedestal. Sheen mourns the fact that modern women, "once our superior, [are] now our equal." He describes mothers as "being patterned noble," meaning there is a natural role for women.[47]

Although being an idealized, "superior" woman offers great power in the heavenly world, where she is an intercessor, it gives her little power in this world. Sheen idealizes Mary, as a woman, by giving her a key role in the story of salvation, but he also goes out of his way to credit other women in the Scriptures. He compares three biblical women to three categories of women in the world of the fifties:

> In the greatest crises of our Blessed Lord there are many instances of men failing, not a single instance of women failing. Peter denied; Judas blistered His lips with a kiss. As regards women, some solaced Him on the way to Calvary. A woman made her way into Pilate's courtroom to plead His case. A woman wiped His face on the road to Calvary and became known as Veronica, "Veronikon," the true image. Then there were the three women at the cross. Their names were the same, Mary. Mary Magdalene, Mary of Cleopas, and Mary of Nazareth, the mother of the Savior. They are the three women we described. They symbolize the three. Mary Magdalene symbolizes the women, those that take hold of the tangled skeins of a seemingly wrecked and ruined life and weave out a beautiful tapestry of saintliness and holiness. Therefore, this woman goes into the political and economic and social order and regenerates and heals the wounds of those who are sick of heart. Then there is Mary Cleopas, the mother of James, the mother who taught such obedience to a son that he became obedient even to wisdom that was the Word. Finally, Mary the contemplative, who left the lights and glamour of the world for the shades and shadows of the cross where saints are made. These are three women who do not fail; we salute them, we toast them not as modern woman once our superior, now our equal. We toast them [as] great women, as women who never fail, women who were closest to the Cross on Good Friday, and first at the tomb on Easter morn.[48]

Not only are women stereotyped here as mothers, but as mothers they are present in crisis and times of struggle, when men fail. Women as mothers are sorrowful mothers, like the "Mater Dolorosa" in the *Stabat Mater.*[49]

Embedded in the text is a description of women who struggled amid sorrows, including the idealized or noble mother. Sheen quotes Elizabeth Leseur, whose husband, as described earlier, tried "to break her faith." Sheen concludes, "As she was dying, she said to her husband, 'Felix, when I am dead you will become a Dominican priest.' Rummaging through her papers, he found her last will and testament, and it read 'I will to you the most precious thing that any wife can will a husband. I will to you nine years of suffering. In 1905 I asked Almighty God to send me sufficient pains and suffering to purchase your soul.'"[50]

Another illustration of this noble suffering is described when the bishop tells the story of a young girl who struggled and survived in war-torn Berlin:

> Finally the American soldiers came in, and she was wooed by one of them. She came to this country, and when she came to this country it was decided perhaps she should marry the American soldier. He became an alcoholic, refused to work, so she lived in an alley in Ohio, the best she could do. She wrote me a letter and said at times she thought she would leave him. "You know, if I take my finger out of the dike, it's not going to mean very much water will be lost, but if every woman in trouble took her finger out, there would be a flood. Civilization will be lost. I'm going to stay in the alley with faith just to preserve civilization."[51]

Note that "it was decided . . . she should marry," which is surprising in light of all the decisions she made to survive the war. Her only decision in this narrative is to suffer by remaining in the marriage. Much like Elizabeth Leseur, the young woman holds on to her ideals and tries to change her husband in spite of his alcoholic addiction.

The issue of alcohol abuse occurred frequently in the programs; women are expected to suffer nobly, as illustrated above. The abuse of alcohol is always described as a characteristic of men, tied to loss of love for wife and family. Sheen never discusses the fact that the alcoholic is harming himself or that the wife is harming herself by staying in the relationship. The emphasis is on living up to role expectations in the relationship rather than individual needs. For example, Sheen says when an "alcoholic man represses his love of alcohol, he is expressing for the moment his love for his wife. If he represses love of his wife, he is expressing his love of alcohol."[52] Not only does Sheen emphasize the fidelity of a relationship here, but he also equates women and alcohol. One can be exchanged for the other.

In another example the spouse of the alcoholic was to "be like the captain who goes down with the ship." Sheen says of the alcoholic, "What are you going to do in a case like that? Stick it out. Why? Suppose a husband instead of being an alcoholic had a pneumonia; would you the wife nurse him and care for him? He has moral pneumonia. He's spiritually sick. Why abandon him? You have a child with polio; do you give up the child? The believing wife sanctifieth the unbelieving husband, the believing husband sanctifieth the unbelieving wife."[53]

Sheen's solution to any problem for women is noble suffering and submission. He expresses this idea through the discourse of Lily, a European princess who suffered with her husband because of Nazi control of her homeland. Sheen quotes her: "I learned to be content with whatever lot the Lord has given you. If he has given us misunderstanding and a kind of crucifixion, even slander and imprisonment, that's our happiness. Then the lily is happy to be in prison." This ideal, in the next quotation, is rooted in the reasoning of natural law that claims that there is a natural order to the world. Natural law makes the world manageable; it clearly defines roles. In this case the woman must be submissive. The princess explains: "You know, I have only one sorrow in life, that is that I do not suffer, I do not suffer more. The happiness of a woman is in a fiat, a surrender, submission. We submit to the universe, to its laws, to its rhythms; we submit to man. And the Heavenly Queen submitted to God; so must we, and that to me is perfect happiness and perfect peace. And somehow or other I would like to pronounce some kind of fiat and say to God, 'Whatever it is, I want to do your will.'"[54] What could a woman do to survive her struggles and suffering? Lily recommends submission and accepting one's fate; but one could also pray. The role of intercessor keeps open the promise of another world that will be better.

Elizabeth Leseur, the sorrowful woman mentioned in an earlier discussion, is much like Lily. Both women prayed, but it wasn't enough. They needed to submit, and because Leseur submits in her own pain and suffering she is able to "purchase" her husband's soul. So too, in the same program, Francis Villon, the sinner who murdered and lusted, asked his mother "every day to go kneel before the statue of Notre Dame and pray for him that he would eventually come back to God."[55]

This message is very different from that of popular Protestant writers of the time, who focused on reward in this world and the elimination of pain. In contrast to Peale's theme of positive thinking, Sheen consistently emphasizes that the role of a woman is to suffer in this world. Prayer and the hope of another world through the example of Mary, the paradigm of woman, can help her to endure. Sheen says, "Tension will be solved only in Heaven, where we will achieve and capture the infinite."[56]

The sorrowful woman is to have "confidence in God." Sheen refers to a letter from the wife of a Methodist minister in Noblesville, Indiana: "She had many trials while her husband was studying for the ministry. One day she went to her sister and shed a few tears. Her four-year-old nephew, who saw her crying, said, 'Don't cry, Auntie! You must never put your trust in men; as Bishop Sheen said, you must put your confidence in God.'"[57]

Speaking of women as roses, Sheen makes it clear that any human sacrifice, "such as being plucked" by the hand of God, might destroy the woman's earthly life, but she in turn receives a reward in a heavenly union. The reward is a sublimated love with God:

> So in the human family a human rose with its own real father and mother and brothers and sisters, its own hopes and aspirations for the future, own real laughter and own real tears. From High Heaven there comes the Hand of the Heavenly Gardener, Who reaches down, plucks her up, and destroys her life as far as human environment is concerned; but there is no injustice done, because as the hand of man is above the rose, so the Hand of God is above the soul, and He may solicit the human heart for perfect love. What favor and blessing ever accrues to the rose that is plucked? Well, this rose plucked is touched by human hands and may even be pressed to human lips, may even be privileged to lay its crimson head alongside the Lady of Love. The rose's life is shortened, yes, but what a beautiful life it now begins to lead with man so all can see it. The young human is put into the vase of consecration, service, and love of God and the refreshing waters of sanctifying grace. Here are lovers. To be in love with God—these are the women who do not fail.[58]

Note that God is the gardener; he has authority over the garden. A woman, although not a mystical rose like Mary, is invited to mystical union by submitting and giving her life to God. In its own way, the image maintains the social order by treating the woman as an object of desire. Sheen's woman is a rose that "may be pressed to human lips," yet this rose has a love that surpasses this world.

As much as Sheen values the roles of family, and especially motherhood, he mentions his own biological mother only a few times. Very noticeable in these examples is that Sheen's mother did not fit the ideal he describes as the Christlike mother. It is the mother's responsibility, according to "How Mothers Are Made," to give the child a "name." This literally did not happen in Sheen's case. In one program he tells how he got his name. Embedded within the story is a contrast between the selfless ideal of motherhood and his own mother, who needed a break from her crying child:

> I am or I was the original and only Prince of Wails! [Applause.] I always hate to meet relatives and friends who knew me as a baby because tradition has it—and tradition must always be respected—tradition has it that I cried for the first three years of my mortal life. Honestly. That's how I got the name Fulton. I was baptized Peter, and I cried and cried so much I was a constant burden to my father and mother, and to get a little relief they used to take me to my grandparents, whose name was Fulton. So I got to be known as Fultons' baby, and that's how I got the name. [Applause.][59]

Sheen's mother plays the masculine role of lawgiver rather than a more feminine role characterized by tenderness and equity:

> I can remember when I was a boy about eight or nine years of age. My brother and I were playing ball in the backyard, and we threw a ball accidentally through the neighbor's window. Mother heard it and she called us in. And she sent us to our piggy bank, and she made us take the money out and go over to the man next door and give him the money for the broken window and also ask him to forgive us. Now, why should we just ask to be forgiven? Well, because we broke a window. . . . We disturb an equilibrium, an order, and that order has to be redressed.[60]

Once again we see the influence of natural law, which claims that there is a balance or equilibrium in nature, an ordered world. However, his own mother's lack of complete conformity to the role suggests that Sheen is speaking of woman more as an ideal than as reality.

In Catholic rhetoric of this era, both men and women had to live up to the constraints of their roles; there is no room for individuality. Tradition, learned within the family, never changes because it comes from nature, which mirrors God's law: "When a child is obedient, he learns wisdom. Not only the wisdom that comes from the experience of parents, . . . the wisdom that comes from the moral and religious training of children, but also the wisdom that comes from tradition. For the family is that which perpetuates the tradition. Then when the child has finally acquired that wisdom by obedience, then later on he can use that wisdom for his own perfection and out of his own freedom, but he has to obey first." For Sheen, the child learned natural law much as the scientist did: "If he is ever to know nature, [the child] has to sit passively before it."[61] For both the scientist and the child, the structure of nature and of the law is there; all one has to do is to preserve the equilibrium.

By centering tradition and the law in the family, Sheen ensured that the status quo of role definition would not change. But Sheen was arguing for more than gender role stability; he was arguing for a way of life that was being threatened. There were movements in the society of the fifties that challenged not only the family structure, but ultimately the way of life advocated by the church. This was a way of life, rooted in Scholasticism, that valued order, hierarchy, and rationality. It was challenged by new ideas that spoke of individual freedom or equality, emotional expression, and no particular standard for the truth.

The best-selling second report published by Alfred Kinsey in 1953, entitled *Sexual Behavior in the Human Female,* claimed that half of six thousand women questioned admitted to having intercourse before marriage and a quarter of them admitted to adulterous intercourse after marriage. The book asserted that women were at least equal to men in sexual responsiveness. The role of wife and mother was threatened by the idea that women had sexual desires and did not see sex solely as a means of having a family. Criticism of the report came from such diverse religious leaders as the popular evangelist Billy Graham and the academic theologian Reinhold Niebuhr of Union Theological Seminary.

Another major threat to the idea of marriage and motherhood was *Playboy,* whose first issue, in 1953, featured a naked Marilyn Monroe. It sold fifty-three thousand copies. The magazine boasted of the high social and business status of its readers and claimed it had to be taken seriously because it showed that the elite of society sought gratification from people like Monroe. The 1955 best-seller *Peyton Place* destroyed the image of family and small-town purity in rural New Hampshire. A series of James Bond books, beginning with *Casino Royale* in 1953, and the Mickey Spillane novels glorified the narcissism of sex and the female body that was the masculine hero's prize.

In sharp contrast to the aristocratic distance of Grace Kelly and Audrey Hepburn or to the strong women of the twenties and thirties—Greta Garbo, Marlene Dietrich, Mae West[62]—actresses such as Monroe, Brigitte Bardot, and Jayne Mansfield expressed a changing view of womanhood. As sex objects, they were to be enjoyed for sexual gratification in itself. Complementing this revolution in sexuality and ultimately gender roles was the introduction of "the pill." By the late 1950s only Massachusetts and Connecticut banned the dissemination of birth control information.

Some religious groups in the fifties—but not the Catholic Church—began to endorse birth control for family planning. What seemed like timeless truths were being questioned. The Church of England sanctioned birth control in 1958. In the United States the Very Rev. James Pike of the Episcopal Church advocated contraceptives as a "positive duty for married couples" during times of unusual or extraordinary stresses, whether that stress was from health, financial, or emotional problems.[63] This change in the churches opened the door for new views of sexuality besides the Catholic view that it was exclusively for procreation and contributed to the changing notions of femininity from the role of motherhood to a new individuality.

There were signs of change taking place in the structure of Catholicism as well, albeit change approved by the hierarchy. Lay people were more involved, through organizations like the Pre-Cana, the Catholic Worker, and the Grail movements. Such organizations got people thinking and organizing for themselves. They were beginning to discover a "vocation distinct from priests and nuns." Even the traditional role of the nun was beginning to change. Pius XII called the superiors of religious women to Rome as early as 1950 to discuss adapting their lifestyles to the needs of a changing world. As one consequence of the resulting 1952 conference, superiors of diverse women's congregations gathered to discuss issues for the training of sisters and began to publish journals such as *The Bulletin Review for Religious, Sponsa Regis* (now *Sisters Today*), which created dialogue among women who had always operated separately. At the same time, nuns who were educators began to bond together to discuss common issues and concerns. These developments might be described as "change within stability; ferment within obedience."[64]

The traditional ideology of the nun kept these women subordinate to the control of the priest and bishop. The religious life of the nun was viewed "in a monastic framework, as a cloister separation from the world."[65] Even though nuns might be involved in a parish, a school, or a hospital, they were expected to maintain a proper distance from lay persons who could be a temptation with respect to their vows. Priests and bishops set the norms for nuns' interactions, regulating their day-to-day lives. Religious women were treated as childlike dependents. Lack of contact with the outside world—radios and newspapers were forbidden—made it difficult for these women to change the status quo.

Sheen's rhetoric preserves not only the status quo of nuns, but also the status quo of the laity in relation to the priest leader. In contrast to Catholic women, Protestant women challenged the authority of the male religious leader. In *The Feminization of American Culture,* Ann Douglas (1977) notes that an increased number of women in Protestant congregations caused theology and religious symbolism to be softened and resulted in more power for women over religious life.

Although both Catholic and Protestant women had religious authority, they had different models for acting out their affiliation. Protestantism since the Reformation had stressed the authority of a home- or family-centered religion, which was in agreement with the Protestant doctrine of the priesthood of the faithful, whereby each believer had a sacred role in religious practice. This was a reaction against the Catholic emphasis on the authority of the priest as mediator between God and the layperson. As a consequence the Protestant family, since Victorian times, had defined the home as a heaven or paradise that reflected the eternal family. Victorians worshiped together in the home through Bible reading and catechetical education. Both parents had religious authority, but the father was associated with the role of priest, leading family and servants at prayer and even preaching, whereas the mother was the teacher of religion to her children.[66]

In Catholicism the woman had religious authority as a "domestic redeemer" through her intercessory prayer, but worship was centered not in the home, but within the institution of the church, where the priest was needed to carry out the rituals. Sheen was preserving the role of the priest in the church, where the laity were becoming more involved. His rhetoric put the Catholic layperson in a subordinate role in the realm of religion, while keeping the priest firmly in charge.

What Sheen was doing here was arguing not just for motherhood but for a very way of life that would maintain the balance between the sacred and the profane. By claiming that emotions and sexuality were not just animalistic emotions, Sheen was contending against a sexual revolution that was beginning and would change society. He wanted to preserve an ordered, hierarchical world.

According to Sheen, men and women are called to live up to their idealized roles, which maintain the established order:

> The level of any civilization is always the level of its womanhood. The reason is that when we know something we always bring it down to our level. That is why we always have to explain things to children by bringing it down to the level of their minds. But when we love something, we always have to go out to meet it. For example, if we love music, we have to meet the demands of music. If we study a foreign language, we have to meet its laws. Even if we study ping pong, we must meet its requirements too. Now inasmuch as a woman is loved, it follows that the nobler a woman is, the nobler the man will have to be to be deserving of that love. That is why the level of civilization is always the level of its womanhood.[67]

Sheen's message fits in well with the ideology that promises a reward for women in an afterlife as long as they remain passive in this world by accepting the law of nature.

In addition to the example of his own mother, there are two other situations in which the gender role stereotypes are broken in Sheen's presentation. The first instance occurs when Sheen uses the analogy of soldier to describe women who become nuns, referring to

> some women who have preserved ideals. So there will always be ideals to which every man can look when he loves a woman. They are those women who dedicate and consecrate themselves in virginal lives to God. They are like soldiers. Who does the most to preserve patriotism? It is not politicians who talk about the country; it is not dramatists who write about it. Those who do most to preserve patriotism in the nation are the soldiers who are prepared to die on the battlefield if need be. Why should there not

be women who will do for love what soldiers do for patriotism? . . . Should there not be some women who will love Divine Love so deeply and profoundly that they will sacrifice all lesser loves in order to preserve, for a weak and sinful and possibly sex-minded world, the real understanding of Love? They keep it pure . . . in order to manifest to citizens that other values are necessary, other values are important compared to great love of country.[68]

Sheen also confuses his gender role stereotypes by referring to himself as a mother. He is talking about how busy he is and the fact that, although some audience members think he is going on a vacation at the end of his TV season, the TV program is not his full-time job: "I'm very much like the mother of sixteen children. And every Thursday night used to go over and sit and read to an old lady from eight to eight thirty on Thursday night. And finally, the old lady recovered her health, and the mother of the sixteen children received a postcard from the old lady saying, 'Happy vacation!' [Laughter.] That's the kind of vacation I have. I'm back with my sixteen children."[69] That in the analogy the audience is the sick old woman says much to the audience about Sheen's salvific role as priest.

Sheen broke his rigid structuring of gender roles only in discussion of priest and nuns. He uses the metaphor of marriage to speak of his role as priest in relation to his church. Pointing to his ring, he says, "This ring is symbolic of my marriage to the spouse the Church, spiritual union to the mystical body of Christ." By bonding to a mystical body rather than a physical one, priests, nuns, and religious brothers could transcend worldly gender roles and (as in the case of the soldier-nuns) "preserve, for a weak and sinful and possibly sex-minded world, the real understanding of Love." [70]

Thus, Sheen places priests and nuns on a higher level than the layperson. He implies this difference several times. After speaking about the spirituality of monasticism, he offers this transition: "Coming back to the level of human beings . . ." In the same program he says, "Tensions are common, in a certain sense, not only to the love of husband and wife, but common even in the higher region of mysticism, the love of God."[71] This transcendence of gender distinctions not only proves the superhumanity of priests and nuns; it maintains Catholicism's traditional bonds of separation between laity and religious.

Speaking of himself as a mother might make Sheen less intimidating for a mixed-gender audience, especially in light of the James Bond stereotype common for men in the fifties. But it also maintains Sheen's status as a bridge between the two worlds. Sheen has to unite with the role of woman and the role of Mary to create a trinity that reinforces his ideology and ultimately the authority of the church in its priests.

How does his uniting with the role of woman and the role of Mary to create a trinity reinforce church authority? The very purpose of womanhood or motherhood is to serve as an intercessor, according to Sheen and tradition. This validates Mary as an intercessor since she too is a mother. And Sheen's depictions argue for the controversial claims of Catholicism representing Mary as a heavenly power.

Women are idealized in this discourse through the use of analogies that also apply to the role of the priest, and often mothers are given priestly functions. Sheen tells about the ideal mother who can "arise to proclaim" the uniqueness of her child. Similarly, the priest proclaims the word of God. In the same program he refers to women's eucharistic role, first noting that "mothers became a living ciborium"—a cup used by the priest at Mass—and then putting the words of Christ that a priest says at Mass into the mouth of mothers: "Mothers say, 'Take, eat. This is my body, this is my blood.'"[72]

A third priestly function is implied in the same program when Sheen notes that a mother "gives a child a name." The priest names the child in the Catholic sacrament of baptism. Sheen gives his own mother a priestly role when he says that as a child she placed him on the altar and dedicated him.[73] In Catholicism the altar rail separated the laity from the altar, which was the realm of the priest. Women were allowed in this area only to clean the space. Sheen gives women another priestly role of "being witness" and "[healing] the wounds of the sick of heart." Women are defined in terms of equity, which is suggestive of the priest's role in the sacrament of penance, where he "reconciles conflicting parties."[74]

Finally, women are given the responsibility of praying for delinquent husbands and troubled children. The priest also has the job of praying. Sheen promises to pray for viewers, saying, "I will spend two hours a day on my knees and ask God to bless you and hear your prayers." This unites both of them with the sacrificial role of Christ. An example is the deathbed prayer of Elizabeth Leseur, who offered her life as a sacrifice for her husband's salvation. Sheen uses the biblical quotation that refers to Christ, but now he inserts "woman" into the statement. He begins by quoting her words to her husband, Felix, in her last will and testament: "'I will to you nine years of suffering . . . to purchase your soul.' No greater love than this no woman has, that she would lay down her life for her husband."[75]

The final attribute of prayer and sacrifice sums up all priestly functions. Prayer and sacrifice are not just for oneself; the priest and the mother pray as mediators or intercessors between worlds. But the woman cannot transcend the gender role unless she is a religious. Therefore, the priest, in this case Sheen, has more authority as an intercessor. The need for mothers to be intercessors, as Sheen defines them, is an argument not only for Mary's authority but for that of the priest. Yet Sheen's argument for gender distinctions also supports the ideology of the priest, and ultimately the church, because it argues for the authority of intercession.

The bond between the role of priest and that of woman is cemented by adding the third member of the trinity, Mary. Sheen's prayer to Mary argues for her authority while giving credibility to his own.

Sheen's discussion of his prayer at Lourdes provides an example of this intercession between worlds and how Sheen and the Madonna reinforce each other's authority. He prays to the Madonna (not to Christ) intimately, as if she were a person he interacted with every day. On one visit he claims he returned to Lourdes with friends to "thank our Lady for introducing us with each other." Later in the program he describes his prayer as selfless, but at the same time very much like an informal conversation. This implies that Sheen and the Lady are on the same level. In fact Sheen's love is described as very sublimated, as the example below makes clear:

> I've been to Lourdes twenty-six times. This particular time I
> wanted a spiritual favor; it would not have profited me in the
> least. And when I left it was not forthcoming. So I was making my
> thanksgiving after mass. It was my last day. And I was talking to
> the Blessed Mother and this is what I was saying: I said, "Now
> listen, I have come over three thousand miles to visit you. It
> doesn't mean anything to me and you refuse to grant it. Now you
> can keep it. Now I don't want it." I said, "If you asked me for
> something, I'd give you anything you wanted. Why don't you give
> something to me?" "I'm mad at you." "Now," I said, "it's all right
> for me to be mad at you, but I don't want you to be mad at me, so
> I'm going to give you another chance to prove you're not mad at
> me." So I said, "I'm going down to the grotto, take a drink of the

water, then I'm going to leave the grounds. I want you to send me
a little girl, aged twelve, dressed in white, who will hand me a
white rose, and I shall take that as a sign that at least you are not
mad at me." I knew she has a thousand reasons to be mad at me,
but I didn't want her to be. So I was about seventy-five feet from
the gate. I didn't see anybody there. "You don't have much time." I
got to the gate and just behind it was a little girl aged twelve and
she handed me a white rose. It reminded me of a line from G.K.
Chesterton, "Her son climbed up her body as a tower of ivory and
kissed upon her lips a mystic rose," and that's what she gave me.[76]

Sheen's petitions—even the most idealized—are never ignored. His
power in bridging the worlds of the real and the ideal offers hope to
women that their own prayers can be answered if they are faithful to
their role in the trinity.

Other than priests, men have no place in this trinity, nor do they
need one, because their role superiority is maintained by the trinity.
Although the average man has little authority in the realm of religion
and the transcendent, men are authoritative because they preside over
the construction of images and roles.

Sheen's program always reminds the viewer of this ideology, even
when he does not state it. He never fails to begin and end the program
by standing beneath the statue of Madonna as if to receive her heavenly blessing as she upholds not just the Child, with the world in
their arms, but a worldview that invokes the status quo. That status
quo is a view of the American dream extended, via Catholicism, to a
transcendent world. The view provides a motive for suffering and
struggle in this world, especially for Catholics climbing the social ladder. At the same time care is taken not to disturb the Protestant majority and its hegemony. As the church used Mary in the past to urge
popular devotion and compliance with hierarchical authority, Sheen
uses similar tactics as he struggles against secularism in the fifties.

As Catholicism nears the twenty-first century, the question of the
role of Mary and women is again central. Pope John Paul II issued
Ordinatio sacerdotalis in 1994, claiming the church cannot ordain
women. He used Scripture as his evidence. This inflamed many in the
Catholic Church. Cardinal Joseph Ratzinger fueled the flames by claiming this was an infallible statement and could not be questioned by
theologians. Recently the Catholic Theological Society issued a strong

rejection of such claims. This occurs at a time when most American Catholics favor women's ordination.

At the same time the number of reported Marian apparitions has increased. Devotion to Mary is renewed in orthodox circles of Roman Catholicism. It is even rumored that the pope is considering a new statement giving Mary the title of coredemptrix, meaning she had a role to play in the redemption of humanity. This would have a significant effect on ecumenical relations. The Vatican has recently denied serious consideration of this title. However, the fact that it became an issue testifies to Mary's power within Catholicism.

Humanae vitae, the Vatican's statement in 1968 against birth control, served as the benchmark event when laity stopped listening to the official church. The implications of recent papal statements are yet to be determined. History shows that devotion to Mary has always been strongest during eras when church authority was in crisis. The difference from the fifties is that the church in the nineties is at crisis within itself and its authority structures. Theologians and the Vatican continue to argue, leaving American Catholics skeptical of church authority and more willing to decide for themselves how they will express their Catholicity.

5

Bishop Sheen's Role Negotiation from Ascetic Bishop to Television Celebrity

Well Sheeing is believing! [Laughter.] At this hour for the American public there are these three: Berle, Hope, and Charity! [Laughter; Sheen pauses; audience applause.] It cost me a hundred dollars to be with you tonight! Really and truly! Last year there was a woman from South Carolina who sent me one hundred dollars to be used for our work. I sent it to a leper colony in India. Then she saw me on television and she said, "You are irretrievably bad on television, and unless you give up television, I insist that you give me back my one hundred dollars!" I said, "Madam, you are not penalizing me. You are penalizing these poor people to whom I sent your money. Will you please reconsider?" She said, "I will not reconsider! Either you stop television or send me back the one hundred dollars!" So I sent back the one hundred dollars. [Applause.] But you look so comfortable in your own homes, I felt it was worth the one hundred dollars to be with you. [Applause.][1]

As Bishop Sheen recognizes in this anecdote, people have expectations for him both as a Catholic priest and as a television celebrity, and he must carefully manage his diverse roles and role expectations when he appears on television. The roles' conflicting demands require him to engage in impression management so as not to disrupt viewers' expectations. Complicating the picture is his need to appeal to differing role prescriptions that Americans had for their clergy in the fifties—including the clergy roles defined in the Protestant tradition, which still held hegemony in American society. The genteel and the ungenteel styles of preacher characterize the role expectations for the Protestant tradition.[2]

Every Protestant preacher could be placed on a continuum between the poles of the genteel and the ungenteel. The genteel style was representative of the early Puritan preacher, especially in the days preceding the American revolution. Genteel implied well-bred or aristocratic—a refined spirit, elegant, stylish, and educated, paralleling the circumstances of the New England colonist. This style of preaching advocated an authoritative rhetorical distance from the congregation. In contrast the ungenteel style emerged in America as immigrants joined the colonies and the nation grew. The community became more diverse, and the social control maintained by the genteel preacher became more difficult. New, ungenteel leaders with little education spoke to congregations that did not value authority, education, or tradition. The Methodist circuit rider is an exemplar of this new style. These itinerants went into rural, less densely populated areas and preached in streets and homes. They were skeptical of institutional authority and education. "Hot gospel" or emotionally stirring preaching was proof that the ungenteel speaker was divinely inspired. Extemporaneous speech, implying a genuineness and divine inspiration, was preferred to the rigorously prepared text of the genteel style. Ungenteel preachers reached people in innovative ways: humor, attacks, storytelling, and intimate, personal experience. This approach was cruder than the rational formality of the genteel style.

By the nineteenth century, with the movement of many Americans from rural to urban areas, from agriculture to industry, these two styles often merged as revivalism became institutionalized. Some more charismatic groups that stressed the ungenteel style moved to gain respectability by building Gothic structures and taking on a genteel appearance. At the same time congregations that valued the genteel style needed to modify themselves to keep their members and attract new ones. What the polar opposites shared was a stress on the personhood of the preacher in relation to the congregation. Parishoners wanted personal contact with the minister and expected frequent visits to the home. The sermon became a means of entertainment as well as education. Attention continued to focus on the preacher's ability to attract listeners as some took to the lecture circuit and became known as "princes of the pulpit." Celebrity preachers such as Charles Finney (1792-1875), Phillips Brooks (1835-93), Dwight Moody (1837-99), Russell Conwell (1843-1925), and Billy Sunday (1863-1935) appealed to people across Protestant denominations, stressing personal conversion over doctrine. The personality of the preacher became a key element of the process as doctrinal differences diminished in Protestantism. This cult of personality would pave the way for radio and television preachers in the Protestant tradition. They could become celebrities without compromising their role in ministry.

Role expectations for the Catholic priest, in sharp contrast, deemphasized personality and individual celebrity, but favored transcendence and otherworldliness. The priest was expected to "die to self" by total service to the institution and its doctrines.[3] His ordination made him an *alter Christus* (another Christ). At the time Bishop Sheen was in the seminary, priests were even warned keep their distance from parishoners. Their formation was much like that of a monk; individuality was discouraged. The seminarian was expected to avoid "particular friendships" with classmates—friendships that could involve an attachment. Every seminarian dressed in a black cassock, whether en route to chapel or shower, and at one seminary it was forbidden to be seen at a window without a cassock on. It was a constant reminder to conform to role.[4] Once the seminarian became a priest, the people, too, placed him at a distance; his vows put him at a higher level of sanctity, and in an ethnic church he might be the only educated person in the congregation.

Unlike his Protestant counterpart, the Catholic priest was not dependent on the congregation to preserve his job; he received his appointment from the bishop. He was expected to serve institutional authority. In 1907 Pius X published his *Pascendi dominci gregis*, condemning theological questioning and decreeing that every priest and seminarian take an oath of loyalty against modernism, which could clash with church tradition. Pius XII, in the apostolic exhortation *Menti nostrae* (September 23, 1950), affirmed the priest's need to detach "from things of the earth." The priest was expected to "live a holier life than the lay people," to converse not with the common and vulgar but with the "angels and with men that are perfect."[5] That focus isolated the priest from the realm of the earthly in much the same way as had been advocated through traditions since the late medieval era. At the same time it created a potential conflict for a priest who also played the role of a television celebrity.

In his comments quoted at the beginning of this chapter, Sheen engages in role management, perhaps unconsciously, and demonstrates his skill at it. He talks to the audience as if he could see them directly,

Sheen and other celebrites roast Milton Berle at the Friars Club. Courtesy of the Sheen Archives, Diocese of Rochester.

through the camera lens, in the comfort of their homes. Here he appears to respond to the role prescriptions for a television personality that suggest personal intimacy with the audience. He finds places for role management where values of the differing audiences intersect with his own role requirements. He uses the double meanings of irony, in these places of intersection, to maintain his roles as Catholic priest and television celebrity. But Sheen also appeals to role definitions for clergy, such as the genteel and ungenteel styles, that are valued by mainstream culture.

Throughout his programs Sheen uses ironic humor to balance conflicting demands. For example, in the quotation above, he associates himself with the celebrity of Milton Berle and Bob Hope—but uses a more neutral term to refer to his program, *charity*, the third quality in the religious formula for the three theological virtues. By leaving it for the audience to fill in his name and credit him with celebrity, Sheen makes the audience participate in the maintenance of his role of priest-celebrity. By not including himself in the celebrity triad, he satisfies the constraints of Catholic role definitions that demanded humility among clergy. At the same time, the word play

"Sheeing" in the opening line heightens the audience's awareness that his name is missing from the list of three television celebrities. In this way Sheen indirectly defines his role as priest and celebrity.

In this chapter I examine (1) how the opening credits and the staging of Sheen's program aid in his impression management, (2) Sheen's role maintenance in light of the demands of the genteel-ungenteel styles of the Protestant preacher, and (3) Sheen's presentation of his role as television celebrity and how he simultaneously maintains the role of Catholic priest. These role categories—genteel, ungenteel, priest, celebrity—are not used rigidly but provide a way to understand the strategies of Sheen's image management that an audience of the fifties would identify with.

The opening credits advertise Sheen as having appeal for all persons. In the early years of the program, an unseen, male announcer tells the audience: "Ladies and gentlemen, we take pride in presenting his excellency, Bishop Fulton J. Sheen, in *Life Is Worth Living,* a program devoted to the everyday life problems of all of us. The entire amount received from this program is applied to the sick and needy of every race, no matter what religion, color, or creed, throughout the world. Bishop Sheen directs the activities of the World Mission Aid Society." [Sheen's New York address appears on the screen.] While the viewer hears the spoken introduction, the camera focuses on a book, placed on the edge of a desk, with bold print showing "Life Is Worth Living" and "Fulton J. Sheen." Present, but in smaller letters, are the words, "his excellency . . . auxiliary bishop of New York."

The spoken introduction makes clear that Sheen's message is not denominational, or for that matter even religious, and that Sheen will discuss problems common to all persons. In addition, it reinforces Sheen's philanthropy and selflessness because it reminds the viewers that he does not personally profit from the program.[6] At the same time, the nonverbal credit—the small letters to denote religious authority—downplays his role as bishop. Although many other hosted programs in early television were named after the lead character or host, Sheen's was not. This may have been another accommodation to satisfy the ascetic expectations for the role of the Catholic priest because it does not give personal attention to the individual.

The musical accompaniment to the credits is also an attempt to manage conflicting role expectations. It is formal, almost classical, suggesting tradition. Church bells give it an otherworldly sound. The upbeat tempo, however, calls to mind a contemporary Broadway stage, which might appeal to those favoring the ungenteel avoidance of tradition.

The stage setting suggests a place for balancing the different expectations for the Catholic priest and the Protestant minister.[7] The library setting features many books against the back wall and a desk. The paneled walls and leather chairs, which imply tradition and masculinity, are in sharp contrast to the modernistic furniture popular in the fifties.[8] A cross suspended over the fireplace also helps to control the image projected. The cross has no corpus, even though Catholicism, with its stress on image and devotion, would have placed one there. Protestantism, rooted in the Reformation, valued the words of Scripture more than images of devotion. The devotional artifacts found in Catholic churches and homes—religious images, statues, blessed candles, holy water, blessed palm—were reminders of ethnic origins in Europe that stressed devotionalism and the mystical graces that were bestowed on the artifacts' owners.

The setting is constructed to appeal to diverse audiences because it is not within the church or liturgical setting of the transcendent priest. At the same time it does not offend viewers favoring the tradition of the genteel style that values education among its gentlemen preachers. In Protestant Victorian homes a library and a parlor were essential elements in conveying a family's respectability; Catholic bishops, too, were expected to be educated men who could teach their flocks. In the ethnic community, still representative of Catholicism, education was all the more esteemed. Catholicism was undergoing a renewal of education in the fifties to improve the status of its people and its own image as a community. Sheen's use of a chalkboard enhances the impression that he is a genteel teacher who happens to be a bishop in the Roman Catholic tradition.

This role definition also suggests to mainstream society the inaccuracy of the ethnic stereotype of Catholics as uneducated buffoons. Just as later television evangelists helped their followers, moving away from their lower-class roots, to see themselves more positively,[9] Sheen's style broke with stereotypes that implied that Catholicism was an ungenteel religion.

Sheen's formality fits the expectations for the genteel preacher, who was aristocratic and well educated. For example, Sheen frequently introduces a topic using the Latin style of address: "Would it please you if tonight we talked about . . . ?" The audience always approves with applause. This language gives the speaker a certain distance from the everyday, helping to maintain the status of genteel aristocrat. On the other hand, the applause suggests the role maintenance of the ungenteel minister who seeks audience approval for, and involvement with, his theme. The home audience gets the clear message that Sheen is speaking to enthusiastic supporters. This interaction with the audience also implies the priestly role of Catholicism, because Sheen's style of address suggests service to a superior at the expense of oneself.

Sheen further maintains his aristocratic, genteel role by mention of personal associations. For example, he prefaces his conversation about a dinner party with friends by telling the audience who was at the table: "I can remember once, being seated at a dinner in Italy. I don't remember what was served; I only remember the conversation. There were at that table a king, his wife, the princess, two friends of theirs, and a colleague of mine, a professor."[10] This gathering not only highlights Sheen as the sophisticated traveler, moving in aristocratic circles of the genteel style, but also embodies class and hierarchy. His association with these European aristocrats can also appeal to the role expectations for the television celebrity, who could take viewers around the world while they sat back on sofas and easy chairs.

Sheen rarely speaks about his years of education and intellectual abilities; doing so would risk compromising the priestly role and open him to accusations of vanity and pride. When he does speak of himself, he is self-deprecating, balancing the roles of genteel educator and priest: "You know, priests are ordained at twenty-four, and when they're ordained they're supposed to know enough to go out and do some work. I was retarded. I was in school till I was twenty-nine. I'll never forget those six years in the third grade. [Laughter.] So I was doing some graduate work at the University of Louvain in Belgium. . . ." Sheen reminds the audience that he is an educated man, but only after making self-deprecating statements. The self-deprecation, a technique Sheen uses often, helps him to maintain the role of the priest as one who is detached from self:

> A couple years in Belgium, then in Rome, then went over to
> England to teach. . . . Then I came back to take an examination
> for a degree called an Agrégé en Philosophie. It was a rather hard

one. The examination is public. It's before the invited professors of
the other universities. It starts at nine in the morning and lasts till
five at night. It's oral and anybody in the auditorium stands up
and asks a question. You're supposed to know the answer. Supposed to know the answer! I was going to the auditorium. . . . I
saw this whole family coming down the street. . . . "Well, the
night before last we all walked eighteen miles to the shrine of our
Lady, and we spent the whole day there yesterday in prayer for
you, and last night we walked back. We hoped you passed." I
passed. [Applause.] Not due to any merits of mine, I assure you. I
passed because some very nice people live in alleys.[11]

Although the anecdote asserts Sheen's role as a genteel educator, it
also highlights the priestly role of detachment from personal reward
because Sheen credits his success to the poor family that prayed at the
shrine. He tells us twice that he passed but twice assures us that it was
not due to his merit. Sheen's rhetoric of self-deprecation leaves little
room for personal credit—but the audience responds with thunderous applause, which Sheen ignores as he begins his next sentence,
making the audience applaud all the longer.

When a speaker stops to allow audience applause, he is generally
acknowledging that the applause is deserved.[12] Sheen rarely does so,
showing that the applause is not solicited and that the information he is
conveying is more important than stopping for applause. This appearance of humility further ingratiates him in the role definition of priest.

Usually Sheen talks only indirectly about his education. In one
program he describes how he prepared for the telecast: "Nothing I say
is written. I merely think about it, do considerable research, pray over
it, meditate over it, and then the night before give it once in French,
and once in Italian. Rehearse it myself, and then you get it in English,
or is it English?"[13] Again we hear both the self-deprecating rhetoric—
is he making sense to the audience?—and the implicit statement of
Sheen's intelligence as someone who speaks French and Italian. Ultimately this enhances his genteel role.

Elsewhere he compares the mind to a house whose upper level is
the place of "art, science, philosophy," whereas the cellar is the place
of "those who just want pleasure and never develop their minds."
Sheen always makes it clear that he lives in the upper level. He does
this literally when he uses the royal "we": "We climb four flights of
stairs three times a day for meals."[14] In another program he describes

a dinner party at which "we talked about relativity, about literature, the philosophy of Communism, world affairs . . ."[15]—conversation in sharp contrast to that of the cellar, where "pleasure" is key.

Sheen maintains the genteel style in another way. He frames the audience as his peers in education, notwithstanding his university degrees. Ultimately this flattering but inaccurate depiction makes the audience even more aware of Sheen the educated man.[16] Everyone wins: Sheen presents the audience in a positive light and leaves it for them to esteem him for his education, thereby remaining self-deprecating.

Even when only a person with technical knowledge in a particular field would be able to identify with his questions and answers, Sheen's rhetoric includes his audience. For example, he says, "We can even pick up the books of the past, the great minds like Sophocles, Aristotle, Aquinas, Bonaventure, Bossuet, and we know something of their character." The audience might know the names of these philosophers, but few will have read them. Elsewhere he says, "Everybody in the audience who knows philosophy will recall the name of the great philosopher he succeeded: Peter Lombard." In another example, "For the three of you in this vast audience who have forgotten their Latin, I will translate."[17] These statements remind the audience of how little they know and of Sheen's role as an educated authority who gives the answers.

Sheen further maintains his role as genteel preacher by demonstrating his mastery of the language of ideologies that he opposes, such as Communism and psychology. He is educated enough to beat his opponents at their own game. For example, he shows the audience Lenin's many volumes, noting, "I read them all." Earlier he wrote on the board the name Vladimir Ilyich Ulyanov and said, "You thought it was going to be about Lenin! It is!"[18] Sheen displays his expertise by showing that he knows not only Lenin's popular name but his name of family origin as well as significant dates connected to his life.

In another program Sheen claims that even Communist listeners will learn from him: "In this particular telecast we will outline and, inasmuch as we have Communist listeners, and we attempt to appeal to all listeners, will give a lesson in Communist philosophy, and for the benefit of the Americans we will tell you what is wrong with their philosophy." He goes on to use the terminology of Communism, such as *false consciousness, proletariat,* and *bourgeois.* He even explains economic determinism with the remark "sounds very, very learned but means simply. . . ."[19]

Sheen uses a similar strategy in his discussion of psychology—a discipline he is not fond of, as is evident by his tendency to make psychologists the butt of his jokes: "Anybody who goes to a psychoanalyst ought to have his head examined." "A psychoanalyst is the one who, when a very pretty woman enters the room, looks at everybody else." He goes on, "You heard the story, didn't you, of the two psychoanalysts who passed each other on the street. One said to the other, 'Good morning!' and the other said, 'I wonder what he meant by that.'" The problem with psychologists is that "they live in a world not of reason but of dreams." Psychologists are quick to identify any moral problem as "unfulfilled sex drives."[20] This statement shows that Sheen knows the technical language of this group as well. He even develops programs such as "The Psychology of the Irish," "How to Psychoanalyze Yourself," and "Inferiority Complex," in which he often speaks of schizophrenia, consciousness, and unconsciousness. By using the language of psychology, he shows his mastery over it, again enhancing his role as the genteel preacher.

Sheen is very direct about his lack of education in only one area: art. He often illustrates his presentations with simple, stick-figure drawings on the board. Once again he is self-deprecating and looks knowingly at the audience before he draws, triggering immediate laughter from them and him. Sheen's inability to draw is an inside joke that builds intimacy with the audience, thus fulfilling the role definition of the television personality. Just in case a viewer does not get the point, Sheen adds, "I draw just as bad this year as I did last year." Similarly, he says, "Did you know an art school offered me a scholarship? I draw so badly really they did. They hated to see art dragged into the mire."[21]

Why does Sheen make such an issue of his inability to draw? He may indeed have been a poor artist, but his is a convenient handicap for the genteel educator in the tradition of Catholicism. Art in the fifties was often associated with the emotions, self-expression, and abstraction rather than realism. That new form of art broke the barriers of tradition. Emotion, individuality, self-expression, and breaking with tradition, although not sinful in Sheen's Catholic ideology, are suspect, as they could lead one away from the superior use of the mind and reason. By discussing his deficiency in art, Sheen, whether or not consciously, helps maintain his role as a genteel educator, while his self-deprecation also satisfies the Catholic role expectations for a priest. A deficiency in art is a minor flaw; the mind is most important. When Sheen presents his hierarchy of scholarly thought, art is always subordinate to philosophy and morals. He often talks about philosophy, connecting himself with the higher realm of the hierarchy.[22]

So far we have discussed the strategies Sheen used to display the role definitions of the genteel educator and how this intersected with the ascetic role of the Catholic priest. Now we will see how he used image management to display his identification with the ungenteel roles of popular culture.

Sheen always begins his television program with a personal and anecdotal ice-breaker—contrasting with the formal request, "Would it please you if . . ." discussed above. His presentation is spiced with humor and anecdotes, always told in the first person. At no particular place in the program's progression does he switch from "we" to "I," but he rarely uses "I" in a way that can be interpreted as self-promoting.

Sheen's humorous anecdotes help to associate him with everyday experiences such as being in bars or department stores, trying to care for children, and enjoying television comics. In contrast to the educated expert implied by the aristocratic genteel style, these anecdotes imply the layperson and worldliness. One night he begins by saying: "This particular individual was stopping at an inn . . . and went into the parlor, and Milton Berle was on. I still belong to the tradition there was no room in the inn. [Laughter and applause.] . . . He went into the bar, where there was a much bigger crowd, and they were listening to me, and the talk was on alcoholism. I probably have been in more bars and done less drinking than any man in the United States."[23] Sheen's statement preserves an element of genteel expectations in that he is not physically in the bar drinking, but at the same time it illustrates that he is popular in places that are stereotypically not religious.

In one program Sheen tells about being in a department store, but even from this everyday anecdote he draws a theological point:

> The other day I was on an elevator in a department store. I was shopping on the fifth floor and wanted to go to the sixth. I went into the elevator, and several other passengers went in with me. Just as the elevator was about to start and the operator said,

"Going up," some woman came rushing out madly and said, "I don't want to go up. I want to go down!" Then turning on me—I don't know why she picked on me [applause and laughter]—but turning to me she said, "I didn't think I'd go wrong following you!" I said, "Madam, I only take people up!" That actually happened.[24]

Another illustration serves a similar strategy, but it debunks the image of Sheen the educator by having a child correct him for his attempt at child care. As the bishop retells it: "This past week I was on an airplane, and a mother with a three- or four-year-old child was opposite me. She put the child alongside me on a vacant seat and asked me to take care of the child as she absented herself. The child took one look at me and started to cry. So I took a few pencils out of my pocket and started doing this [Sheen waves his hands] and saying, 'daa, daa' and so forth. The child looked up at me and said, 'Don't be silly.'"[25]

In each example Sheen uses the opening phrase "this past week" or "the other day" to help build an impression of intimacy that fulfills the role of the television celebrity. He is letting his audience in on the events of his everyday life. Sheen also takes care to read letters from various places around the country, both rural and urban, which helps frame him as very popular to a wide audience. Just as a successful revival preacher in the ungenteel tradition has many converts, Sheen has many viewers.

In the following example Sheen begins, as usual, with the ungenteel and intimate address to the viewers as "friends." Here is a place of intersection between the television personality and the ungenteel definitions of role. Sheen notes that this letter is from a Protestant minister, and he goes out of his way to praise it. Sheen often refers to ministers from various Protestant denominations as evidence of his authority in and positive respect for differing audiences. He says:

Friends! During this past week we received a very beautiful and lovely letter from a Presbyterian minister and his wife from Paulsboro, New Jersey. It concerned their little four-year-old daughter named Becky. It seemed Becky wanted to see television, so the mother turned on first Bob Cummings. No she didn't want to see Bob Cummings. So the mother turned on Groucho Marx. No she didn't want to see Groucho. "Well, who do you want to see?" "I want to see the man who uses the chalk and blackboard and tells funny stories." So the mother turned me on for the four-year-old Becky. What do you think I was talking about that night? Melancholy and sadness! Sorry, Becky.[26]

Anecdotes such as that evoke the ungenteel or the popular layperson, and Sheen is aware that they sometimes debunk the role of the genteel aristocrat. For example, the "purpose of buttons on sleeves is not to prevent men from wiping their nose. [Laughter from Sheen and the audience.] I didn't mean to say it, but now I've said it." Not only does Sheen tell humorous stories, but he also enjoys the humor of other television personalities: "I often marvel at the theatrical power of Sid Caesar. How that man can carry on all alone. Sometimes without any words at all when he just simply does pantomime."[27]

Sheen displays himself in the tradition of the ungenteel style of ministry not only by his claims to popularity and his personal anecdotes, but also by his extemporaneous style of delivery, which was a hallmark of the ungenteel Protestant preacher and suggested sincerity. Sheen is not unaware that some viewers expect this and often goes out of his way to note that he never uses "idiot cards" or a TelePrompTer:[28]

> There are various ways of treating subjects you do not know by heart. Just as teachers say there are various ways of cheating on an examination, there are also ways of cheating on a stage and on television. For example, one way that is very often used is to have cards in front of you. You . . . in your homes cannot see these cards, but the one who is talking looks down and he reads off: joke one, joke two. Then a new card is put in. And then one other system is to have a prompter offstage. But the one system that is best of all to fool the audience at home with is the TelePrompTer. It is set on top of a television camera. We do not have one here. And the message unrolls. You can generally tell the man who has a TelePrompTer because he dares not take his eye off it. . . . I've always been afraid to use one. I heard once of a politician who was giving a speech and said, "All of us of course are grateful to that great man who fought so valiantly at Valley Forge, who crossed the waters of the Delaware . . . who became the first president of the United States." And the thing got stuck and to this day he doesn't know the next line. [Laughter.][29]

In both the ungenteel and the genteel styles of role definition, the minister who could cite the Bible was respected. The Scripture was the primary source of authority in the Protestant traditions. Sheen often weaves into his delivery scriptural texts, which he can recite extemporaneously. For example: "God has spoken. . . . All you need to do is turn over the pages of the Old Testament, and you will find written there the speech of God. . . . Take, for example, those great commandments which were given to the Jews, and which have been the fabric of the world's civilization ever since: I am the Lord thy God; thou shalt not have any strange gods before Me. Thou shalt not take in vain the name of the Lord thy God. . . . Thou shalt not covet thy neighbor's goods."[30] Not only can Sheen recite biblical passages from memory, but he notes that these are God's words, giving him all the more credibility.

Sheen uses several techniques to maintain the role expectations of a television personality. The extemporaneous quality of his presentation—he uses no notes—enables him to have direct eye contact with the camera. The camera is positioned in the place of the viewer, making it appear that Sheen is looking at the viewer at home. The entire program is filmed with variations of the close-up that help Sheen appear as an intimate to the viewer. However, despite some ungenteel traits that suggest the ordinary layperson and a certain degree of equality, overall Sheen's role is not that of an equal but a superior. That superiority is shown in his role as the teacher instructing an audience of students and, as we will see, in his display of paternalism as a priest.

The fact that Sheen speaks from the intimate personal space of a member of the clergy must have been very compelling. Catholicism treated its bishops with great distance, awe, and reverence, but Sheen's audience is invited into his personal space. The opening camera shot slowly captures each element of the library—books, statue, doorway, chair, desk—in much the same way that one would scan an office while waiting for an important person to arrive. The camera eventually positions the audience as if seated at the edge of Sheen's desk. This suggests intimacy with a very revered person who introduces himself by saying "Friends" and concludes, "Thank you for allowing me to come into your homes" or "Bye now, God love you!"

The intense intimacy is balanced by the three-quarter shot of Sheen posing with his hands opened wide or resting on his chest. Both poses create distance by focusing on the bishop's robes as he stands in authoritative silence. The less conversational, dramatic tone of voice, often used as he reaches his climactic conclusion, also contributes to a distancing. Sheen always concludes by bowing as if he is a Shakespearean actor from a bygone era.

Sheen speaks before a live studio audience in the Adelphi Theater. There is no editing of the program's flow. The home viewer never
sees the theater audience, but that audience's applause and laughter
encourage the viewers to feel they are part of it.

Sheen also breaks down the barrier of the proscenium between
him and his viewers by reflecting on the process of television itself.
This enables the viewer to psychologically step in front of the camera
in the spirit of the parasocial relationship that connects the television
speaker directly with each viewer. Sheen says:

> Television . . . is one of the greatest of all inventions inasmuch as
> it brings all kinds of sights and sounds into your own room. It is
> not a particularly easy medium, that is to say for those who are on
> it. Those of you who are looking at home, you see now for
> example only me. But you do not see all these people on the front
> of the stage: sound men, one man holding a pipe camera, sound
> boom, cameras, lights, engineers, technicians. All of those are
> hidden from your view. Now when you have somebody on stage
> with you it is much easier because you can talk to him. This is a
> lonely place if you have nobody with you. . . . Television, however,
> makes it very difficult for the speaker from the point of view of
> the audience because you can always test the sincerity of the
> speaker. You can always tell if he has a TelePrompTer in front of
> him.[31]

Sheen's openness about what is usually hidden in television gives the
viewer a sense of being privileged with inside information about the
program.

Often Sheen draws attention to the cameras in front of him. For
example, he says, as he walks to the camera, in an extreme close-up,
"If I stole the watch of one of these operators here, if I could get close
enough to this camera man here and steal his watch [laughter]. . . ."
Another time he comments that the camera in front of him has no red
light. He asks, "Is it because it is Saint Patrick's Day and [you're] afraid
to show red?" He adds, as he sees the light go on, "There it is."[32]

In one of the very first programs, Sheen begins by stating, "This
week I received several inquiries, 'Was I nervous at the conclusion of
the program as my eyes wandered?' No. I was not nervous on stage.
There are two cameras and a clock, here, on stage. There are two parts
of every speech: a beginning and an end. In something not memo-
rized, such as this, it is good to time yourself from the end and say to

yourself, 'I will allow so many minutes [to conclude].' You always finish right on the nose."[33] As in the other illustrations, here Sheen affirms that he is comfortable with the role expectations of the television celebrity, and he continues to treat the viewer as an insider.

Sheen's role management as a television personality is, most likely, very appealing for a sponsor in the fifties; his fierce patriotism and anti-Communism make him a safe personality in an era of McCarthyism. Although he makes viewers feel that they are participating in a world mission by watching a program that is dedicated to the world's poor, Sheen uses the respectability of his own role as priest to enhance his sponsor's image:

> This is the last of our series, and I wish to thank the Admiral
> Corporation for its sponsorship, which indeed has been very
> cordial and genial. There is no corporation in the United States
> which over so long a period of time had given so much to the
> poor of the world as Admiral. They have done this because the
> one they had on this program never took anything for himself. All
> was passed on to the Eastern part of the world where poverty
> reigns. If there is ever an ethical bond that develops between
> sponsor and those who watch the program and the program itself,
> Admiral stands before you as a corporation of integrity, and I trust
> you will always be grateful to it and continue to support it as I am
> grateful![34]

Sheen never becomes a salesperson for Admiral directly, but he does reflect on its qualities as his corporate sponsor. Elsewhere he uses humor to advertise for Admiral:[35] "And certainly a mark has been left upon the younger generation for Admiral which will take a long time to erase. This is a true story that comes to us from Boston. This mother's little girl came home from catechism class, and the mother thought she would see if she knew the lesson, and she said to the child, 'Who are the first parents?' And the little girl answered, 'Admiral and Eve.'" [Laughter and applause.][36]

As he does here, Sheen frequently uses references to children, usually under four years old, to gain legitimacy. This story not only sells the sponsor, as a television celebrity is expected to do, but also shows that Sheen possesses the asceticism of the priest, who associates with the innocent and sexually pure. In another example Sheen describes "a letter from Pittsburgh in which a mother told me every Tuesday night when I finish television, her four-year-old daughter goes up and kisses the screen so I always get the greeting through an Admiral. [Laughter and applause.]"[37]

It is not uncommon for Sheen to subtly promote the sponsor through humor. "I hope you remember who is sponsoring this! Last year someone went into an appliance store and asked for a Bishop Sheen refrigerator. They must have been listening to *Life Is Worth Freezing*!" Another time he says, "A tube gives out on a radio set and you buy another tube—unless it's an Admiral; then you don't have to buy one. [Laughter and applause.]"[38] In these examples Sheen can fulfill the role requirements both of a celebrity, who must sell a product, and a priest, who is expected to be detached from worldliness.

Because the priest is not supposed to seek fame, Sheen uses humor to balance the role expectations of priest and television celebrity. He says, "I bumped into a boy in the street this week who said, 'I always listen to you on Tuesday night. My father makes me!' [Laughter.] I told him he ought to have his father watch *Howdy Doody*." In another, typical example, Sheen begins, "Let no one returning to TV exaggerate his importance. In Boston, two little girls walked ten miles to see me, and I took them out for ice cream. One little girl said, 'You are the second most important person I ever met.' 'Who is the first?' 'The keeper at the Boston zoo.'"[39] Sheen shows that he is recognized as a celebrity (often by a child), yet his celebrity is then compared to that of a person or a concept that threatens to lower his prestige. This challenges Sheen's distanced persona as a scholar and a representative of high culture.

Humor draws the audience close to Sheen by showing his humanity and his ability to laugh at himself, but ultimately it also serves to remind the audience that he is a celebrity—a celebrity who can step down to the level of the everyday. Sheen's humor is often corny,[40] such as "Long time no Sheen" or "I see you're back to have your faith lifted." Corny humor usually focuses attention on the speaker; we laugh at the joke-teller's attempt at humor rather than at the joke itself.

Sheen's humor serves another important purpose: it encourages the audience to elevate him so that he can fulfill the transcendent nature of his priestly role definition:[41] "When someone who commands an elevated position and employs an elevated style almost unexpectedly does use the everyday language of the man in the street, there is a special response. For if the posture of elevation can produce awe, that of equality from the elevated can produce affection and love. A touch of the ordinary from the great makes the latter seem somehow greater."[42]

Sheen's self-deprecating and corny humor therefore elevate him. The audience knows he is not an ordinary person, so his ability to relate intimately to them makes him all the more extraordinary. This might be problematic for a Catholic *priest,* but as a Catholic *bishop* Sheen is expected to have an extraordinary Christlike quality. Self-deprecation therefore helps him manage his dual images as intimate celebrity and priest-bishop.

The charisma that Sheen builds through his self-deprecating and corny humor also helps him negotiate his dual roles. Even though he walks a tightrope between those two role expectations, Sheen is never in danger with the church, because he has proven his loyalty by years of service. His charisma, though it is a personal quality, reflects positively on the role of priest.

Significant physical attributes that imply a charisma also help Sheen bridge the roles of priest and television celebrity.[43] Although only five feet eight inches tall, Sheen appears larger than life in his cape. He moves about the stage with dramatic gestures, the camera always following. His costume, eyes, and movements command attention.

Sheen's eyes, a key to his presentation, give the impression that he is an ascetic priest, but they also have the intimate directness of a charismatic television celebrity. His blinking seems to be controlled, and though he rarely looks at the theater audience, he does look directly at the camera and thus maintains intense eye contact with the home audience.

Sheen's makeup man, Bob Obradovich, highlighted Sheen's eyes so that with makeup and lighting, the eyes stood out as burning coals. *Time* described them as "one of the most remarkable pairs of eyes in America" and noted, "Strong men have been known to flinch before that gaze."[44] In the context of his smile and the close-up of the camera, however, Sheen's eyes invite the audience to come closer.

But Sheen ultimately is not intimate in the sense of being an equal; his charisma places him above the audience. Even animals and little children are captivated by it:

> I was afraid you would not believe me if I told you, so may I read
> verbatim from a Philadelphia paper. [He reads:] "This came as an
> awful blow to us, but a reporter must follow the news, however
> painful. Eleanor Flynn of the Philadelphia navy yard has a cat, Mr.

Gerrity, that is smart in two ways. He hates TV except when he hears the televised voice of Bishop Sheen. Then he trots down the stairs from his diggings and sits fascinated. As soon as the bishop finishes he goes back to his diggings." A letter comes from a little girl, in the Bronx, who tells us that her canary never sings except when I am on the air. I want you to know I have the highest rating in television among the cats, dogs and birds. [Laughter and applause.][45]

In the same program he tells of a letter from the mother of a four-year-old Toledo girl who came in and sat quietly through the telecast just to hear him say, "God love you." In Catholic hagiography saints are recognized for their ability to draw animals and little children. Through these many anecdotes about children, Sheen alludes to the innocent asceticism of the priest who is untainted by sexual relations or sin. The anecdotes draw the audience to Sheen, but they also distance him as one with charismatic qualities.

Sheen presents himself as possessing saintlike qualities. He generously gives all money earned from the program to the poor. He concludes one program by noting, "If I brought one soul to peace in God, that's why I am on TV."[46] A little girl asks him for a horse; he says he will help pay not only for the horse but for a saddle as well. He describes missing a train in Lourdes to counsel a suicidal young woman who approached him for advice.[47]

Sheen is a man of prayer and humility. We see this when he says: "I remember, some years ago (this happened during the last war), a movie company called me and asked me to go to Saint Patrick's Cathedral [and] kneel before the main altar so they could get a picture of me praying for peace. I said, 'Do you know the parable of the pharisee and the publican?' 'Yes,' he replied. 'Then you know that the Lord criticized the pharisee because they wanted him to go up in the front of the church so Fox News could take a picture.'" Sheen goes on to note that he could become filled with pride if he decided he was good on the telecast; but "tomorrow I might wake up and find that the good Lord took away all the gifts."[48] The guises of humility, prayerfulness, and generosity all emphasize qualities similar to those of the saints.

On Sheen's program of February 24, 1953, he predicted the death of Stalin by using dramatic quotes from Shakespeare's *Julius Caesar,* substituting the names of Russian leaders for the Romans. When Stalin died unexpectedly nine days later, some suggested that Sheen's words may have been responsible. This gave Sheen the aura of a visionary as he exhibited the sainted qualities of a charismatic celebrity.[49]

Ascetic detachment from self and adherence to role requirements of the institution differentiated the priest from his Protestant counterparts in the genteel and ungenteel traditions of ministry. The Catholic priest was expected to be in the world but not of it. On Sheen's stage this expectation is represented by a solitary chair next to a fireplace—a traditional symbol of American family and community, suggesting warmth, security, and belonging. (Franklin Roosevelt used a similar prop in his "fireside" radio chats.) Although Sheen invites us to the warmth of his television fireplace, the solitary chair suggests that when the camera is not on, he is alone. In the priestly role, Sheen has no family because he is an *alter Christus* (another Christ), a status that sets him off from the ordinary person. He further elaborates on his priestly role when he describes himself as a "poor stub of a pencil" or as a mendicant and as a servant of God.[50] He humbly asks the audience to pray for him and refers to himself as a beggar.[51] These qualities suggest the priestly role of the monk who is detached from the world.

Sheen's initial appearance each week leaves no doubt that he understands the expectation of detachment for the priestly role. He walks onto the stage quickly and purposefully as the camera focuses on his entire body. He is attired in the robes of a Catholic bishop, with cross, cape, and zucchetto (skull cap). His robes clearly establish his religious affiliation and position of high status. He turns on a spot that seems predetermined and bows slightly and formally to the audience. His face is for the most part serious; a polite smile suggests that he is distanced from the thunderous applause that greets him. That distanced facial expression and his determined pace suggest a detachment from the moment and a need to get on with his task.

The robes make Sheen look not like the ungenteel intimate but rather like a mystic who transcends this world. They cover his body and help mask his humanity. The cape fills the space around him, distancing anyone who might want to get close. The camera frames him in such a way that the viewer generally looks up at Sheen. In later programs light from above creates a halo effect around him. The lighting, the robe, and the detached facial expression support the role expectation of the transcendent priest.

Lest the audience forget his priestly role definition, the camera sometimes frames him posing with his body angled away, suggesting a distance from a more regal presence. His eyes, which continue to make direct contact with the audience, have an authoritative, mystical quality that contrasts with the intimacy of the full body pose of directness.

In light of this role expectation of the otherworldly priest, it is interesting that Sheen's only companion on stage is his metaphorical angel. Sheen playfully pretends that his angel provides unseen assistance throughout the program. The imaginary angel helps construct the transcendent nature of the priestly role, but this is balanced so as not to disturb those who would have little use for a spiritual realm.

The image management is achieved through the strategy of humor. Sheen always speaks of the angel in a humorous light, making it in effect the straight man for Sheen's jokes: "Now while my angel is cleaning off the board [a stagehand erases the board whenever Sheen puts the chalk down and moves away]—and my angel is back with me again this year. Incidentally, you can never see the angel on television. Not even with an Admiral! [Laughter.] But we have a drawing of the television. When I left last year, Dick Brown drew a cartoon of the angel bidding me good-bye. This is a picture of the little angel. Now that's the way the angel really looks." Sheen's description of his angel as "little" implies the innocence of a transcendent being. At the same time he connects his angel with a worldliness when he says, invoking his sponsor's name, "Our little angel is working very much faster now [erasing the board]. He found that he swabbed decks too quickly last week, so our angel, the admiral, has acquired much more dexterity."[52] Yet, by playing with extensions of a nautical metaphor to describe the way his angel erases the board, Sheen provides a distance from the sponsor because of the alternative meaning of *admiral*. Associating the angel with his sponsor lets Sheen manage the television personality's requirement to promote the commercial sponsor while preserving the transcendence of the priestly role.

At one point Sheen makes a serious and explicitly Catholic aside: "There are angels. I have one of them with me on this program. You've got one of them too, if you only knew it, incidentally."[53] He is able to add such potentially divisive comments because his discussion of the angel respects all audiences. Talk about the angel gives a sense of spontaneity and humor that appeals to the ungenteel and the expectation of intimacy in the television celebrity. Sheen seems to be letting the audience backstage become acquainted with his unseen partner.

Sheen in the spotlight. Courtesy of the Sheen Archives, Diocese of Rochester.

Even though Sheen associates with the otherworldly angel, he maintains his own image as very much in the everyday world. For example, he begins one program by telling the audience that his angel has been drawing on the board. He says, as he walks to the board:

> This is probably humiliating for me . . . [On the board is a cartoon picture of Sheen and the angel with the following caption.] "What will you do for me until the fall?" "What fall?" I tell you what I will do for him: He's been cleaning my blackboard all year. I will use a long feather duster to clean his wings [Sheen draws on the board]. I wonder if he will let me use his halo for the summer. How will he look in my beanie? [Sheen draws a halo on his own head and a beanie similar to his own zucchetto.] He looks all right in a beanie. I wonder how I look in a halo. [Applause.] You see, I'm not ready for a halo yet. I'll be back in the fall.[54]

Once again Sheen is being self-deprecating in suggesting that he is not ready for a halo. He de-emphasizes his religious zucchetto by calling it a beanie, a term that would be more popular with ungenteel listeners. Again, however, the audience is invited to help Sheen maintain his priestly role by applauding to demonstrate their belief that a halo would fit him quite well.

Sheen's priestly asceticism is also present, but he does not talk baldly in terms of celibacy or penitential practices. He uses humor and implicit codes to balance the expectations of diverse audiences. For example, whenever he speaks about himself eating, he tells the audience that he is rarely aware of what he eats. Describing a dinner at his home where John McCormack, the famous tenor, was present, he discusses the behavior of a man who served the dinner while on a "moral holiday" (that is, drunk): "He came in to serve the table, and there was a roast served that night. Ordinarily I do not remember what we have to eat, but he got down on both knees and bowed and the roast waved perilously from side to side, and I was saying to myself, 'Gee, I hope John McCormack doesn't think that's the way I trained him.'"[55] Here Sheen is associating himself with the celebrity of his dinner guest, satisfying the role expectations for the television celebrity by showing that he associates with the famous. He also appears to be letting us in on his inner thoughts, again implying an intimacy suited to the television role and to the genuineness of the ungenteel minister, through his use of the informal "gee." But there is a distancing here as well, because in sharp contrast to the emphasis on classlessness in the fifties, Sheen has servants who wait on his table. Sheen also distances himself from the waiter's poor moral habits, but in a humorous way so as not to offend the mundane or earthly mentality of the ungenteel.

Sheen's acknowledgment that he rarely recalls what he eats implies an ascetic avoidance of immediate pleasure and gratification. In Sheen's ideology eating has attributes similar to those of sexual lust: "There are those in our contemporary world, for example, who would say, speaking of the emotion of love in the form of sex, 'There's nothing wrong with sex. There's nothing to be ashamed of it.' Certainly not, if you mean it as a gift of God for the propagation of the human species. In that sense we would say there is nothing wrong with eating. Why be ashamed at that! Is there something wrong with slobbering at the table, though we have the instinct to eat?" Yet to give ungenteel legitimacy to this priestly asceticism, he balances it through humor. He reminds listeners that this asceticism was a trait of Abraham Lincoln, of whom Sheen says, "He hardly ever knew what he ate."[56] In this way he points out the civil religious legitimacy of his role enactment.

Another time he jokes, "We climb four flights of stairs for breakfast, lunch, and dinner. During Lent it is not worth it."[57] He tells us about the Catholic asceticism of fasting during the religious season of Lent, but he does so through ungenteel humor. He appears to be letting the audience inside his home to learn about his personal habits, fulfilling the television role expectation of intimacy, but at the same time he maintains a distance by his asceticism.

In this last illustration Sheen uses the pronoun *we*, as he often does. He is very ambiguous as to its meaning. The Catholic role definition of priest-bishop frowned on its clergy speaking in their own name. Yet Sheen could not speak explicitly about "we" as the hierarchical church because many in his audience appreciated Protestant styles of ministry. If he used the pronoun *I* too often, his own church would have been critical. Sheen tries to balance the needs of a diverse audience by alternating between the pronouns *I* and *we*. He always uses *we* when expounding on his philosophy of life. Depending on the codes of a particular audience, "we" could mean the church, the production crew, or the philosophical Western tradition and its thinkers.

To avoid alienating those in the audience who might have little tolerance for the royal "we" or the asceticism of a priest, Sheen stresses

the professionalization of his role of priest. On one of the few occa-
sions when Sheen talks directly about the clergy, he says, "I know
someone in my profession, really and truly, his sermon was found on
the pulpit Monday morning by the janitor. He had written in the mar-
gin of a typewritten sermon, 'Argument weak, shout like the deuce.'"[58]
By using "deuce," a slang term for the devil, Sheen helps uphold his
ungenteel image. Yet his anecdote makes a genteel criticism because
shouting is a behavior of the ungenteel preacher, and in this case Sheen
implies that it accompanies a weak argument. More to the immediate
point, though, his use of "professional" helps to ground the clergy in
an everyday, less transcendent status. "Professional" ties in with the
Protestant work ethic and the American postwar corporate structure,
which valued work and professionalization.

Even humility, a primary priestly attribute, is transformed in that
it involves not taking credit for work undone. Again using Lincoln for
legitimacy, Sheen says, "Do you ever notice today how often people
will . . . contradict themselves and say, 'Well, I'm very proud, and I say
it in all humility'? I've heard dozens of people receiving awards say
this. Lincoln would never accept an award or an honorary chairman-
ship without some kind of work behind it."[59]

As a priest Sheen needs to show detachment. He does this baldly
by stating that he does not like to talk about himself. Yet when he
does talk about himself, he makes his selflessness known in a way
that indicates the same pride shown by those whom he criticizes for
false humility. These are the people who, in his words, employ the
rhetoric of accepting rewards "proudly but with all humility." He is
guilty of this false humility when he says:

> Now I come to a very unhappy part of the program for me. I
> receive so many requests for copies of our telecasts, and tele-
> grams. . . . May I tell you, all of our telecasts are published at the
> end of every year. Now, we published the first year in a book
> called *Life Is Worth Living,* and the second, *Life Is Worth Living,*
> and last year in *Thinking Life Through.* . . . Thank God that's over. I
> hated to do this because I don't like to talk about anything I've
> written. I did it because I don't get anything out of these books
> anyway; all the royalties go to the poor. Now that's finished. I
> received all kinds of cards from people wishing me a happy
> vacation. Vacation, mind you, now that I'm off television! Remem-
> ber television is purely incidental in my life. I'm very much like

the mother of sixteen children. And every Thursday night she used to go over and sit and read to an old lady from eight to eight thirty on Thursday nights. And finally, the old lady recovered her health, and the mother of the sixteen children received a postcard from the old lady saying, "Happy vacation!" [Laughter.] That's the kind of vacation I have. I'm back with the my sixteen children.[60]

Sheen de-emphasizes his celebrity role by noting that television is incidental in his life but boasts that all the money from the program goes to the poor and that he has no vacation because of his immense responsibilities. There is little genuine humility here.

Similarly, when discussing his years at Louvain, he describes his actions at a particular Christmas: "I decided the best way to enjoy Christmas was to visit the poor. . . . I had visited twenty families. The twentieth family was without food or financial resources. . . . I went out and bought necessities and what to them must have seemed as luxuries. They depended on me more or less. I got a job for the blind father, employment for the two children. . . . [They] always, always, came to me and begged. I barely made it through the university. I didn't have much but I held onto them [the family]."[61] This does not indicate humility but rather a paternalism that helps to construct Sheen in the image of a charitable, selfless person. It fits well with the role definitions of the priest, who is expected to embody selflessness. Reading between the lines, we can also see the solitariness of the priestly role. Even on Christmas, Sheen does not have family and friends to celebrate with, but must go out to the poor to find family. Sheen exemplifies the ideal priest in that he is part of the family of humankind on Christmas. But he describes the family as if they were objects—"I held onto them"—and the fact that they came to him "always, always," and begged implies a very subordinate relationship.

Even Sheen's decision to visit the poor on Christmas seems to indicate that the poor have a specific role at that season. Sheen's decision that "the best way to celebrate Christmas was to visit the poor" points to the contemporary presence of the poor Jesus in the Bethlehem stable—which is where Sheen's story is leading on this particular night. Poverty is very much a part of Sheen's social system. It is an opportunity for charity and a metaphoric reminder of Jesus. It was not a social evil to be eliminated, as it was according to the ideology of some Protestant groups that viewed the gospel as a call to social change. Sheen's role is to show God's love in the midst of poverty; the family remains dependent.

This illustration not only provides insight into Sheen's priestly role but also suggests his theology of ministry. He tells us that he visited twenty families on Christmas eve; the visits must have been very brief. Perhaps Sheen gave blessings to the families, seeing himself as a sacramental presence bringing Christ into their lives. This must have helped him to preserve the role expectation of the *alter Christus*.

But Sheen transforms the *alter Christus* from the suffering Christ into the glorified Christ of the successful priest. He associates with the poor—the cab driver, the people in the back alley, the suicidal woman—not as a wounded healer but as a spiritual father who can solve problems and eliminate doubt. His fatherly role encourages the audience to put him on a pedestal as a hero. Ultimately his friends or peers are the princess, the educated, the celebrity such as John McCormack. He is no peer of the suffering.

Sheen is not genuinely humble, but the audience nonetheless seems attracted to his enactment of role. Why is Sheen so popular and the audience apparently uncritical? One explanation is that his visual presence is so compelling that the audience is overwhelmed by appearance.[62] Or perhaps genuine humility was no longer part of the role expectations of Catholic clergy. In that golden era for Catholics, when their pastors were builders of parishes in the new suburbs and their bishops princes, Catholics were throwing off the image of humble immigrant. It could be that American Catholics were finding reasons for pride in their new American status but holding on to nostalgic images of their immigrant past. Such a community might be expected to be sensitized to the mere appearance of humility and be *less* critical of false humility.

In this light, Sheen's role management succeeds because his Catholic audience gets the best of both worlds. Sheen enacts the role of the humble priest but not the reality, to conform to the expectations of his situation. This makes him the embodiment of the morality play because he knows how to enact a script that assures the audience that the world is in order—or, at least, that a priest is the exemplar of Christlike perfection for this world and by implication that pure goodness and innocence do exist in the world.

On the other hand, the reality of Sheen's life as an aristocrat who presents the glorified Christ serves as a charismatic symbol that Catholics can make it in American society and achieve all the promises of the American dream. Ultimately this charismatic symbol is not a threat to the church but gives new status to the priest, as a professional who can integrate differing definitions of ministry by adapting his role to fit the American experience.

Still another possibility is that the mere enactment of a role is all-important for viewers in the fifties. Role conformity—keeping up with appearances, ensuring the order, and not going out of character or against institutional ideology—was the standard expectation for the newly emerging corporate world. Sheen's enactment of the priestly role and the audience's lack of critical discernment may suggest the great need of fifties audiences for symbols to enact idealized goodness even in a world filled with nuclear and secular corruption. The reality does not matter as much as the ideal and the symbol that his role creates. Sheen therefore is popular despite his boastful pride under the guise of humility.

We have seen how Bishop Sheen integrated a number of often-conflicting role requirements. These include ungenteel versus genteel; classless versus aristocratic; mundane versus transcendent; anecdotal versus educational; formal versus informal; charismatic versus ortho-dox; humorous versus reserved; close versus distant; low culture ver-sus high culture; Protestant versus Catholic; grand versus ascetic; self-promoting versus self-deprecating; religious versus secular; and patriotic versus global. Sheen successfully balances all these compet-ing tensions of role expectations. Like Aristotle's *phronimos,* a person who can be sympathetic to his neighbor but keeps his distance so as not to be controlled by eros,[63] Sheen has an outlook on life that stresses that emotion is natural but must be balanced by a sense of reason. Where there was potential conflict in role expectations, Sheen used the ambiguity of language to construct his image and maintain the image of a *phronimos.* Ironic humor reminded his audience of his ex-traordinary celebrity status; at the same time he could appear to be humble or self-deprecating.

Sheen outlined his belief in the ideal *phronimos* when he talked about Abraham Lincoln, one of the deities of American civil religion: "No character is ever born great. Characters become great. Some people's lives are flat and dull. And others have a tension and pull. There are opposites in them like the positive and negative poles of electricity. Moses, for example, was not always a meek man. He once killed an Egyptian. He had to become meek. . . . So there was some great tension in Lincoln. He became great because he was able to reconcile those opposites."[64]

Image management by balance fits well with Sheen's own Catholic ideology because he believed that within each person was a tension that needed to be balanced. This was very much the spirit of medieval Scholasticism, and Sheen presented himself as a contemporary Thomas Aquinas. Like Aquinas, he could be the otherworldly monk while answering the complex questions of living in a secular world. He could live an ascetic life while managing a corporate fundraising office for the church that managed moneys sent around the world. He could show knowledge of a more spiritual world while dining with the rich and famous. He could appear to represent the values of high culture while presenting himself on television, the medium of popular culture. Like Aquinas, Sheen outlined how the spiritual was integrated into the material and how the ascetic monk could provide insight into the ethics of society.

Sheen's synthesis of his role also ties in with the spirit of the medieval morality play, whose characters journeyed to a better, spiritual world. In the morality play the respected scholar often had the last word after the climax of the drama. He was the one to resolve the tensions of the two worlds that the play's characters struggled with. He was able to do this because he, like the *phronimos,* could experience emotion yet keep his head in the higher realm of reason. In this way he could give answers and make judgments on the meaning of ethics and belief.

Bishop Sheen was central to the formation of the television preacher. His presence on TV encouraged other preachers to preach an electronic gospel. Robert Schuller's blue academic gown and his dramatic gestures suggest the impact of Sheen's style. Jim and Tammy Bakker's creation of the talk show format and Pat Robertson's *700 Club* in a news broadcast format are reminiscent of Sheen's attempt to meet the wider culture halfway.

Nonetheless, the days of Sheen's aristocratic genteel style are gone. Contemporary preachers have shown themselves to be all too human. Oral Roberts's plea in 1986 and 1987 became the object of humor when he claimed that God would call him home to heaven if he failed to raise money for his ministries. Jimmy Swaggert's confession of his adultery in 1988 and Jim and Tammy Bakker's misuse of donations have contributed to skepticism in the way people treat television religion.

Today we live in a society where credibility is achieved not so much by role and its authority structure but by personal charisma. There is less social distance between people, which suggests that Bishop Sheen's ascetic distance would be less persuasive for most modern viewers.

The role of the Catholic priest has adapted to a changed society. Vatican II allowed for more individuality. Seminaries placed emphasis on psychological development of their candidates and integration within society, rather than distance from it. Some blame the decline of priestly vocations to this. However, even Bishop Sheen, as bishop of Rochester, created one of the first seminaries where psychological testing and personal growth were the norm. One outcome was that individual priests could now dissent publicly with the authority of their bishops over issues from Vietnam to doctrine. The priest became more humanized. Media charges of pedophilia brought the role of the priest down to earth in a way that threatened the image of the priest as "another Christ." In short, the role of the Catholic priest moved closer to that of his Protestant counterpart. The priest came to be seen as human.

This has not been without conflict. Bishop Sheen spoke from a church of uniformity. Catholic leaders in the 1990s speak from a very different place, one of diversity over the very meaning of being American Catholic in the nineties. That diversity has been praised by those on the liberal side of the conflict but mourned by those who, from a more conservative perspective, seek solidarity in the midst of a changing world.

The situation of the nineties might explain why no Catholic preacher has taken Bishop Sheen's place. Individual bishops, such as Cardinal John O'Connor of New York, have hosted regional programs. Father Andrew Greeley has become a media figure for his best-selling novels. Mother Angelica's EWTN television network is the largest religious network in the world. But none of these media celebrities has universal appeal in the way Sheen did in the fifties. Ironically, at a time when the role requirements of the Catholic priest are least in conflict with his Protestant counterpart and the role definitions of a television celebrity, Catholicism itself is in conflict over the role definition of the priest.

This chapter began by quoting Sheen saying, "Sheeing is believing." The statement sums up Sheen's role. He rarely spoke explicitly about theology, but his enactment of role was itself a theological statement that showed the way to believe in a secular society by way of a unified role structure in the Catholic Church.

6

Bishop Sheen as Harbinger of an American Camelot

In the late fifties, the immigrant dream of America as a land of opportunity seemed to have become a reality. Communism appeared, temporarily, to be contained. American aid programs were eliminating poverty, and the world was a safer place. Mainstream society knew abundance as a baby boom generation matured. Youth continued America's millennial tradition as ambassadors of peace to the world in the new army, the Peace Corps. Technology would soon enable Americans to embark on a journey to the moon. The White House would soon be inhabited by a young World War II hero whose election symbolized a new religious toleration and a coming of age for the American Catholic.

Bishop Sheen popularized that coming of age, not by carving out new theologies within Catholicism but by showing that it was possible for the Catholic to be fully American. He shaped a vision of an American Camelot that in John Kennedy became a reality.

Sheen embraced the diversity of the American religious tradition, helping to pave the way for an era of ecumenism that would emerge within Catholicism after Vatican II. His message seemed to embody mystical limitlessness and values that promised enduring happiness in a perfect society. He mapped out a world of clear-cut boundaries between good and evil. Like the medieval morality play, his message respected natural hierarchies and saw moral change as coming from within the individual, who was in a constant struggle to turn to the good. Since good was defined by a law greater than the individual, it was always certain that good would win; law would maintain order.

Fearful of a technological world order that had so recently emerged from the ashes of the Depression and two world wars, the outer-directed American of the fifties valued tradition and the guarantee of order that it provided. At the same time the emphasis on order made sense to the many Americans whom postwar abundance had delivered into the ranks of the middle class.

America, still a young nation but now a world power, was continuously inspired by the myths of popular civil religion that suggested a noble destiny. Evil—especially Communism—would be overcome by American values of the good. Sheen's message guaranteed this mythic dream even if it was partially qualified by the addition of elements unique to Catholicism.

Earlier chapters showed that Sheen's worldview looked to the medieval past as the key to salvation and the ideal for the American way of life. His medieval city, where justice on earth would be established by respect for law and order, mirrored the heavenly kingdom that was being established by God. Sheen spoke approvingly of America's sacred quest to overcome Communism, an evil borne of a secular society that had forgotten God's kingdom. Secularism, as Sheen labeled it, threatened the freedom and innocence that were guided and inspired by the medieval cathedral principle.

Sheen himself represented the tension between the secular and the spiritual. He provided a bridge between them by making his persona a roadway to unite earth and heaven. He described himself as a mendicant, a reference to the medieval monk who traveled the roads and brought the gospel message to those in need of conversion. For audiences who did not know what a mendicant was, Sheen acted out the role. He could speak eloquently of the beauty of a more heavenly world and angelic messengers while using humorous anecdotes to show his appreciation of the everyday world of hard-working people and human imperfection. Sheen knew the ways of the world yet could inspire his listeners to the values of a more ethereal kingdom. He could play the mystical scholar or the television comic. His presentation of self offered something for everyone.

Sheen delivered his message in a society that had often been in open conflict with the Catholic theology he represented. Yet through the images he presented and in the words he spoke, he never compromised his Catholic belief. For example, despite an anti-Catholic movement to have American bishops declared foreign ambassadors of a Roman pope, he appeared on stage in the robes of a Catholic bishop; his stage props included a statue of the Madonna and Child. Although Protestants were critical of Catholic Marian theology, Sheen used metaphors that could be described as culturetypes unique to Catholicism, such as describing women in terms of rosaries or ciboriums.

Consciously or unconsciously, however, Sheen avoided controversy by using ambiguous language and by balancing his presentation with American metaphors such as destiny and freedom. He showed that he was a patriot who shared American hatred of Communism. Instead of referring to Mary's assumption or stressing her virginal role, he emphasized her motherhood—another quality much valued in American society of the fifties. Furthermore, Sheen balanced his role as bishop by showing that he could also fill the roles of both the genteel and the ungenteel styles of the Protestant minister. Through five years on national television, he avoided making explicit statements of Catholicism, though they were always embedded in his anecdotes and metaphors.

Progress was a sacred term in the fifties, yet the decade was also an age of fear brought about by rapid social change. Sheen's call to return to the past and tradition guaranteed a stability or rootedness for which many Americans longed in the Cold War era. More precisely, Sheen's message provided a rationale for incorporating the past into a future that was timeless because, in the ideology of Scholasticism, the law and its values never changed. Sheen was one of the first American clergy to speak through the popular medium of television, an icon of American progress, at a time when more conservative religious groups saw television as sinful because it promoted secular values.

Sheen's presence on television implicitly blessed America's future. He stepped away from his altar and through technology came into listeners' homes. His commercial sponsor, the Admiral Corporation, sold televisions and electrical appliances that encouraged Americans to be part of a consumer society.

Sheen gained popularity by synthesizing the needs of a rapidly changing culture and finding a place for God and religion within it. His Scholastic philosophy taught that the earth was filled with the sacred and thus that the earth and materialism were blessed. He emphasized the incarnation—the human birth, suffering, and death of Jesus—as both human and divine. He told humorous anecdotes about the mundane events of living and the spiritual possibilities in those events. He emphasized that the presence of the divine could be found in Mary, who showed that all individuals contained in their humanity a bit of the divine to which all women witnessed. He spoke about faith in economic terms as something that could be purchased, thereby suggesting that the secular had sacred possibilities.

In this way Sheen's message contrasted sharply with the traditional values of mainstream Protestantism, which taught that the world was evil. It is no surprise that the traditional theology of Protestantism was in crisis because as America became a global authority, it needed to legitimate its newfound abundance and provide a rationale for seeking more in a consumer society. Billy Graham helped bridge this gap by offering an unqualified blessing on America while continuing to preach the Calvinistic notion of the sinful world. At the other end of the spectrum, Norman Vincent Peale offered an unqualified blessing to the individual and claimed that sin could be overcome by positive thinking. Sheen's message was a synthesis between the two. He challenged American greatness by giving the nation a salvific role while recognizing the need to turn to God and the cathedral principle. He recognized both the sacredness and the evil present in the world. He recognized the holiness within the individual and the tendency to sin.

Sheen's timely message filled the void that had been deepening within popular American ideology. He showed that America was still a nation chosen by God. His jeremiad called the individual, not the institution, to take responsibility for America's failure to bring about the millennial end of evil. Sheen's message helped keep alive the sentimental innocence that had been part of the American ideology.

In the process Sheen provided a rationale for the newly organized corporate culture. Although he might describe himself as a humble mendicant, Sheen led a corporate organization in charge of fund-raising for Catholic world missionary efforts. In his unfolding morality play, hierarchy was to be respected and authority never questioned. Thus he validated the organizational structure of the corporate world. That world was a man's world; women were responsible for the spiritual realm. At the same time, even though the individual was subordinate to the institution, Sheen's message adopted the myth of the American dream that an individual who acted in the right way—one that showed respect for the system—could climb the ladder and achieve success.

Sheen blessed the new leisure industry of American abundance by his puns and joking, delivered with seeming intimacy into the television camera. His message depicted religion not as an oppressor to be feared but as a positive help in achieving success, if not in this world, then in the next. That ties in well with the expression of popular religiosity that portrayed church membership as an American virtue yet uncritically guaranteed God's benevolence to the person who lived righteously. His message helped people to feel good about themselves if they observed the letter of the law.

Sheen never fully embraced the new secularism, nor was he uncritical of American society. Secularism was the root of all the world's problems, but it emerged not from the material world but from an inner forgetfulness of God. Sheen's concept of sin explained the disorder that at times was a part of the secular world. His view must have had broad appeal because the fifties valued popular religiosity and the suggestion that there was room for tolerance as long as one was on the noble quest for God's truths.

Although Sheen's worldview stressed tolerance, his message always gave unspoken priority to Catholic belief, the religion valued by his ideal medieval world. He made compromises with Catholicism and the culture, but they were minor and paralleled changes occurring within the American Catholic Church. For example, Sheen did make room for women in the workplace, but as "spiritual mothers" they had limited possibilities in this realm. Sheen also showed that Catholic clergy were very much a part of the world, not distanced from it. As Catholicism moved to the suburbs, the priest began to be viewed less as an ascetic and more as a pragmatic builder, fund-raiser, and community organizer.

The fact that Sheen had to compromise little suggests that the Catholic was coming of age in American society. Sheen's very presence on television represented this. His good humor, appreciation of tradition, and patriotic values demonstrated that Catholics were not out to overthrow the American way of life but to be a part of it. His message reassured that revolution was against Catholic teaching. His respect for authority and hierarchy showed an acceptance of the status quo that was necessary to the natural order.

For the American Catholic Sheen's message had special significance. He professed orthodoxy within the institutional church, and as a bishop he had much authority. Here was one of their very own who was a celebrity on television, which through its advertising and messages was a primary transmitter of American values. Sheen was everything a Catholic in the fifties could be proud of. He was a religious person at a time when Americans valued clergy, yet his head was not in the clouds. He was an educated man when American Catholics were placing great value on education. He was friend of the little person; but he also dined with European nobility at a time when America was becoming a global power. His aristocratic bearing suggested rootedness and tradition. Sheen's presence on TV suggested that Catholics were the true Americans.

All of this makes sense in light of the fact that, thanks to postwar abundance, Catholics were moving up the socioeconomic ladder, from the lower class toward parity with Protestants. By 1961 Catholics were attending graduate schools in greater numbers than Protestants.[1] In 1955 there were ten Catholics in the U.S. Senate and seventy-two in the House of Representatives; by January 1967 they were the single largest religious group, with fourteen senators and ninety-four members in the House. A similar trend was taking place in the business world.[2] Bishop Sheen embodied that movement because he showed the Catholic listener how to keep one foot in the spiritual world and the other in the secular world. He also embodied not only spiritual success (as a priest) but worldly success (as a television celebrity) as well. Television, the symbol of American utopian dreams, promised the tools and technology for the individual to achieve greatness without leaving his or her own living room.

Sheen's charismatic personality, representing television's promise, was marked by a sense of discipline and a certain element of compromise that ultimately sustained and did not question the American way of life. It tied very much into the Protestant work ethic. At the same time Sheen provided a service for the Catholic Church because in a secular age his rhetoric gave a prime role to the priest, who functioned as a bridge between the secular and the spiritual world. If the priest and the institution he represents are to survive from one generation to the next, he must have the support of the laity. Sheen implicitly pointed out the church's need to keep order in a society where individuals could choose between using the material to sin or to attain sanctity.

Television has been characterized as a liminal or in-between place, one that helps the individual or group to transcend the ordinary and meaningless in order to discover new meaning and identity by discovering new codes and symbols. The medieval traveler went on pilgrimage in crisis and returned home with the crisis resolved; the young person made the transition to adulthood through ritualized drama.

The in-between place is a place of experimentation where the social order can be treated in a ludic way. Ironically, this ludic play sometimes restores the rules of the society, hence revitalizing the culture.[3]

Sheen's television program enacted a ritual of revitalization by showing that the Catholic could have a place in American society. His humor, puns, and word play showed that an aristocratic, educated bishop could humble himself and even laugh at himself. To accommodate a hegemonic Protestant ethic that was suspicious of too much leisure and confined its play to the use of words, his ritual downplayed image and stressed the power of words.

For the Catholic, a priest was a person on a pedestal. Bishop Sheen came down from his pedestal to demonstrate that the Catholic could make it in American society in much the same way as he had made it on TV. Sheen led the viewer in this status elevation ritual, in which a person of higher status allows one of lower status to see him removed—temporarily—from his or her pedestal. Ultimately the order is restored. Through his play on words and humor, Sheen laughs at his aristocratic status and role as a prince of the church. His presentation begins and ends with a genteel formality, but he moves in and out of the ungenteel style, inviting the audience members to an intimacy that would lead to identification; if the audience identified with Sheen in the ungenteel, they could then feel part of the genteel as well.

Sheen also stressed that the humble would be exalted in the kingdom of heaven, thereby encouraging those who were socially humble to respect the order because they would ultimately gain their reward. Sheen's self-deprecation suggested a classlessness, but ultimately it enacted a ritual message of respect for the class system and of assurance that Catholics would not upset that system's balance. Sheen showed those concerned with the genteel tradition that Catholics were educated and possessed aristocratic qualities. He showed those who favored the ungenteel tradition that Catholics were ordinary people who could fit into American society. His own balancing act showed Catholic viewers how to become assimilated as they struggled in the liminal passage of climbing the social ladder.

Sheen did little to change church doctrine. His significance is that he popularized it by reading the signs of his times and using rhetoric to show how the Catholic fit into American society. He paved the way for ecumenism.

Life Is Worth Living went off the air in 1957. In an interview in the

New York Times Sheen said he sought in retirement "to devote more time to my first duty [as leader of Propagation of the Faith], which is to be a beggar with a tin cup in my hand for the poor of the world."[4] No definitive reason why his television series was canceled is available. An unofficial biographer has claimed that because of an argument between Sheen and Cardinal Spellman, his superior in New York, Spellman ordered Sheen off the air. Sheen would in fact later have several other series,[5] but they were syndicated rather than released nationally, suggesting that his message was not as marketable as it had been in the fifties.

A more likely explanation for Sheen's going off the air is that in the late fifties major networks, recognizing the financial potential of television advertising, decided to market their own programs that could appeal to multiple sponsors. Networks turned to Hollywood to bring action films to their audiences. Hollywood filmed television programs that were more captivating than live television programs, many of which were canceled in 1957.

Another explanation for the demise of Sheen's program is that he had fulfilled the need of his audience in an age of insecurity. As Americans became more confident and Catholics more accepted in American society there was less need for his message. In addition, as the sixties approached, people began to question Sheen's ideology.

According to the myth of the Broadway play *Camelot,* its reality "lasted for one shining moment." Similarly, the death of John Kennedy destroyed the myth that good always triumphs over evil and seemed to open a door to America's dark side that had been repressed in the fifties. For the first time black leaders such as Martin Luther King and Malcolm X came into national prominence, pointing to America's crimes related to racism, poverty, and the war in Vietnam. The youth would begin to challenge the fifties' unspoken rule that authority was never to be questioned.

Even within the Catholic Church, the myth of the stability and certitude of a Camelot-like world began to be shaken as the new pope, John XXIII, called Catholic leaders from around the world to Rome in Vatican Council II. For the first time Catholics would witness their clergy openly challenging one another over definitions of good and evil. Clergy and religious who had vowed to be harbingers of the kingdom would no longer choose to represent the "better life." Fathers

Philip and Daniel Berrigan would become national symbols of dissent against the Vietnam War.

Sheen's message of reasoned order would have been challenged in this age of innovation and experimentation. The institution and the ideals of Camelot and Sheen's natural law were open to question as an age of subjectivity rebelled against the narrow constraints of the past.

It has been said that the priest is concerned with maintaining the religious institution that empowered him, whereas the more charismatic prophet can set new pathways that bring change. Sheen was always very much the priest. He never forgot that he had been empowered by the institution to enact the rituals that would preserve it. He led the Catholic to a coming of age but was concerned with giving answers, not with teaching his viewers how to live with questions. His message implied that by following clear-cut formulas people would achieve success and attain salvation. Sheen claimed that his ideology was not just a construction of the church but came directly from God. But when Americans in the sixties began to question their institutions and their preachers, they therefore also questioned the very existence of the God that Sheen claimed had ordered the world.

Chapter 5 described the *phronimos* of ancient Greece as the person who could balance practical judgment and wisdom. Sheen balanced the needs of the fifties by being either the ungenteel or the genteel preacher while displaying the asceticism of the priest. He could not balance the changing relationships of a changing society, however, because he could not see forms of wisdom other than his own, firmly rooted in the past. His ideology blessed the status quo and provided a place for the church in a secular society but at the same time compromised the values that his ideology promoted. He never spoke about racism or institutional sin or economic or militaristic oppression in his telecasts because he was preoccupied with maintaining the order of his worldview.

Today there is a credibility problem in the message of the Catholic Church. The message of an ordered world preached by Bishop Sheen has had to make room for a new world order with the fall of Communism in Russia and the tumbling of the Berlin wall. Within Catholicism voices on the right and on the left have spoken out on the role of women and the laity in the church order. The position of Catholic clergy is being questioned. A young Catholic rock star has become a new Madonna to provide meaning for a new generation, blurring the boundaries of gender definition and of morality. The path of the journey mapped out by Sheen is no longer clear.

Yet Bishop Sheen's message is being viewed with new interest by some within popular culture, because it appeals to a yearning for a more secure time. Others such as Mother Angelica on the Eternal Word Television Network have tried to fill the gap Sheen left, but no one has succeeded. Sheen's era called forth that "one shining moment" when innocence seemed to triumph over evil and justice reigned. His message contributed to the construction of that shining moment when the situation of American culture intersected with Catholic assimilation into society and set the stage for an American Camelot.

Notes

Introduction

1. McGreevy, "Thinking on One's Own."

2. R. Miller, *Paladin of Liberal Protestantism*, 434.

3. "My Day in the Lion's Mouth"; Hennessey, *American Catholics*, 298; O'Brien, *Public Catholicism*, 214.

4. O'Dea, *American Catholic Dilemma*, 158.

5. J.R. Oakley, *God's Country*, 326.

6. Whitfield, *Culture of the Cold War*, 83.

7. D.T. Miller, "Popular Religion in the 1950s," 66; Whitfield, *Culture of the Cold War*, 83.

8. Whitfield, *Culture of the Cold War*, 86.

9. Ibid., 83.

10. Pierard and Linder, *Civil Religion and the Presidency*, 191.

11. MacDonald, *Television and the Red Menace*, 109.

12. Whitfield, *Culture of the Cold War*, 87.

13. Pierard and Linder, *Civil Religion and the Presidency*, 196. Elsewhere Eisenhower declared that America's government "makes no sense unless it is founded on a deeply felt religious faith—and I don't care what it is" (Herberg, *Protestant, Catholic, Jew*, 97). Eisenhower was the only president ever to be baptized while in the White House; he told Graham that the American people would not follow anyone who was not a member of a church. On Flag Day, June 14, 1954, he signed into law the addition of "one nation under God" to the Pledge of Allegiance.

14. Speaking about the program in the *New York Times*, Sheen said, "I went on television to help my sponsor, the good Lord" (Adams, "The Bishop Looks at Television," 13).

15. Hadden and Swann, *Prime Time Preachers*, 83.

16. Parker, Barry, and Smythe, *Television-Radio Audience*, 211.

17. Quoted in Conniff, *Bishop Sheen Story*, 12.

18. Conniff, *Bishop Sheen Story*, 11.

19. Fiske and Hartley, "Bardic Television."

20. Marc, *Demographic Vistas,* 30.

21. McLuhan, *Understanding Media,* 320, 317-18.

22. See Mann, "Spectacularization of Everyday Life," 59. For more information on the "exotic personality," see Cluett, "Telegenic Colloquies."

23. Burke, *Philosophy of Literary Form,* 304.

24. Osborn, "Rhetorical Depiction," 81.

25. This discussion is based on Osborn and Ehninger, "Metaphor in Public Address." The quotation is from p. 233.

I. The Shaping of a Medieval Knight for a Modern World

1. Sheen, *Treasure in Clay,* 356.

2. Ibid., 63.

3. Ibid., 10.

4. Ken Crotty, "Bishop Sheen Star As College Debater," *Boston Post,* 15 May 1953, 10.

5. Ibid., 42.

6. In one instance of controversy, Sheen clashed with New York psychiatrists in 1947 over a sermon he preached at Saint Patrick's Cathedral that was seen as demeaning the profession. Sheen qualified his statements, noting that he was being critical of Freudian psychiatry, not the field itself (Riley, "Bishop Fulton J. Sheen," 325-29). For more on Sheen's treatment of psychiatry, see chapter 2.

7. See the discussion in chapter 4 of the *Life Is Worth Living* episode entitled "Why Some Become Communists."

8. Ellis, *Catholic Bishop,* 81.

9. Cooney, *American Pope,* 254.

10. Noonan, *Passion of Fulton Sheen,* and Murphy, *La Popessa,* also discuss this incident.

11. Ellis, *Catholic Bishop,* 80.

12. Bishop Edwin Broderick, interview by author, New York City, June 20, 1996.

13. Broderick interview.

14. "Video Debut."

15. Broderick interview.

16. Palmer, "Bishop Sheen on Television," 79.

17. Sheen, *Treasure in Clay,* 69.

18. Sheen, *Treasure in Clay,* 259.

19. "Bishop Cloys as Critic," 1413.

20. In his autobiography Milton Berle said, "Steal one line from his writer and a bolt of lightening hits you where you sit!" (Berle, *B.S. I Love You,* 195).

21. "Bishop's Shift."

2. Quest for Stability in the Midst of Change

1. The seven virtues have polar opposites in the seven vices. The pairs are charity versus envy, meekness versus pride, patience versus wrath, generosity versus covetousness, abstinence versus gluttony, chastity versus lechery, and industry versus sloth.

2. Hopper and Lahey, *Medival Mystery Plays,* 157-158.

3. Both metaphors are archetypal because they refer to "experiences common to . . . many races and ages—experiences revived by each generation anew" (Osborn and Ehninger, "Metaphor in Public Address," 229).

4. Although "as late as 1946, 66 percent of the Catholic population could be classed as members of the lower class as opposed to 45 percent for most Protestant groups of the same class," new opportunities delayed by war enabled great numbers of Catholics to enter the middle class in the fifties (Greeley, *Church and Suburbs,* 51).

5. See Miller and Nowak, *The Fifties,* 129; Meyer, *Positive Thinkers,* 171, 192; Riesman, Denney, and Glazer, *The Lonely Crowd.*

6. See Postol, "Reinterpreting the Fifties," 42; J.R. Oakley, *God's Country,* 231; Pearce, *Fifties Sourcebook,* 30.

7. When Walt Disney produced a series of three hour-long programs on Davy Crockett in 1955, he opened the door for a $300 million industry that sold everything from dolls to coonskin caps.

8. If the psychologist could not solve an individual's problem, an answer might be found in the $5-million-a-year industry of selling 1.2 million pounds of tranquilizers (J.R. Oakley, *God's Country,* 313).

9. Sheen, "Psychological Effects of the Hydrogen Bomb."

10. Sheen, "Pain and Suffering"; Sheen, "Meet a Perfect Stranger"; Sheen, "Reparation."

11. Sheen, "Role of Communism."

12. Sheen, "Psychological Effects of the Hydrogen Bomb"; Sheen, "Inferiority Complex."

13. Sheen, "Fig Leaves and Fashions."

14. Sheen, "Role of Communism."

15. Sheen, "Meet a Perfect Stranger"; Sheen, "Three Degrees of Intimacy."

16. Sheen, "My Four Writers."

17. Sheen, "Desert Calls a Playboy"; Sheen, "East Meets West."

18. Sheen, "Greatest Trial in History"; Sheen, "Glory of the Soldier."

19. Sheen, "How Traitors Are Made."

20. Sheen, "Greatest Trial in History."

21. Ibid. The cult of reassurance, which will be discussed later, was influenced by these thinkers.

22. Sheen, "Psychological Effects of the Hydrogen Bomb."

23. Sheen, "Why Some Become Communists." Sheen refers to teachers

as custodians and asks, "What greater joy is there in the world than to mold young minds, young wills in the way of truth and goodness" ("Why Some Become Communists"). This implies that truth and the knowledge of truth came prepackaged and that all one had to do was to act as an artist in shaping it.

24. Sheen, "Why Some Become Communists."

25. Sheen, "Message to Youth"; Sheen, "Philosophy of Communism."

26. Sheen, "Message to Youth."

27. Sheen, "Fig Leaves and Fashions."

28. Sheen's view of this era is clearly idealized. The high medieval era saw the horrors of the black death and the plague, political upheaval both within and between warring kingdoms, the corruption of wealth within the church, and heresies, many in response to the church's materialism and wealth. For more information on the medieval morality play see Gibson, *Theater of Devotion;* and Harris, *Medieval Theatre in Context.*

29. Ong, *Frontiers in American Catholicism,* 6; Halsey, *Survival of American Innocence,* 66.

30. Sheen, "Stones of Notre Dame Cry Out."

31. Ibid.

32. Ibid.

33. Sheen, "Something Higher."

34. Sheen, "East Meets West." The mendicant was a bridge between the spiritual and the secular kingdoms. In medieval times mendicant lifestyles emerged in the cities as an alternative to the rural monastic sites. In this time of geographical movement to the suburbs, Sheen is describing himself in terms of a form of spirituality that was proper to medieval city life. Catholics were predominantly city dwellers until the fifties. In using the drama metaphor, Sheen self-deprecatingly describes his own place in this drama: "I shall be grateful that almighty God has used this poor stub of a pencil to write and engrave on the letters of your soul his words of truth and his emotion of love" ("East Meets West"). Sheen's depiction of himself as only a tool being used by God is in keeping with Scholastic thought's discouragement of individuals from seeking any credit for themselves.

35. Sheen, "Psychology of the Irish"; Sheen, "Glory of the Soldier"; Sheen, "Greatest Trial in History."

36. Sheen, "East Meets West."

37. Sheen, "Pain and Suffering."

38. Sheen, "Meet a Perfect Stranger."

39. Ibid.

40. Sheen battled with New York psychiatrists openly in the *New York Times* in 1947, after he preached a sermon at Saint Patrick's Cathedral that was critical of psychoanalysis. The sermon text was never written. Sheen

publicly denied the accusation. He wrote his own version of Liebman's *Peace of Mind,* which began the cult of reassurance, entitled *Peace of Soul,* in which he admitted that psychiatry was not wrong, but he said religion was a more potent solution to the world's troubles because it appealed to the soul, not just the mind (Riley, "Bishop Fulton J. Sheen," 325-32).

Sheen took legitimacy away from psychology both explicitly and implicitly. Implicitly he equates psychology with "modern." In "Meet a Perfect Stranger," he says, "Within the last fifty, seventy-five years our modern world has developed a new branch of psychology in which it is believed that now we have plunged into the abyss of the self." But though he is more explicit, Sheen is sensitive not to stir up the anger of psychiatry, nor of the society that was embracing it in the fifties: "Now there is no doubt about it: this science of psychiatry has done a great deal of good. It is a science. It has a place and it is competing indeed for this other kind of wisdom, 'know thyself.' But what we want to bring out tonight is, we're not talking about psychiatry. We're not saying it is not valid. We are saying, however, that for normal people, normal people, this is the better wisdom." He concludes that program by stressing the "superiority of knowledge of self" over psychology, noting that psychology "is very valid and necessary and useful, but inasmuch as we are here concerned with normal people and the development of character, we are pleading for the superiority of knowledge of self." Similarly, in "How to Psychoanalyze Yourself," he states that "serious cases of mental illness . . . must be taken care of by a psychiatrist, and psychiatry belongs in the domain of medicine and not in the domain of psychology." Sheen also often makes psychologists the butt of his jokes, as described in chapter 5.

41. Sheen, "Something Higher."
42. Sheen, "Human Passions."
43. Ibid.; Sheen, "How to Be Unpopular"; Sheen, "Stones of Notre Dame Cry Out."
44. Sheen, "Something the Princess Could Never Forget."
45. Sheen, "Fig Leaves and Fashions."
46. Sheen, "For Better or Worse."
47. Sheen, "How to Psychoanalyze Yourself."
48. Ibid.; Sheen, "Meet a Perfect Stranger."
49. Sheen, "Pain and Suffering"; Sheen, "Reparation."
50. Sheen, "Message to Youth."
51. Sheen, "Three Degrees of Intimacy."
52. Spigel, *Make Room for TV,* 52.
53. Sheen, "Fig Leaves and Fashions."
54. Sheen, "Best Town in Which to Be Broke."
55. Ibid.
56. Sheen, "How to Psychoanalyze Yourself."

57. Sheen, "Best Town in Which to Be Broke."

58. Sheen, "Stones of Notre Dame Cry Out."

59. Sheen continued to keep a daily one-hour prayer vigil in his private chapel throughout his priesthood (Sheen, *Treasure in Clay,* 187).

60. Gordon Liddy claimed that his Catholic upbringing taught him discipline; FBI director J. Edgar Hoover looked for recruits from Notre Dame because they were well disciplined. See J.T. Fisher, *Catholic Counterculture in America,* 154.

61. Ong, *Frontiers in American Catholicism,* 29.

62. Sheen, "Pain and Suffering."

63. Sheen, "Psychological Effects of the Hydrogen Bomb."

64. Television became a national pastime, and the fifties also saw the establishment of a permanent hobby industry in the United States. Paperback novels were widely circulated. Americans coping with life in a nuclear era were especially fascinated with science fiction and the search for UFOs. The fantasy worlds of comic books attracted a monthly circulation of 100 million persons (Postol, "Reinterpreting the Fifties," 53).

The new leisure/fantasy world was epitomized by Disneyland, opened by Walt Disney in 1955. Disneyland opened simultaneously with the related television series *Disneyland*—a first in that respect. It was designed not by architects but "imagineers," the same people who had given the world Mickey Mouse. To "sell" happiness, Disney established clear-cut physical and social boundaries that defined an ideal view of American life, blending the rural town and the futuristic Tomorrowland. Disneyland made the world manageable; even the buildings were constructed at seven-eighths their normal size. A kind of antique shop in reverse, Disneyland was a place where "the buildings are old fashioned, the products for consumers modern"; where, on Main Street, "nothing is dirty, where everything is manageable and life-size, where sex and social conflict are eliminated, where the family never changes except to receive more goods and services" (Susman, "Did Success Spoil the United States," 33).

65. Wollen, *Readings and Writings,* 79-81; Witten, "Narrative and the Culture of Obedience."

66. Jamieson, *Eloquence in an Electronic Age,* 116.

67. Similarly, Ronald Reagan often used personal asides and humor. These not only helped him constructed a mythos the audience could identify with, such as the myth of the American dream, they also gave him the opportunity to make statements that were weak on logic (Lewis, "Telling America's Story," 296).

68. Sheen, "Why Some Become Communists."

69. Sheen, "Should Parents Obey Children?"

70. Sheen, "Something the Princess Could Never Forget."

71. Black, *Rhetorical Questions,* 115.
72. Hunter, *Culture Wars,* 57, 108-16.

3. The Medieval City and the Crusade for the American Ideal

1. Winthrop, "Model of Christian Charity," 83.
2. The jeremiad was a Puritan preaching style for adapting to change. Just as the prophet Jeremiah had warned the people of Israel that they were straying from God and were in danger of sin, in times of social disorder the Puritan jeremiad warned people that God was punishing their failure to live up to their destiny. It chastised them to restore the principles of the American ideology in order to ensure the fulfillment of the promise. The jeremiad became institutionalized in American ideology over time and was used by politicians and preachers to remind Americans of their mythical roots as a chosen people. See Bercovitch, *American Jeremiad.*
3. Sheen, "Stones of Notre Dame Cry Out."
4. Chapter 4 describes how Mary's role as mediator was another point of disagreement between Catholicism and Protestantism.
5. Sheen, "Stones of Notre Dame Cry Out."
6. Sheen avoids controversy in "Psychological Effects of the Hydrogen Bomb" when he quotes Pius XII but does not refer to him by function or by role or name. Mentioning the name of the pope would have fired the anger of critics suspicious of the loyalty of Catholic bishops. For example, Paul Blanshard wanted Catholic bishops declared foreign ambassadors because of their loyalty to the pope. Aware of this, Sheen tactfully begins, "What we have to be mindful of are two great warnings that were given to us, one on February 11, 1943, and the other on Easter Sunday 1954, in which it was said that such explosive power would eventually bring catastrophe to the planet itself." Sheen describes the two warnings as "great" but leaves it at that. An exception to his policy was made when he used the same quote in "Three Times in a Nation's History" and did name the pope. And in the published version of "Psychological Effects of the Hydrogen Bomb," which had a less diverse audience, Sheen uses the name Pope Pius XII.
7. Sheen, "Stones of Notre Dame Cry Out."
8. Sheen, "Why Some Become Communists."
9. Cardinal Spellman, the commander of all Catholic military chaplains, often referred to God as "father of America," even in a prayer at the United Nations. For him patriotism was not just a defensive posture but a source of identity. For an analysis of American bishops' rhetoric that claimed that the American spirit was inherently Catholic, see Dohen, *Nationalism and American Catholicism.*
10. In fact, Feeney criticized Sheen often in 1952 for promoting inter-

faith relations (Pepper, *The Boston Heresy Case,* 36). For information on Feeney, see Pepper (1988) and Cuddihy, *No Offense.* For more information on Murray, see Hennessey, *American Catholics,* 257; O'Brien, *Renewal of American Catholicism,* 66-69; Fogarty, *The Vatican,* 368-85.

11. Sheen, "Should Parents Obey Children?"

12. Sheen, "Greatest Trial in History." Anti-Communism became a safe turf on which American Catholics could form an alliance with the government and prove their loyalty. Catholicism in Eastern Europe was in grave danger. The Vatican reported twelve thousand priests killed, imprisoned, or exiled by Communist regimes behind the Iron Curtain. Cardinal Joseph Mindszenty of Hungary and Archbishop Aloysius Stepinac of Yugoslavia, senior members of the Catholic hierachy, were arrested and accused of treason. American Catholic missionaries were not exempt from similar treatment. Passionist Bishop Cuthbert O'Gara and Maryknoll's Bishop James Walsh were imprisoned and tortured in China; another Maryknoll bishop, James Ford, died in a Chinese prison. For more information see "Other Side of the Curtain" and Crosby, *God, Church and the Flag,* 10-13.

13. Sheen, "Reparation"; Sheen, "Philosophy of Communism."

14. Catholicism had emphasized sacrament over preaching partly as a reaction against Protestantism. Catholic priests received little formal training in preaching. As Catholicism grew rapidly with immigration and then the growth of the suburbs, priests put energy into being builders and administrators rather than preachers. One critic described Catholic preaching as a "veritable cure for insomnia." See Dolan et al., *Transforming Parish Ministry,* 145.

15. Sheen does use the image of a tabernacle in "Some Nice People Live in Alleys"; he says that "divinity is tabernacled among us." He uses the word not in the special Catholic sense but to refer to the presence of God with the Jewish people in the desert. He says it is an allusion to the "wanderings of the Jews in the desert, during which Yahweh dwelt in a tent, or tabernacle." He goes on to note that the "tabernacle of the Old Testament was a material prefigurement of the great truth of the Incarnation." In this statement he places Judaism in a positive light as the root of the major Christian religions, because of the association of Judaism with the tabernacle spoken of in the Hebrew Scriptures. The word *prefigurement* ultimately gives more authority to the incarnation, which was a Christian event, than to the "material" Jewish event. Sheen places higher value on the incarnation because it is both material and spiritual. The word *tabernacle* is a culturetype metaphor that has powerful associations with the sacramental emphasis of Catholicism, which differentiates it from Protestantism. Ultimately, Catholic sacramentality is emphasized as the higher tabernacle or dwelling of God, which Judaism prefigures. Every Catholic Cathedral has a tabernacle where it is believed that God dwells.

16. Sheen, "Reparation."

17. Sheen, "Stones of Notre Dame Cry Out."

18. Like the medieval city, Sheen's land is surrounded by a protective wall that represents natural law's guarantee of basic human freedoms. This wall contrasts with the egalitarian emphasis of the American ideological mythos in which structures are flexible. Sheen develops this metaphor in "Liberation of Sex":

"In the midst of a great sea there was an island with a great wall, a high wall. On that island lived children, who sang, danced, and played. One day some men came to the island in a rowboat. They called themselves liberators and said to the children, 'Why put up these walls? Who built up these barriers? Can you not see that they are restraining your freedom and your liberty? Tear them down. Be free.' The children tore down the walls. Now if you go back you will find all the children huddled together in the center of the island, afraid to sing, afraid to play, afraid to dance, afraid of falling into the sea. Protect your civilization with law and order. The greatest freedom in America is America's freedom to obey the law. The greatest freedom of the soul is to be a saint of God."

19. Sheen, "Psychology of the Irish."

20. Sheen, "How Traitors Are Made."

21. Sheen, "Glory of the Soldier."

22. Cherry, *God's New Israel,* 129.

23. Sheen, "East Meets West."

24. Ibid.

25. Sheen, "Role of Communism."

26. Ibid.

27. Sheen, "Stones of Notre Dame Cry Out."

28. Kaledin, *Mothers and More,* 7.

29. Sheen, "Role of Communism."

30. Ibid.

31. Sheen, "Three Times in a Nation's History."

32. Sheen, "War as the Judgment of God."

33. Sheen, "Psychological Effects of the Hydrogen Bomb."

34. Sheen, "War as the Judgment of God."

35. Sheen, "Meet a Perfect Stranger."

36. Sheen, "Three Degrees of Intimacy."

37. In "Three Times in a Nation's History," Sheen notes that "Christ is God in the essence of man."

38. Sheen, "Some Nice People Live in Alleys."

39. Ibid.

40. Sheen, "Pain and Suffering."

41. Sheen, "Greatest Trial in History"; "Meet a Perfect Stranger."

42. In retelling the life of Jesus, Sheen emphasizes not Jesus' actions but rather the moral response to his presence. "Greatest Trial in History" focuses on Herod, Pilate, and their modern-day counterparts who fail to recognize the truth. "Pain and Suffering" concerns the response of the two thieves to the crucifixion of Jesus. "How Traitors Are Made" focuses on the sinfulness of Judas and traitorous activity. "Meet a Perfect Stranger: Yourself" recounts the story of a Pharisee and a Publican, suggesting the proper moral attitude that is needed in prayer. Even when Sheen mentions in passing the miracle of the multiplication of the loaves and fishes, the focus is on the reaction of those in receipt of it and their desire to make Christ king in a worldly sense. Sheen's God is concerned with moral behavior, with telling people how to act. However, as is true of the distanced God of the American mythos, this God's will can be easily interpreted, because even He is subject to moral law.

In "Three Times in a Nation's History," Sheen tells us that Jesus "wept three times in his life. Once at the death of a friend when he saw the dissolution of a body, the penalty of sins. He wept once again for the death of souls in the garden of Gethsemane. . . . The third time he wept was over a civilization. Maybe our times will draw tears from the God-man." The focus here is not on the miraculous and unconditional love of God in raising Lazarus from the dead but His grief over material life that forgets the spiritual. Again, Sheen's God rarely works outside the law but mourns the fact that someone disobeys the law, resulting in both spiritual and material death. The focus is not on God's mercy but on our need to observe the law.

43. Sheen, "Greatest Trial in History."

44. Sheen, "How to Psychoanalyze Yourself."

45. Sheen, "Greatest Trial in History."

46. Sheen, "How Traitors Are Made."

47. Sheen, "Some Nice People Live in Alleys."

48. Sheen, "Why Some Become Communists"; Sheen, "How to Psychoanalyze Yourself."

49. Even the death of Jesus was described as an economic transaction. Sheen uses the extensions of this root metaphor in "Philosophy of Communism," explaining that "Jesus comes to pay a debt." Along a similar line, he adds in "Something Higher," "It costs so much; Heaven must be won," and in "My Four Writers," he concludes, "The Cross must be purchased eternally." He tells us in "Greatest Trial in History" that "Pilate was eager at the chance of dismissing the business"; in "How Traitors Are Made," when he gives America a Christic role by analogy, he says, "One can sell Christ as Judas did, but one cannot buy Him; one can sell America, but one cannot buy America, because love is not for sale."

50. Sheen, "Philosophy of Communism."

51. Sheen, "Something Higher."

52. Sheen, "Liberation of Sex"; Sheen, "Something Higher."
53. Sheen, "Desert Calls a Playboy."
54. Sheen, "Something Higher."
55. Sheen, "Why Some Become Communists."
56. Sheen, "Some Nice People Live in Alleys."
57. Sheen, "Something Higher."
58. Ibid.
59. Ibid.
60. Sheen, "Best Town in Which to Be Broke."
61. Sheen, "Something Higher."
62. Sheen, "Human Passions."
63. Sheen, "Something the Princess Could Never Forget."
64. Sheen, "Stones of Notre Dame Cry Out."
65. Sheen, "Role of Communism."
66. Sheen, "Philosophy of Communism.
67. Sheen, "Role of Communism"
68. Ibid.
69. Ibid.
70. Sheen, "East Meets West."
71. Sheen, "Something Higher."
72. Sheen, "Three Times in a Nation's History"; Sheen, "Something Higher."
73. Sheen, "War as the Judgment of God"; Sheen, "Role of Communism."
74. Sheen, "East Meets West."
75. Sheen, "War as the Judgment of God."
76. Sheen, "Something Higher."
77. Sheen, "Philosophy of Communism."
78. Sheen, "How Traitors Are Made."
79. Sheen, "War as the Judgment of God."
80. In "Abraham Lincoln," Sheen offers a distinctly Catholic interpretation of Lincoln's life in which Lincoln participates actively in his own death by a confession of faith—not through the lips but by his life or action: "And Lincoln, who had never openly quite confessed the redemption with his own lips, now confessed redemption with his own life. For he often said, 'Our concern is not whether God is on our side, but whether we are on His!' George Washington will always be the father of our country, but Abraham Lincoln will always be its savior!" Unlike the Protestant belief in faith alone as the way to salvation, Catholicism states that the believer gains merit through good works.
81. Sheen, "Human Passions." At least since the nineteenth century, America embraced an ideology that became less inwardly spiritual and more

action oriented (Bellah, "Civil Religion in America," 34; McLoughlin, *Revivals, Awakenings, and Reforms,* 79; Albanese, *America Religion and Religions,* 253). Sheen's call to action was more inward because the purpose was to change the individual so that he or she could achieve salvation.

82. Sheen, "Reparation."
83. Ibid. Recall that earlier Sheen described God as a physician.
84. Sheen, "East Meets West."
85. Sheen, "Reparation."

4. A Television Troubadour Sings His Medieval Lady's Praise

A version of this chapter appeared in *The Journal of Communication and Religion* 20, no. 2 (Sept. 1997).

1. Sheen, "Psychological Effects of the Hydrogen Bomb."
2. Sheen, "Three Times in a Nation's History."
3. "Assumption Dogma."
4. Sheen, "Best Town in Which to Be Broke."
5. Burke, *Philosophy of Literary Form,* 70-71.
6. Sheen, "How Mothers Are Made."
7. Marian devotions were an integral part of the American Catholic Church. In 1846 the Sixth Catholic Provincial Council of Baltimore proclaimed the feast of the Immaculate Conception as the patronal feast of the United States.

In the United States, an actress won an Academy Award for her role as the young visionary at Lourdes in the 1944 movie *The Song of Bernadette.* Pilgrimages and devotions to Mary were common, as were reports of Marian apparitions. Anti-Communism and Marian devotion became more and more connected. In 1946 John Haffert, editor of *Scapular* magazine, began publicizing devotion to Fatima in America. In 1950 Haffert and Msgr. Harold Colgan, a pastor from Plainfield, New Jersey, who had recovered from a heart attack after making a vow to the Lady of Fatima, organized the Blue Army. This organization was approved by church authorities, and its message was communicated through *Soul* magazine, whose monthly circulation rose from three thousand in 1950 to seventy thousand in 1951. It was an army that used the rosary as a weapon against Communism.

8. Sheen, "Best Town in Which to Be Broke."
9. Ibid.
10. Ibid.
11. Note that once again Sheen divides the world in two. The pope wants Leseur to remain "in the world" rather than becoming a priest in the heavenly world.

12. McGuire, "Order of Presentation."

13. Sheen, "My Four Writers."

14. Sheen, "Stones of Notre Dame Cry Out."

15. Sheen, "Best Town in Which to Be Broke."

16. Ibid.

17. Sheen, "Stones of Notre Dame Cry Out."

18. Sheen, "Some Nice People Live in Alleys."

19. Ibid.

20. Ibid.

21. Ibid.

22. Ibid.

23. Ibid.

24. Sheen, "How Mothers Are Made."

25. Sheen, "Something Higher."

26. Sheen, "Something the Princess Could Never Forget"; Sheen, "Some Nice People Live in Alleys."

27. E.T. May, *Homeward Bound,* 78-79. This book is an excellent source of information on the family in post–World War II America.

28. Sheen, "Women Who Do Not Fail."

29. Ibid.; Sheen, "Children."

30. Sheen, "Children."

31. Sheen, "For Better or Worse."

32. Sheen, "Fig Leaves and Fashions."

33. Sheen, "For Better or Worse."

34. Sheen, "Fig Leaves and Fashions."

35. Ibid.

36. Sheen, "Liberation of Sex."

37. Sheen, "Women Who Do Not Fail."

38. Sheen, "Should Parents Obey Children?"; Sheen, "How Mothers Are Made."

39. Sheen, "For Better or Worse."

40. Sheen, "Human Passion."

41. Sheen, "Liberation of Sex."

42. Sheen, "For Better or Worse."

43. Sheen, "Women Who Do Not Fail."

44. Ibid.; Sheen, "How Mothers Are Made."

45. Sheen, "Should Parents Obey Children?"

46. Sheen, "How Mothers Are Made."

47. Sheen, "Women Who Do Not Fail"; Sheen, "How Mothers Are Made."

48. Sheen, "Women Who Do Not Fail."

49. The Franciscans led in promoting devotion to Mary as the sorrowful mother. From the eleventh century onward, Mary was seen as a coredemptrix

who actively participated in redemption by standing by her son in death. The tears of the sorrowful mother offered not only comfort to the believer but also the possibility of cleansing and rebirth through her supplication. By the thirteenth and fourteenth centuries, a time of violence in society and corruption within the church, society looked for more humanized objects for devotion. Mary was stripped of her royal regalia, and the notion of a sorrowful mother had much appeal.

50. Sheen, "Best Town in Which to Be Broke."

51. Sheen, "Some Nice People Live in Alleys."

52. Sheen, "How to Psychoanalyze Yourself."

53. Sheen, "For Better or Worse."

54. Sheen, "Something the Princess Could Never Forget."

55. Sheen, "Best Town in Which to Be Broke."

56. Ibid.

57. Sheen, "East Meets West."

58. Sheen, "Women Who Do Not Fail."

59. Sheen, "Children."

60. Sheen, "Pain and Suffering."

61. Sheen, "Women Who Do Not Fail."

62. Dyer, *Heavenly Bodies,* 56-57. Another crack in the stability of the fifties outlook was rock and roll, criticized by "proper" society as "the Kinsey Report set to music" (J. Hart, *When the Going Was Good,* 131). Elvis's pelvis gyrating on television was the male expression of sexual liberation, but Elvis's songs, unlike James Bond's, suggested tenderness and care for the woman he loved rather than promiscuity.

63. May, *Homeward Bound,* 151.

64. Dolan et al., *Transforming Parish Ministry,* 252; Kenneally, *History of American Catholic Women,* 203.

65. Schneider, "American Sisters," 70.

66. McDannell, *The Christian Home,* 93-109. This is an excellent source on gender roles in Protestantism and Catholicism at the dawn of the twentieth century.

67. Sheen, "Women Who Do Not Fail."

68. Ibid.

69. Sheen, "East Meets West."

70. Sheen, "Something the Princess Could Never Forget"; Sheen, "Women Who Do Not Fail."

71. Sheen, "For Better or Worse."

72. Sheen, "How Mothers Are Made."

73. Sheen, "Best Town in Which to Be Broke."

74. Sheen, "Women Who Do Not Fail"; Sheen, "Stones of Notre Dame Cry Out."

75. Sheen, "East Meets West"; Sheen, "Best Town in Which to Be Broke."
76. Sheen, "Best Town in Which to Be Broke."

5. Bishop Sheen's Role Negotiation from Ascetic Bishop to Television Celebrity

1. Sheen, "Three Degrees of Intimacy."
2. Bormann, *Force of Fantasy,* extensively analyzes the two Protestant genres of ministry.
3. Cardinal William O'Connell, archbishop of Boston in the early 1940s, had declared: "There is no such thing as the personality of the bishop or the personality of a parish priest. Personal qualities are subject to change. These are transient things on which depend nothing of the certainty of the Catholic faith" (quoted in Dolan et al., *Transforming Parish Ministry,* 9).
4. Murnion, *The Catholic Priest,* 26.
5. Pius XII, *Menti nostrae,* in Liebard, 52-53, 56.
6. This ties in well with American popular religion's respect for philanthropy (Wuthnow, *Acts of Compassion,* 9, 50). Sheen's message is coactive because the audience did the work of making this identification (Simons, *Persuasion,* 121-38).
7. For a discussion of how the stage set was determined, see chapter 1.
8. The architecture of the period stressed spaciousness and mobility, not clearly defined, objective boundaries that anchored life. Saucer-shaped designs were popular, as in the mobiles of Paul Boomerang or the TWA building at New York's Idlewild (now Kennedy) Airport, a bird with massive wings, whose "open spaces soared" (Hine, *Populuxe,* 162).
9. Hoover, *Mass Media Religion,* 180.
10. Sheen, "Something the Princess Could Never Forget."
11. Sheen, "Some Nice People Live in Alleys."
12. Atkinson, *Our Masters' Voices,* 99.
13. Sheen, "My Four Writers."
14. Sheen, "Something Higher."
15. Sheen, "Something the Princess Could Never Forget."
16. Incongruity shows the absurdity of an idea by contrasting it with its opposite (Burke, *Attitudes toward History,* 308-13).
17. Sheen, "Three Degrees of Intimacy"; Sheen, "Stones of Notre Dame Cry Out"; Sheen, "Should Parents Obey Children?"
18. Sheen, "Life and Character of Lenin."
19. Sheen, "Philosophy of Communism."
20. Sheen, "How to Psychoanalyze Yourself."
21. Sheen, "Psychological Effects of the Hydrogen Bomb"; Sheen, "For Better or Worse."

22. Sheen, "Philosophy of Communism."

23. Sheen, "My Four Writers."

24. Sheen, "Something Higher."

25. Sheen, "Greatest Trial in History."

26. Sheen, "Message to Youth."

27. Sheen, "Fig Leaves and Fashions"; Sheen, "Three Degrees of Intimacy."

28. Sheen, "Should Parents Obey Children?"

29. Sheen, "Macbeth."

30. Sheen, "Three Degrees of Intimacy."

31. Ibid.

32. Sheen, "Pain and Suffering"; Sheen, "Psychology of the Irish."

33. Sheen, "War as the Judgment of God."

34. Sheen, "East Meets West."

35. The fact that Sheen speaks on a commercial medium was one of the criticisms made against him by conservative Protestantism ("Bishop Cloys as Critic"). This was less a rhetorical problem for Catholicism because Catholicism stressed the goodness of all the created order, including technology (Ong, *Frontiers in American Catholicism,* 29).

36. Sheen, "East Meets West."

37. Sheen, "Human Passions."

38. Sheen, "Psychological Effects of the Hydrogen Bomb"; Sheen, "Nurses and Doctors."

39. Sheen, "Why Some Become Communists"; Sheen, "Psychological Effects of the Hydrogen Bomb."

40. Van Horne, "Bishop versus Berle," 65; "Microphone Missionary," 72; Conniff, *Bishop Sheen Story,* 4.

41. Kaufer, in "The Ironist and Hypocrite as Presidential Symbols," looks at the interplay of humor and irony in the construction of the public persona of John Kennedy. He shows that Kennedy's self-disparaging remarks elevate him in the eyes of his audience.

42. Willner, *Spellbinders,* 59.

43. Lindholm, in *Charisma,* an excellent resource on charisma, provides contemporary illustrations of charisma being enacted.

44. Noonan, *Passion of Fulton Sheen,* 56; "Microphone Missionary," 78.

45. Sheen, "Human Passions."

46. Sheen, "East Meets West."

47. Sheen, "Should Parents Obey Children?"; Sheen, "Best Town in Which to Be Broke."

48. Sheen, "Meet a Perfect Stranger."

49. Milton Berle wrote in his autobiography of this incident, "As if on cue, Stalin had a stroke. A week later Stalin was dead. One of my writers said,

'Why can't you do something like that.' A second writer replied what for? They'll say Milton stole the bit" (Berle, *B.S. I Love You*, 195).

50. Sheen, "East Meets West."

51. Sheen, "Philosophy of Communism"; Sheen, "Should Parents Obey Children?"

52. Sheen, "Three Degrees of Intimacy"; Sheen, "War as the Judgment of God."

53. Sheen, "Some Nice People Live in Alleys."

54. Sheen, "Role of Communism."

55. Sheen, "Three Degrees of Intimacy."

56. Sheen, "Human Passions"; Sheen, "Abraham Lincoln."

57. Sheen, "Something Higher."

58. Sheen, "Message to Youth."

59. Sheen, "Abraham Lincoln."

60. Sheen, "East Meets West."

61. Sheen, "Some Nice People Live in Alleys."

62. Voters are often persuaded by candidates' visual images that are created on television rather than by the candidates' logic (Jamieson, *Eloquence in an Electronic Age*, 116).

63. Beiner, *Political Judgment*.

64. Sheen, "Abraham Lincoln."

6. Bishop Sheen as Harbinger of an American Camelot

1. For demographics see Glenn and Hyland, "Religious Preference and Worldly Success"; and Greeley, *Religion and Career*, 49.

2. Ellis, *American Catholicism*, 152.

3. For more on ritual see Wallace, "Revitalization Movements"; and the work of Victor Turner (Turner, *The Ritual Process*; Turner, *From Ritual to Theatre*; Turner and Turner, *Image and Pilgrimage in Christian Culture*, 1-39).

4. Adams, "The Bishop Looks at Television."

5. Noonan, *Passion of Fulton Sheen*.

Bibliography

Adams, Val. "The Bishop Looks at Television." *New York Times,* April 6, 1952, sec. 2, 13.

Agonito, Joseph. *The Building of an American Catholic Church.* New York: Garland Publishing, 1988.

Ahlstrom, Sydney. *The Religious History of the American People.* New Haven, Conn.: Yale Univ. Press, 1972.

Albanese, Catherine. *America Religion and Religions.* Belmont, Calif.: Wadsworth Publishing, 1981.

———. *Sons of the Fathers: Civil Religion of the American Revolution.* Philadelphia: Temple Univ. Press, 1976.

Allen, Robert C., ed. *Channels of Discourse.* Chapel Hill, N.C.: Univ. of North Carolina Press, 1987.

Allit, Patrick. "American Catholics and the New Conservatism of the 1950s." *U.S. Catholic Historian* 7, no. 11 (1988): 15-38.

American Business Consultants. *Red Channels.* New York, 1950.

Appleby, R. Scott. "In the Church but Not of the World: Pioneer Priests of the Eve of Vatican II." *U.S. Catholic Historian* 11 (1993): 83-100.

Aristotle. *Nichomachean Ethics.* Trans. M. Ostwald. Indianapolis: Bobbs-Merrill, 1965.

"Assumption Dogma to Be Announced." *Christian Century,* Aug. 30, 1950, 1012.

Athans, Mary C. "Mary in the American Catholic Church." *U.S. Catholic Historian* 8, no. 4 (1989): 103-16.

Atkinson, Clarissa, Constance Buchanan, and Margaret Miles. *Immaculate and Powerful: The Female in Sacred Image and Social Reality.* Boston: Beacon Press, 1985.

Atkinson, Max. *Our Masters' Voices.* London: Methuen, 1984.

Barnouw, Eric. *The Golden Web: History of Broadcasting in the United States.* Vol. 2. New York: Oxford Univ. Press, 1968.

———. *The Tube of Plenty.* New York: Oxford Univ. Press, 1975.

Barthes, Roland. *Mythologies*. New York: Hill and Wang, 1957.

Beiner, Richard. *Political Judgment*. Chicago: Univ. of Chicago Press, 1983.

Bellah, Robert. "Civil Religion in America." In *American Civil Religion*, ed. Donald G. Jones and Russell Richey, 21-44. San Francisco: Harper and Row, 1974.

Benko, Stephen. *Protestants, Catholics and Mary*. Valley Forge, Pa.: Judson Press, 1968.

Bercovitch, Sacvan. *The American Jeremiad*. Madison: Univ. of Wisconsin Press, 1978.

Berger, Peter L. *The Sacred Canopy*. New York: Doubleday, 1967.

Berle, Milton. *B.S. I Love You*. New York: McGraw-Hill, 1988.

Berle, Milton, and Haskel Frankl. *Milton Berle*. New York: Delacorte Press, 1974.

Bevington, David. *Medieval Drama*. Boston: Houghton Mifflin, 1975.

"Bishop Cloys as Critic." *Christian Century*, Dec. 5, 1956, 1413.

"Bishop Sheen's Gesture." *Commonweal*, March 15, 1968, 704.

"The Bishop's Shift." *Newsweek*, May 9, 1955, 85.

Bitzer, Lloyd. "The Rhetorical Situation." *Philosophy and Rhetoric* 1 (1968): 1-14.

Black, Edwin. "A Note on Theory and Practice in Rhetorical Criticism." *Western Journal of Speech Communication* 44 (fall 1980): 331-36.

———. *Rhetorical Criticism*. 2d ed. 1965. Reprint, Madison: Univ. of Wisconsin Press, 1978.

———. *Rhetorical Questions*. Chicago: Univ. of Chicago Press, 1992.

———. "The Second Persona." *Quarterly Journal of Speech* 56 (April 1970): 109-19.

Blankenship, Jane. "Toward a Developmental Model of Form: ABC's Treatment of the Reagan Inaugural and the Iranian Hostage Release as Oxymoron." In *Form, Genre, and the Study of Political Discourse*, ed. Herbert W. Simons and Aram A. Aghazarian, 246-77. Columbia: Univ. of South Carolina Press, 1986.

Blanshard, Paul. *American Freedom and Catholic Power*. Boston: Beacon Press, 1949.

———. *The Irish and Catholic Power*. Boston: Beacon Press, 1953.

"Blessings of Television." *Newsweek*, Nov. 19, 1956, 108.

Boddy, William. *Fifties Television*. Chicago: Univ. of Illinois Press, 1990.

Boorstin, Daniel, and Ruth Boorstin. *Hidden History*. New York: Harper and Row, 1987.

Bormann, Ernest. "Fantasy and Rhetorical Vision: The Rhetorical Criticism of Social Reality. *Quarterly Journal of Speech* 58 (1972): 396-407.

———. *The Force of Fantasy*. Carbondale: Southern Illinois Univ. Press, 1985.

Boss, George. "Essential Attributes of the Concept of Charisma." *Southern States Communication Journal* 41 (1976): 300-313.

Brieg, James. "And Now a Word with His Sponsor." *U.S. Catholic,* Feb. 1980, 24-28.

Brooks, Phillips. *Lectures on Preaching.* New York: E.P. Dutton, 1877.

Bruce, Steve. *Pray TV.* New York: Routledge, 1990.

Brummett, Barry. "Burke's Representative Anecdote as a Method in Media Criticism." *Critical Studies in Mass Communication* 1 (1984): 161-76.

———. "The Representative Anecdote as a Burkean Method, Applied to Evangelical Rhetoric." *Southern Speech Communication Journal* 49 (fall 1984): 1-23.

Burke, Kenneth. *Attitudes toward History.* 1937. Reprint, Berkeley: Univ. of California Press, 1984.

———. *Dramatism and Development.* Barre, Mass.: Clark Univ. Press, 1972.

———. *A Grammar of Motives.* Berkeley: Univ. of California Press, 1945.

———. *Language as Symbolic Action.* Berkeley: Univ. of California Press, 1966.

———. *Permanence and Change.* New York: Bobbs-Merrill, 1935.

———. *Philosophy of Literary Form.* 1941. Reprint, Berkeley: Univ. of California Press, 1973.

———. *A Rhetoric of Motives.* Berkeley: Univ. of California Press, 1950.

———. *The Rhetoric of Religion.* Berkeley: Univ. of California Press, 1961.

Burns, Jeffrey. "Catholic Laywomen in the Culture of American Catholicism in the 1950s." *U.S. Catholic Historian* 5, nos. 3-4 (1986): 385-400.

Camille, Michael. *The Gothic Idol.* Cambridge: Cambridge Univ. Press, 1989.

Carter, Paul. *Another Part of the Fifties.* New York: Columbia Univ. Press, 1983.

Castel, Robert, Franocoise Castel, and Anne Lovell. *The Psychiatric Society.* Trans. A. Goldhammer. New York: Columbia Univ. Press, 1982.

Charmaz, Kathy. "The Grounded Theory Method: An Explication and Interpretation." In *Contemporary Field Research,* ed. Robert Emerson, 109-26. Prospect Heights, Ill.: Waveland Press, 1983.

Cherry, Conrad. *God's New Israel: Religious Interpretation of American Destiny.* Englewood Cliffs, N.J.: Prentice Hall, 1971.

Chinnici, Joseph P. *Living Stones.* New York: Macmillan, 1989.

Christian Prayer: The Liturgy of Hours. New York: Catholic Book Publishing, 1976.

"Churches Should Be Depots for the Poor." *National Catholic Reporter,* July 17, 1968, 3.

Clarke, Peter. "John England: Missionary to America, Then and Now." In Gerald Fogarty, *Patterns of Episcopal Leadership,* 68-84.

Cluett, Richard. "Telegenic Colloquies: Paradigms of Society in the TV Talk

Show." In *Meanings of the Medium,* ed. Katherine Henderson and Joseph Mazzeo, 3-16. New York: Praeger, 1990.

Cohn, Howard. "Bishop Sheen Answers His Fan Mail." *Collier's,* Jan. 24, 1953, 22-24.

Connelly, Joseph, ed. *Hymns of the Roman Liturgy.* New York: Longmans, Green, 1957.

Conniff, James. *The Bishop Sheen Story.* Greenwich, Conn.: Fawcett, 1953.

Cooke, Bernard. *Ministry to Word and Sacraments.* Philadelphia: Fortress Press, 1976.

Cooney, John. *The American Pope.* New York: Times Books, 1984.

Crosby, Donald. *God, Church and the Flag: Senator Joseph McCarthy and the Catholic Church.* Chapel Hill: Univ. of North Carolina Press, 1978.

Crotty, Ken. "Bishop Sheen Born Above Dad's Store." *Boston Post,* May 8, 1953, 1, 14.

———. "Bishop Sheen Liked Books as Child of 5" *Boston Post,* May 9, 1953, 1, 2.

———. "Bishop Sheen's Devotion Recalled." *Boston Post,* May 10, 1953, 1, 26.

———. "'Spike' Nickname for Bishop Sheen." *Boston Post,* May 11, 1953, 1, 12.

———. "Bishop Sheen Recalled as Top Scholar in Class." *Boston Post,* May 12, 1953, 4.

———. "Bishop's T.V. Program Makes 'Family Night.'" *Boston Post,* May 13, 1953, 6.

———. "Bishop Sheen Star of Play at School." *Boston Post,* May 14, 1953, 3.

———. "Bishop Sheen Star as College Debater." *Boston Post,* May 15, 1953, 10.

———. "Bishop Sheen Bible Guided His Boyhood." *Boston Post,* May 16, 1953, 2.

———. "Dictatorships Are the Result, Not the Cause, of Emotional Disorders that Plague World." *Boston Post,* May 17, 1953, 36.

———. "Bishop Sheen Quick with Quip Always." *Boston Post,* May 18, 1953, 6.

———. "Bishop Sheen Feels Everyone Important." *Boston Post,* May 19, 1953, 8.

Cuddihy, John M. *No Offense.* New York: Seabury Press, 1978.

Daly, Mary. *The Church and the Second Sex.* New York: Harper and Row, 1968.

deWulf, Maurice. *Philosophy and Civilization in the Middle Ages.* Princeton: Princeton Univ. Press, 1924.

Diggins, John. *The Proud Decades.* New York: W. W. Norton, 1988.

Dohen, Dorothy. *Nationalism and American Catholicism.* New York: Sheed and Ward, 1967.

Dolan, James. *The American Catholic Experience*. Garden City, N.Y.: Doubleday, 1985.

―――. *The Immigrant Church*. Baltimore: Johns Hopkins Univ. Press, 1975.

Dolan, James, R. Scott Appleby, Patricia Byrne, and Debra Campbell. *Transforming Parish Ministry*. New York: Crossroad Books, 1989.

Dorsett, Lyle. *Billy Sunday and the Redemption of Urban America*. Grand Rapids, Mich.: W.B. Eerdmans, 1991.

Douglas, Ann. *Feminization of American Culture*. New York, N.Y.: Knopf, 1977.

Durkheim, Emil. *The Elementary Forms of Religious Life*. Trans. J. Swain. New York: Free Press, 1965.

Dyer, Richard. *Heavenly Bodies: Film Stars and Society*. New York: St. Martin's, 1986.

Eckardt, A. Roy. "The New Look in American Piety." *Christian Century,* Nov. 17, 1954, 1395-98.

―――. *The Surge of Piety in America*. New York: Association Press, 1958.

Eisler, Benita. *Private Lives: Men and Women of the Fifties*. New York: Franklin Watts, 1986.

Ellens, J. Harold. *Models of Religious Broadcasting*. Grand Rapids, Mich.: W.B. Eerdmans, 1974.

Ellis, John Tracy. "The American Catholic and the Intellectual Life." *Thought* 30, no. 18 (1955): 351-88.

―――. *American Catholicism*. Rev. ed. Chicago: Univ. of Chicago Press, 1969.

―――. *Catholic Bishop: A Memoir.* Wilmington, Del.: Michael Glazier, 1983.

Ellis, Susan J., and Katherine H. Noyes. *By the People: A History of Americans as Volunteers*. San Francisco: Jossey-Bass, 1990.

Farina, John. *An American Experience of God: The Spirituality of Isaac Hecker.* New York: Paulist Press, 1981.

Ferguson, George W. *Signs and Symbols in Christian Art*. New York: Oxford Univ. Press, 1959.

Fichter, Joseph. *Dynamics of a City Church*. Chicago: Univ. of Chicago Press, 1951.

―――. *Social Relations in the Urban Parish*. Chicago: Univ. of Chicago Press, 1954.

Fiedler, Leslie. *An End of Innocence*. Boston: Beacon Press, 1952.

Fish, Stanley. *Is There a Text in This Class?* Cambridge, Mass.: Harvard Univ. Press, 1980.

Fisher, James T. *The Catholic Counterculture in America, 1933-1962*. Chapel Hill: Univ. of North Carolina Press, 1989.

Fisher, Walter. *Human Communication as Narration*. Columbia: Univ. of South Carolina Press, 1987.

————. "Rhetorical Fiction and the Presidency." *Quarterly Journal of Speech* 66 (1980): 119-26.

Fiske, John. *Television Culture.* London: Methuen, 1987.

Fiske, John, and J. Hartley. "Bardic Television." In *Television, the Critical View,* ed. Horace Newcomb, 600-612. New York: Oxford Univ. Press, 1987.

"Flaw in Good Deed." *America,* April 6, 1968, 429.

Flitterman-Lewis, Sandy. "Psychoanalysis, Film, and Television." In Robert Allen, *Channels of Discourse,* 172-210.

Fogarty, Gerald. *Patterns of Episcopal Leadership.* New York: Macmillan, 1989.

————. *The Vatican and the American Hierarchy from 1870 to 1965.* Wilmington, Del.: Michael Glazier, 1985.

Forest, Jim. *Love Is the Measure.* New York: Paulist Press, 1986.

Foss, Sonja. *Rhetorical Criticism.* Prospect Heights, Ill.: Waveland Press, 1989.

Frady, Marshall. *Billy Graham, a Parable of American Righteousness.* Boston: Little, Brown, 1979.

Frankl, Razelle. *Televangelism.* Carbondale: Southern Illinois Univ. Press, 1987.

Fransen, Piet. "Some Aspects of the Dogmatization of Office." In *Office and Ministry in the Church,* ed. Bastiaan van Iersel and Roland Murphy, 97-108. New York: Herder and Herder, 1972.

George, Carol. *God's Salesman: Norman Vincent Peale and the Power of Positive Thinking.* New York: Oxford Univ. Press, 1993.

Gibson, Gail McMurray. *The Theater of Devotion.* Chicago: Univ. of Chicago Press, 1989.

Gilson, Etienne. *Christian Philosophy of St. Thomas Aquinas.* New York: Random House, 1956.

————. *History of Christian Philosophy in the Middle Ages.* New York: Random House, 1955.

Gleason, Philip. *Keeping the Faith.* Notre Dame, Ind.: Univ. of Notre Dame Press, 1987.

Glenn, Norval, and Ruth Hyland. "Religious Preference and Worldly Success: Some Evidence from National Surveys." *American Sociological Review* 32 (Feb. 1967): 73-85.

Goethals, Gregor T. *The Electronic Golden Calf.* Cambridge, Mass.: Cowley Publications, 1990.

Goffman, Erving. *The Presentation of Self in Everyday Life.* Garden City, N.Y.: Doubleday, 1959.

Goldman, Eric F. *The Crucial Decade and After: America, 1945-1960.* New York: Vintage Books, 1960.

Graef, Hilda. *The Devotion to Our Lady.* New York: Hawthorne Books, 1963.

————. *Mary: A History of Doctrine and Devotion.* 2 vols. New York: Sheed and Ward, 1963-65.

Greeley, Andrew. *The Church and the Suburbs*. New York: Sheed and Ward, 1959.

———. *The Mary Myth: On the Femininity of God*. New York: Seabury Press, 1977.

———. *Religion and Career*. New York: Sheed and Ward, 1963.

Gregg, Richard. "The Criticism of Symbolic Inducement: A Critical-Theoretical Connection." In *Speech Communication in the 20th Century*, ed. Thomas Benson, 41-62. Carbondale: Southern Illinois Univ. Press, 1985.

Grob, Gerald N. *From Asylum to Community*. Princeton, N.J.: Princeton Univ. Press, 1991.

Hadden, Jeffrey, and Charles Swann. *Prime Time Preachers*. Reading, Mass.: Addison-Wesley, 1981.

Halberstam, David. *The Fifties*. New York: Villard Books, 1993.

Halsey, William. *The Survival of American Innocence: Catholicism in an Era of Disillusionment, 1920-1940*. Notre Dame, Ind.: Notre Dame Univ. Press, 1980.

Hanford, William J. "A Rhetorical Study of the Radio and Television Speaking of Bishop Fulton J. Sheen" (Ph.D. diss., Wayne State Univ.). *Dissertation Abstracts International* 30, no. 1 (1965): 422A.

Harris, John Wesley. *Medieval Theatre in Context*. New York: Routledge, 1992.

Hart, Jeffrey. *When the Going Was Good*. New York: Crown Publishers, 1982.

Hart, Nelson. "Bishop Sheen's Television Techniques." *Today's Speech* 10, no. 3 (1962).

Hart, Roderick. *Modern Rhetorical Criticism*. Glenview, Ill.: Scott, Foresman, 1990.

Hastings, Arthur. "Metaphor in Rhetoric." *Western Journal of Speech Communication* 34 (1970): 181-94.

Hatch, Nathan. *The Democratization of American Christianity*. New Haven, Conn.: Yale Univ. Press, 1989.

———. *The Sacred Cause of Liberty*. New Haven, Conn.: Yale Univ. Press, 1977.

Heldenfels, R.D. *Television's Greatest Year: 1954*. New York: Continuum Books, 1994.

Hennessey, James. *American Catholics*. New York: Oxford Univ. Press, 1981.

Herberg, Will. "America's Civil Religion: What It Is and Whence It Comes." In *American Civil Religion*, ed. Donald G. Jones and Richard Richey, 76-88. San Francisco: Harper and Row, 1974.

———. *Protestant, Catholic, Jew*. New York: Doubleday, 1955.

———. "Religion and Culture in Present Day America." In *Roman Catholicism and the American Way of Life*, ed. Thomas McAvoy, 4-19. Notre Dame, Ind.: Univ. of Notre Dame Press, 1960.

Hine, Thomas. *Populuxe*. New York: Knopf, 1986.

Holifield, E. Brooks. *History of Pastoral Care in America.* Nashville, Tenn.: Abingdon Press, 1983.

Hoover, Stewart M. *Mass Media Religion.* Newbury Park, Calif.: Sage Publications, 1988.

Hopper, Vincent F., and Gerald Lahey. *Medieval Mystery Plays, Morality Plays and Interludes.* Woodbury, N.Y.: Barron's Educational Series, 1962.

Horton, Donald, and Richard R. Wohl. "Mass Communication and Para-Social Interaction: Observation on Intimacy at a Distance." *Journal of Psychiatry* 19 (Aug. 1956): 215-29.

Houdijk, Marinus. "A Recent Discussion about the New Testament Basis of the Priest's Office." In *Office and Ministry in the Church,* ed. Bastiaan van Iersel and Roland Murphy, 137-47. New York: Herder and Herder, 1972.

Hudson, Winthrop. *American Protestantism.* Chicago: Univ. of Chicago Press, 1961.

————. "The Ministry in the Puritan Age." In *The Ministry in Historical Perspectives,* ed. H. Richard Niebuhr and Daniel Day Williams, 180-206. New York: Harper and Row, 1956.

Hughes, Richard, and Crawford Allen. *Illusions of Innocence.* Chicago: Univ. of Chicago Press, 1988.

Hunter, James. *Culture Wars.* New York: Basic Books, 1991.

Hutchinson, Paul. "Have We a "New" Religion?" *Life,* April 11, 1955, 138-58.

"I Could Have Gone Higher." *National Catholic Reporter,* Nov. 5, 1969, 2.

In Praise of Mary. Middlegreen, Minn.: St. Paul Productions, 1981.

Ivie, Robert. "Metaphor and the Rhetorical Invention of Cold War 'Idealists.'" *Communication Monographs* 54 (June 1987): 165-82.

Jamieson, Kathleen H. *Eloquence in an Electronic Age.* New York: Oxford Univ. Press, 1988.

Jeffrey, Kirk. "The Family as Utopian Retreat from the City." *Soundings* 55 (1972): 21-41.

Jewett, Robert. *The Captain America Complex.* Santa Fe, N.Mex.: Bear, 1984.

Jezer, Marty. *The Dark Ages: Life in the United States 1945-1960.* Boston: South End Press, 1982.

Jungmann, Josef. *The Early Liturgy.* Notre Dame, Ind.: Univ. of Notre Dame Press, 1959.

Kaledin, Eugenia. *Mothers and More: American Women in the 1950s.* Boston: Twayne, 1984.

Kane, John J. "Protestant-Catholic Tensions." *American Sociological Review* 16, no. 5 (Oct. 1955): 663-72.

————. "The Social Structure of American Catholics." *Sociological Analysis* 16, no. 1 (March 1951): 23-30.

Kaufer, David S. "The Ironist and Hypocrite as Presidential Symbols: A Nixon-Kennedy Analog." *Communication Quarterly* 27 (fall 1979): 20-26.

Kauffman, Christopher J. *Tradition and Transformation in Catholic Culture.* New York: Macmillan, 1988.

Keen, Maurice. *Chivalry.* New Haven, Conn.: Yale Univ. Press, 1984.

Kenneally, James J. "Eve, Mary, and the Historians." In *Women in American Religion,* ed. Janet Wilson James, 191-206. Philadelphia: Univ. of Pennsylvania Press, 1980.

————. *The History of American Catholic Women.* New York: Crossroad Books, 1990.

Kennelly, Karen, ed. *American Catholic Women.* New York: Macmillan, 1989.

Kisseloff, Jeff. *The Box: An Oral History of Television 1920-1961.* New York: Viking, 1995.

Klapp, Orin E. *Collective Search for Identity.* New York: Holt, Rinehart, and Winston, 1969.

————. *Symbolic Leaders.* Chicago: Aldine, 1964.

Kselman, Thomas, and Steven Avella. "Marian Piety and the Cold War in the United States." *Catholic Historical Review* 72, no. 3 (July 1986): 403-25.

Lakoff, George, and Mark Johnson. *Metaphors We Live By.* Chicago: Univ. of Chicago Press, 1980.

Langer, John. "Television's Personality System." *Media, Culture and Society* 4 (1981): 351-65.

Lannie, Vincent. "Catholics, Protestants and Public Education." In *Catholicism in America,* ed. Philip Gleason, 45-57. San Francisco: Harper and Row, 1970.

Laurentin, Renâe. *The Question of Mary.* New York: Holt, Rinehart, and Winston, 1965.

Leclercq, Jean. *The Love of Learning and the Desire for God.* New York: Fordham Univ. Press, 1961.

Leclercq, Jean, Francois Vandenbroucke, and Louis Bouyer. *The Spirituality of the Middle Ages.* New York: Seabury Press, 1968.

Leff, Michael. "In Search of Ariadne's Thread: A Review of the Recent Literature on Rhetorical Theory." *Central States Speech Journal* 29 (1988): 73-91.

————. "Interpretation and the Art of the Rhetorical Critic." *Western Journal of Speech Communication* 44 (fall 1980): 337-49.

————. "Textual Criticism: The Legacy of G. P. Mohrmann." *Quarterly Journal of Speech* 72 (1986): 377-89.

LeGoff, Jacques. *Medieval Civilization.* Cambridge: Basil Blackwell, 1988.

Leuchtenburg, William. *A Troubled Feast: American Society since 1945.* Boston: Little, Brown, 1983.

Lewis, Peter. *The Fifties.* New York: J.B. Lippincott, 1978.

Lewis, William F. "Telling America's Story." *Quarterly Journal of Speech* 73 (Aug. 1987): 280-302.

Lindholm, Charles. *Charisma*. Cambridge: Basil Blackwell, 1990.

Liptak, Dolores. *Immigrants and Their Church*. New York: Macmillan, 1989.

Lucaites, John L., and Celeste M. Condit. "Reconstructing [Equality]: Culturetypal and Counter Cultural Rhetorics in the Martyred Black Vision." *Communication Monographs* 57, no. 1 (1990): 5-24.

Lucas, Stephen. "The Renaissance of American Public Address: Text and Context in Rhetorical Criticism." *Quarterly Journal of Speech* 74 (May 1988): 241-60.

Lynne, Robert. "Civil Catechetics in Mid-Victorian America: Some Notes about American Civil Religion." *Religious Education* 68, no. 1 (Jan.-Feb. 1973): 5-27.

Mabillon, John. *The Life and Works of St. Bernard*. Vol. 2. Trans. Samuel Eales. New York: Burns and Oates, 1889.

MacDonald, J. Fred. *Blacks and White TV*. Chicago: Nelson-Hall, 1983.

————. *Television and the Red Menace*. New York: Praeger, 1985.

Male, Emile. *The Gothic Image*. New York: Harper Torchbooks, 1958.

Mann, Denise. "The Spectacularization of Everyday Life: Recycling Hollywood Stars and Fans in Early Television Variety Shows." *Camera Obscura* 16 (Jan. 1988): 49-77.

Marc, David. *Demographic Vistas*. Philadelphia: Univ. of Pennsylvania Press, 1984.

Marchand, Roland. "Visions of Classlessness, Quests for Dominion: American Popular Culture, 1945-1960." In *Reshaping America,* ed. Robert H. Bremner and Gary Reichard, 163-90. Columbus: Ohio State Univ. Press, 1982.

Marling, Karal A. *As Seen on TV: The Visual Culture of Everyday Life in the 1950s*. Cambridge, Mass.: Harvard Univ. Press, 1994.

Maron, G. "Mary in Protestant Theology. In *Mary in the Churches,* ed. Hans Kung and Jurgen Moltmann, 40-47. New York: Seabury Press, 1983.

Marsden, George. *Religion and American Culture*. New York: Harcourt Brace Jovanovich, 1990.

Martin, William C. *A Prophet with Honor: Billy Graham*. New York: Morrow, 1991.

Martos, Joseph. *Doors to the Sacred*. Garden City, N.Y.: Image Books, 1982.

Marty, Martin. *Modern American Religion*. Vol. 2, *The Noise of Conflict: 1919-1941*. Chicago: Univ. of Chicago Press, 1991.

May, Elaine Tyler. *Homeward Bound: American Families in the Cold War Era*. New York: Basic Books, 1988.

May, Lary, ed. *Recasting America*. Chicago: Univ. of Chicago Press, 1989.

McAvoy, Thomas. *The History of the Catholic Church in the United States*. Notre Dame, Ind.: Univ. of Notre Dame Press, 1969.

McBrien, Richard. *Catholicism*. Minneapolis: Winston Press, 1981.

McDannell, Colleen. "Catholic Domesticity, 1860-1960." In Kennelly, *American Catholic Women*, 48-81.

———. *The Christian Home in Victorian America, 1840-1900*. Bloomington: Indiana Univ. Press, 1986.

———. "True Men as We Need Them: Catholicism and the Irish American Male." *American Studies* 27, no. 2 (1986): 19-36.

McGreevy, John T. "Thinking on One's Own: Catholicism in the American Intellectual Imagination, 1928-1960." *Journal of American History* 84, no. 1 (1997): 97-131.

McGuire, William J. "Order of Presentation as a Factor in 'Conditioning' Persuasiveness." In *The Order of Presentation in Persuasion*, ed. Carl Hovland, 98-114. New Haven, Conn.: Yale Univ. Press, 1957.

McLoughlin, William. "Changing Patterns of Protestant Philanthropy 1607-1969." In *The Religious Situation*, ed. D.R. Cutler, 538-614. Boston: Beacon Press, 1969.

———. *Revivals, Awakenings, and Reforms*. Chicago: Univ. of Chicago Press, 1978.

McLuhan, Marshall. *Understanding Media*. New York: McGraw-Hill, 1964.

Mead, Sidney. *The Nation with the Soul of a Church*. New York: Harper and Row, 1975.

Meagher, Timothy J. "Sweet Good Mothers and Young Women out in the World: The Roles of Irish American Women in Late Nineteenth and Early Twentieth Century Worcester, Massachusetts." *U.S. Catholic Historian* 5, nos. 3-4 (summer-fall 1986): 325-44.

Medhurst, Martin. "Public Address and Significant Scholarship: Four Challenges to the Rhetorical Renaissance." In *Texts in Context*, ed. Michael Leff and Fred Kauffeld, 29-42. Davis, Calif.: Hermagoras Press, 1989.

Meyer, Donald B. *The Positive Thinkers: A Study of the American Quest for Health, Wealth and Personal Power from Mary Baker Eddy to Norman Vincent Peale*. Garden City, N.Y.: Doubleday, 1965.

Meyrowitz, Joshua. "Television and Interpersonal Behavior: Codes of Perception and Response." In *Inter Media*, ed. Gary Gumpert and Robert Cathcart, 253-72. New York: Oxford Univ. Press, 1986.

Michaelson, Robert. "The Protestant Ministry in America: 1850-1950." In *The Ministry in Historical Perspectives*, ed. H. Richard Niebuhr and Daniel Williams, 250-88. New York: Harper and Row, 1956.

"Microphone Missionary." *Time*, April 14, 1952, 72-79.

Miles, Margaret. *Image as Insight*. Boston: Beacon Press, 1985.

Milis, Ludovicus. *Angelic Monks and Earthly Men*. Rochester, N.Y.: Boydell Press, 1992.

Miller, Douglas T. "Popular Religion in the 1950s." *Journal of Popular Culture* 9, no. 1 (1975): 66-76.

Miller, Douglas T., and Marion Nowak. *The Fifties: The Way We Really Were.* New York: Doubleday, 1977.

Miller, Robert. *Paladin of Liberal Protestantism: Bishop G. Bromley Oxnam.* Nashville, Tenn.: Abingdon Press, 1990.

Morrison, Chester. "Religion Reaches Out." *Look,* Dec. 14, 1954, 41-46.

Morse, Margaret. "Talk, Talk, Talk: The Space of Discourse in Television News, Sportscasts, Talk Shows, and Advertising." *Screen* 26, no. 2 (March-April 1985): 1-15.

————. "The Television News Personality and Credibility." In *Studies in Entertainment,* ed. Tania Modleski, 55-79. Bloomington: Indiana Univ. Press, 1986.

Murnion, Philip. *The Catholic Priest and the Changing Structure of Pastoral Ministry.* New York: Arno Press, 1978.

Murphy, Paul. *La Popessa.* New York: Warner, 1983.

Murray, John C. *We Hold These Truths.* New York: Sheed and Ward, 1960.

"My Day in the Lion's Mouth." *Time,* Aug. 1, 1949, 11.

Newcomb, Horace, and Robert Alley. *The Producer's Medium.* New York: Oxford Univ. Press, 1983.

Niebuhr, H. Richard. *Christ and Culture.* New York: Harper and Row, 1951.

————. *Pious and Secular America.* New York: Scribner's, 1958.

Noonan, Daniel P. *The Passion of Fulton Sheen.* New York: Dodd, Mead, 1972.

Oakley, Francis. *The Medieval Experience.* New York: Scribner's, 1974.

Oakley, J. Ronald. *God's Country: America in the Fifties.* New York: Dembner Books, 1986.

O'Brien, David. *American Catholics and Social Reform.* New York: Oxford Univ. Press, 1968.

————. "Civil Religion in America: A Roman Catholic Perspective." In *Civil Religion and Transcendent Experience,* ed. Ralph Wood and John E. Collins, 35-64. Macon, Ga.: Mercer Univ. Press, 1988.

————. *Public Catholicism.* New York: Macmillan, 1989.

————. *The Renewal of American Catholicism.* New York: Oxford Univ. Press, 1972.

O'Dea, Thomas. *American Catholic Dilemma: An Inquiry into the Intellectual Life.* New York: Sheed and Ward, 1958.

Olson, John Frederick. "A Protestant Views the Assumption." *Christian Century,* Oct. 4, 1950, 1161-62.

O'Meara, Thomas F. *Mary in Protestant and Catholic Theology.* New York: Sheed and Ward, 1966.

O'Neill, William. *American High: America in War and Peace, 1945-1960.* New York: Free Press, 1986.

Ong, Walter. *Frontiers in American Catholicism.* New York: Macmillan, 1961.

Orsi, Robert. *The Madonna of 115th Street: Faith and Community in Italian Harlem, 1880-1950.* New Haven, Conn.: Yale Univ. Press, 1985.

Osborn, Michael. "Archetypal Metaphor in Rhetoric: The Light-Dark Family." *Quarterly Journal of Speech* 63 (1967): 115-26.

——. "The Evolution of the Archetypal Sea in Rhetoric and Poetic." *Quarterly Journal of Speech* 63 (1977): 347-63.

——. "Rhetorical Depiction." In *Form, Genre, and the Study of Political Discourse,* ed. Herbert W. Simons and Aram A. Aghazarian, 79-107. Columbia: Univ. of South Carolina Press, 1986.

Osborn, Michael, and Donald Ehninger. "The Metaphor in Public Address." *Speech Monographs* 29 (1962): 223-34.

Osborn, Michael, and Suzanne Osborn. *Public Speaking.* 2d ed. Boston: Houghton Mifflin, 1991.

"The Other Side of the Curtain." *Time,* Aug. 7, 1950, 26.

Overstreet, R. Larry. "Understanding Charisma through Its History." *Central States Speech Journal* 29 (winter 1978): 275-82.

Palmer, Gretta. "Bishop Sheen on Television." *Catholic Digest,* Feb. 1953, 75-80.

Palmer, James C. "An Analysis of the Themes of Bishop Fulton J. Sheen's TV Talks." *Southern States Speech Journal* 30 (1965): 223-30.

Parker, Everett C., David Barry, and Dallas Smythe. *The Television-Radio Audience and Religion.* New York: Harper, 1955.

Pearce, Christopher. *Fifties Sourcebook.* Seacaucus, N.J.: Chartwell Books, 1990.

Pelotte, Donald. *J. Courtney Murray: Theologian in Conflict.* New York: Paulist Press, 1976.

Pepper, George B. *The Boston Heresy Case in View of the Secularization of Religion: A Case Study in the Sociology of Religion."* Lewiston, N.Y.: Edwin Mellen Press, 1988.

Pfliegler, Michael. *Pastoral Theology.* Trans. J. Drury. Westminister, Md.: Newman Press, 1966.

Picklesimer, Dorman. "I Hate Communism but I Love the Communist." In *Great Speeches for Criticism and Analysis,* 2d ed., ed. Lloyd Rohler and Roger Cook, 324-34. Greenwood, Ind.: Alistar Press, 1993.

Pierard, Richard, and Robert Linder. *Civil Religion and the Presidency.* Grand Rapids, Mich.: Zondervan, Academie Books, 1988.

Pius XII. *Fulgens corona.* In *Papal Encyclicals, 1939-1958,* ed. Claudia Carlen. 1953. Reprint, Wilmington, N.C.: McGrath Publishers, Consortium Book, 1981.

——. *Menti nostrae* [The development of holiness in the priestly life] (1950). In *Official Catholic Teachings: Clergy and the Laity,* ed. Odile M. Liebard, 49-87. 1950. Reprint, Wilmington, N.C.: McGrath Publishers, Consortium Book, 1978.

Pollenberg, Richard. *One Nation Divisible.* New York: Viking, 1980.

Pope, Barbara C. "The Marian Revival in the Nineteenth Century." In Clarissa Atkinson, Constance Buchanan, and Margaret Miles, *Immaculate and Powerful,* 173-200.

Postol, Todd. "Reinterpreting the Fifties: Changing Views of a 'Dull' Decade." *Journal of American Culture* 8, no. 2 (summer 1985): 39-45.

Quebedeaux, Richard. *By What Authority.* San Francisco: Harper and Row, 1982.

Real, Michael. *Mass Mediated Culture.* Englewood, N.J.: Prentice Hall, 1977.

Richardson, Christine, and Jackie Johnston. *Medieval Drama.* London: Macmillan, 1991.

Richardson, Herbert "Civil Religion in Theological Perspective." In *American Civil Religion,* ed. Donald G. Jones and Russell Richey, 161-84. San Francisco: Harper and Row, 1974.

Riesman, David, Renel Denney, and Nathan Glazer. *The Lonely Crowd.* New Haven, Conn.: Yale Univ. Press, 1950.

Riley, Kathleen Fields. "Bishop Fulton J. Sheen: An American Catholic Response to the Twentieth Century" (Ph.D. diss., Univ. of Notre Dame). *Dissertation Abstracts International* 49, no. 7 (1988): 1859A.

————. "A Life of Mystery and Adventure." *U.S. Catholic Historian.* 11 (winter 1993): 63-82.

Ritter, Kurt W. "American Political Rhetoric and the Jeremiad Tradition: Presidential Nomination Acceptance Addresses, 1960-1976." *Central States Speech Journal* 31 (fall 1980): 153-70.

"Rochester's Loss Is TV's Gain." *National Catholic Reporter,* Oct. 22, 1969, 2

Roddy, Joseph. "A Talk with Bishop Sheen." *Look,* Jan. 27, 1953, 38-41.

Rodman, Gilbert B. *Elvis after Elvis.* New York: Routledge, 1996.

Schillebeeckx, Edward. *The Church with a Human Face.* New York: Crossroad Books, 1985.

Schneider, Louis, and Sanford Dornbusch. *Popular Religion.* Chicago: Univ. of Chicago Press, 1958.

Schneider, Mary L. "American Sisters and the Roots of Change: The 1950s." *U.S. Catholic Historian* 7, no. 1 (1988): 55-72.

Schultze, Quentin. "Evangelical Radio and the Rise of the Electronic Church, 1921-1948." *Journal of Broadcasting and Electronic Media* 32, no. 3 (1988): 289-306.

————. *Televangelism and American Culture.* Grand Rapids, Mich.: Baker Book House, 1991.

Scott, Donald M. *From Office to Profession.* Philadelphia: Univ. of Pennsylvania Press, 1978.

Seldes, Gilbert. *The Public Arts.* New York: Simon and Schuster, 1964.

Self, Lois. "Rhetoric and Phronesis: The Aristotelian Ideal." *Philosophy and Rhetoric* 12, no. 2 (spring 1979): 130-45.

Shaw, Richard. *Dagger John*. New York: Paulist Press, 1977.
Sheen, Fulton J. *Life Is Worth Living*. Recorded television episodes. Sheen Productions, Inc., Victor, N.Y. Kinescopes.
"Abraham Lincoln," 1956-57 season.
"The Best Town in Which to Be Broke," 1956-57 season.
"Children: Burdens or Joy," 1953-54 season.
"The Desert Calls a Playboy," 1956-57 season.
"A Dreamer in the Streets of London," 1956-57 season.
"East Meets West," 1955-56 season.
"Fig Leaves and Fashions," 1956-57 season.
"For Better or Worse," 1952-53 season.
"The Glory of the Soldier," 1954-55 season.
"The Greatest Trial in History," 1954-55 season.
"How Mothers Are Made," 1952-53 season.
"How to Be Unpopular," 1954-55 season.
"How to Psychoanalyze Yourself," 1956-57 season.
"How Traitors Are Made," 1953-54 season.
"Human Passions," 1954-55 season.
"Inferiority Complex," 1953-54 season.
"Juvenile Delinquency," 1954-55 season.
"The Liberation of Sex," 1953-54 season.
"The Life and Character of Lenin," 1956-57 season.
"Macbeth," 1954-55 season.
"The Man Who Knew Communism Best—Dostoyevsky," 1956-57 season.
"Meet a Perfect Stranger: Yourself," 1955-56 season.
"Message to Youth," 1955-56 season.
"My Four Writers," 1954-55 season.
"Nurses and Doctors," 1953-54 season.
"Pain and Suffering," 1952-53 season.
"The Philosophy of Communism," 1952-53 season.
"The Philosophy of Communism," 1953-54 season.
"The Psychological Effects of the Hydrogen Bomb," 1954-55 season.
"The Psychology of the Irish," 1952-53 season.
"Reparation," 1952-53 season.
"The Role of Communism and the Role of America," 1952-53 season.
"Should Parents Obey Children?" 1956-57 season.
"Some Nice People Live in Alleys," 1956-57 season.
"Something Higher," 1952-53 season.
"Something the Princess Could Never Forget," 1956-57 season.
"The Stones of Notre Dame Cry Out," 1956-57 season.
"Three Degrees of Intimacy," 1953-54 season.
"Three Times in a Nation's History," 1953-54 season.

"War as the Judgment of God," 1952-53 season.

"Why Some Become Communists," 1953-54 season.

"Women Who Do Not Fail," 1953-54 season.

————. *Life Is Worth Living, First Series.* Garden City, N.Y.: McGraw-Hill, 1953.

————. *Life Is Worth Living, Second Series.* Garden City, N.Y.: McGraw-Hill, 1954.

————. *Life Is Worth Living, Fourth Series.* Garden City, N.Y.: McGraw-Hill, 1956.

————. *Life Is Worth Living, Fifth Series.* Garden City, N.Y.: McGraw-Hill, 1957.

————. *Thinking Life Through, Third Series.* Garden City, N.Y.: McGraw-Hill, 1955.

————. *Treasure in Clay.* New York: Doubleday, 1980.

"Sheen Asks Priests' Advice on Top Post—and Follows It." *National Catholic Reporter,* Feb. 1, 1967, 1.

"Sheen on TV Screen." *Life,* March 24, 1952, 92-94.

"Sheen Sets Up Lay Board." *National Catholic Reporter,* May 24, 1967, 3.

Shipley, Orby. *Carmina Mariana.* New York: Burns and Oates, 1894.

Simons, Herbert. *Persuasion.* 2d ed. New York: Random House, 1986.

————. "Requirements, Problems, and Strategies: A Theory of Persuasion for Social Movements." *Quarterly Journal of Speech* 57, no. 1 (Feb. 1970): 1-11.

Spigel, Lynn. "Installing the Television Set: Popular Discourses on Television and Domestic Space, 1948-1955." *Camera Obscura* 16 (1988): 11-47.

————. *Make Room for TV.* Chicago: Univ. of Chicago Press, 1992.

Stark, Werner. *The Sociology of Religion.* Vol 4. New York: Fordham Univ. Press, 1970.

Stout, Harry. *The New England Soul.* New York: Oxford Univ. Press, 1986.

Susman, Warren. "Did Success Spoil the United States? Dual Representations in Postwar America." In *Recasting America,* ed. Larry May. Chicago: Univ. of Chicago Press., 1989.

Swidler, Leonard. "People, Priests and Bishops in U.S. Catholic History." In *Bishops and People,* ed. Leonard Swidler and Arlene Swidler. Philadelphia: Westminister Press, 1970.

Tambasco, Anthony. *What Are They Saying about Mary?* Paulist Press Ramsey, N.J.: Paulist Press, 1984.

Taylor, Charles. *Sources of the Self.* Cambridge, Mass.: Harvard Univ. Press, 1989.

Taylor, Tim. "Fulton Sheen: Verities on Television." *Cue,* Nov. 22, 1952.

Thompson, W. *The Process of Persuasion.* New York: Harper and Row, 1975.

Tichi, Cecelia. *Electronic Hearth.* New York: Oxford Univ. Press, 1991.

Timberg, Bernard. "The Rhetoric of the Camera in Television Soap Opera." In *Television: The Critical View,* ed. Horace. Newcomb, 164-78. New York: Oxford Univ. Press, 1987.

Turner, Victor. *From Ritual to Theatre: The Human Seriousness of Play.* New York: Performing Arts Journal Publications, 1982.

———. *The Ritual Process.* Ithaca, N.Y.: Cornell Univ. Press, 1969.

Turner, Victor, and Edith Turner. *Image and Pilgrimage in Christian Culture.* New York: Columbia Univ. Press, 1978.

Tuverson, Ernest L. *Redeemer Nation.* Chicago: Univ. of Chicago Press, 1968.

Van Horne, Harriet. "The Bishop versus Berle." *Theatre Arts,* Dec. 1952.

Veroff, Joseph, Richard Kulka, and Elizabeth Douvan. *Mental Health in America: Patterns of Help-Seeking from 1957 to 1976.* New York: Basic Books, 1981.

"Video Debut." *Time,* Feb. 25, 1952, 72.

Wallace, Anthony F. C. "Revitalization Movements." *American Anthropologist* 58 (1956): 264-81.

"The Wall of Separation." *Time,* Feb. 7, 1949, 68.

Ware, B.L., and Wil A. Linkugel. "The Rhetorical Persona: Marcus Garvey as Black Moses." *Communication Monographs* 49 (March 1982): 50-62.

Warner, Marina. *Alone of All Her Sex.* New York: Knopf, 1976.

Warner, W. Lloyd. *The Living and the Dead.* New Haven, Conn.: Yale Univ. Press, 1959.

Watson, Mary Ann. "And They Said 'Uncle Fultie' Didn't Have a Prayer." *Television Quarterly* 16 (winter 1993): 16-21.

Weaver, Richard. *The Ethics of Rhetoric.* Chicago: Henry Regnery, 1953.

Weber, Max. *The Sociology of Religion.* 4th ed. Boston: Beacon Press, 1963.

White, James Boyd. *When Words Lose Their Meaning.* Chicago: Univ. of Chicago Press, 1984.

White, Theodore H. *In Search of History.* New York: Harper and Row, 1978.

Whitfield, Stephen. *The Culture of the Cold War.* Baltimore, Md.: Johns Hopkins Univ. Press, 1991.

Whyte, William H. *The Organization Man.* Garden City, N.Y.: Doubleday, 1956.

Wickham, Glynne. *The Medieval Theatre.* New York: St. Martin's, 1974.

Wilkins, Eithne. *The Rose-Garden Game.* New York: Herder and Herder, 1969.

Williams, Peter W. "Fulton Sheen." In *Twentieth Century Shapers of American Popular Religion,* ed. Charles Lippy, 381-93. New York: Greenwood Press, 1989.

Willner, Ann R. *The Spellbinders.* New Haven, Conn.: Yale Univ. Press, 1984.

Wills, Garry. *Bare Ruined Choirs.* Garden City, N.Y.: Doubleday, 1971.

Wilson, James F. "Common Religion in American Society." In *Civil Religion and Political Theology,* ed. Leroy S. Rouner, 111-24. Notre Dame, Ind.: Univ. of Notre Dame Press, 1986.

————. "A Historian's Approach to Civil Religion." In *American Civil Religion,* ed. Donald G. Jones and Russell Richey, 115-38. San Francisco: Harper and Row, 1974.

————. *Public Religion in American Culture.* Philadelphia: Temple Univ. Press, 1979.

Winthrop, Jonathan. "A Model of Christian Charity." In *The American Puritans,* ed. Perry Miller, 78-85. Garden City, N.Y.: Doubleday, Anchor Books, 1956.

Witten, Marsha. "Narrative and the Culture of Obedience at the Workplace." In *Narrative and Social Control,* ed. Dennis Mumby, 97-118. Newbury Park, Calif.: Sage, 1993.

Wollen, Peter. *Readings and Writings: Semiotic Counter Strategies.* London: Thetford Press, 1982.

Wuthnow, Robert. *Acts of Compassion.* Princeton, N.J.: Princeton Univ. Press, 1991.

————. "Religion and the Voluntary Spirit in the United States: Mapping the Terrain." In *Faith and Philanthropy in America,* ed. Robert Wuthnow and Virginia A. Hodgkinson, 3-21. San Francisco: Jossey-Bass, 1990.

————. "Religious Discourse as Public Rhetoric." *Communication Research* 15, no. 3 (June 1988): 318-38.

————. *The Restructuring of American Religion.* Princeton, N.J.: Princeton Univ. Press, 1988.

Yablonsky, Mary Jude. "A Rhetorical Analysis of Selected Television Speeches of Archbishop Fulton J. Sheen on Communism, 1952-1956" (Ph.D. diss., Ohio State Univ.). *Dissertation Abstracts International* 35, no. 11 (1974): 7434A.

Zahn, Gordon. "The Content of Protestant Tensions." *American Catholic Sociological Review* 16, no. 1 (1955): 12-22.

Zimdars-Swartz, Sandra. *Encountering Mary.* Princeton, N.J.: Princeton Univ. Press, 1991.

Index

in the fifties, 91, 113, 123, 146-
47, 168 n 14; related to celebrity,
120, 123, 124, 129, 135-40, 145;
related to other clergy, 120, 123,
124, 125, 130, 142-45, 148
Propagation of the Faith, 21-22, 63,
101
Protestant-Catholic tensions, 2-4, 60,
87-89, 95, 152
Protestantism, 95, 109, 120-21, 171 n
80; Bible, 94, 125, 132; divisions
within, 34, 68, 83, 84; Mary, 88-
89, 98, 99; material world, 52,
154; religious images, 125;
structure of congregation 61,
113; Victorian home, 125
psychology, 28, 45, 92, 128, 129, 149,
162 n 6; controversy with New
York psychiatrists, 163 n 8, 164-
65 n 40

rationality, 75
reason, 47, 103
rhetoric, 12-13
Rochester, N.Y., 28-29, 149
rosary, 90
Rosenbergs, 68, 83

sacrifice, 117
St. Bernard, 91
St. Joseph, 96-97
saints, 138
St. Thomas Aquinas, 19, 73, 128, 148
Scholasticism, 27, 32-84, 111, 148;
early influence on Sheen, 19-20;
history, 19-20; love as a virtue,
75; opposed to ideology of
Communism 84; physical body,
90; reason, 103; related to
religions other than Catholicism,
61; role of God, 69
self-deprecating rhetoric, 126-30,
137, 142, 147, 164 n 34

seminarian, 28, 122, 149
sexuality, 90, 104, 111-12, 114, 143,
174 n 62
Sheen, Bishop Fulton J.: bibliographic
data, 15-31; bishop of Rochester,
28-29; children and, 91, 130,
131, 135-36, 137-38; criticisms
of, 16, 26-27, 29, 176 n 35;
parents and family, 17-18;
physical attributes and clothing,
137-39; radio, 20; storyteller, 38,
55-6; student, 18-20; university
teacher, 20
Sheen, Martin, 27
Social Gospel, 83
Spaulding, Bishop John, 15-16, 20
Spellman, Cardinal Francis, 3-4, 22-
23, 158, 167 n 9
sponsor (*see also* Admiral Corporation), 136, 161 n 14
Stalin, 138, 176 n 49
stoicism, 87
storytelling, 38, 55-56
suffering, 48, 71, 72, 108

TelePrompter, 18, 132
televangelism, 7-8, 125, 148-49, 160
television, 8-11, 33, 100, 166 n 64,
blessed by Sheen, 37, 44, 87,
134, 153-54; liminality, 156-57;
live television, 9; sheen on
television, 7-8, 23-27; technology and direct address, 8-11
television advertising, 34
television camera, 18, 46, 54-56, 96,
123, 133
television celebrity role, 8-10, 120;
examples in Sheen presentation,
123-24, 126, 129, 131-33, 135-
37, 139-40, 145
Theotokos, 87, 99
tradition, 40
troubadour, 89